Finding Atlantis

ET NOS HOMINES

Like a physician dissecting in his anatomy theater, Olof Rudbeck cuts open a map of the modern world and reveals the secret history of Sweden. Homer, Plato, Aristotle, and many other well-known figures of antiquity sit around the dissection table like students. The philosopher Plato strains to take a closer look, and the scholar Apollodorus slaps his head in surprise. Ptolemy, who is so often criticized by Rudbeck for faulty geography, looks away in disgust.

Finding Atlantis

A True Story of Genius, Madness, and an
Extraordinary Quest for a Lost World

DAVID KING

THREE RIVERS PRESS
NEW YORK

Published in the United States by THREE RIVERS PRESS, an imprint of the
Crown Publishing Group, a division of Random House, Inc., New York.
www.crownpublishing.com

THREE RIVERS PRESS and the Tugboat design are registered trademarks of
Random House, Inc.

Originally published in hardcover in the United States by Harmony Books,
an imprint of the Crown Publishing Group, a division of Random House Inc.,
New York, in 2005.

Library of Congress Cataloging-in-Publication Data
King, David, 1970–
Finding Atlantis : a true story of genius, madness, and an extraordinary quest for a
lost world / David King.
Includes bibliographical references and index.
1. Atlantis. 2. Rudbeck, Olof, 1630–1702. 3. Natural history—Sweden—
17th century. 4. Civilization, Ancient. I. Title.
GN751.K56 2005
001.94—dc22
2004024127

ISBN-13: 978-1-4000-4753-6
ISBN-10: 1-4000-4753-6

Printed in the United States of America

DESIGN BY LAUREN DONG

1 3 5 7 9 10 8 6 4 2

First Paperback Edition

TO SARA

*If you are ever in a gathering of your friends
and want to get some attention, wait until a suitable
pause occurs in the conversation and then toss out the phrase
"Well, how about Atlantis?"*

—HENRY M. EICHNER

Contents

Finding Atlantis

INTRODUCTION

May 16, 1702

OST OF UPPSALA was in flames. Strong winds had carried the fire swiftly through the winding alleys of wooden houses. Shortly after midnight, it seemed as if fire rained from the heavens. And now, with the brigades unable to reach the old town, the blaze threatened to turn the cathedral, the castle, and the rest of the university into little more than embers and ash.

As legend has it, a lone figure was seen scaling a building in the path of the ever-rising flames. When he reached the top, the roof already alight, he started to shout orders to the panic-stricken townsmen. His baritone voice rang out over the roar, and his long gray hair blew amid the sparks. There was no doubt about it: this was the seventy-two-year-old professor of the university, Olof Rudbeck.

Only five years before, the Stockholm royal palace had burned to the ground. Along with it, the country had lost untold treasures. Rallying the terrified below with word and deed, Rudbeck wanted to do everything in his power to prevent a repetition of this catastrophe. But suddenly a messenger arrived with the news that Rudbeck's own house would soon be engulfed in the flames.

The professor was advised to make haste to his home; there was still time to remove selected valuables. The townsmen who shared the front lines of the battle also encouraged Rudbeck to go, but the old man refused to abandon his position. Instead, he made his own horses available so that his neighbors might salvage their belongings.

After fourteen exhausting hours, the unlikely firefighters had managed to control the blaze. Despite the ruined bell tower, the collapsed roof, and a lake of water on the inside, the cathedral had been saved. The castle and the university had also just barely survived the inferno. The old professor, however, was not so fortunate. He had lost almost everything he owned.

UPPSALA CATHEDRAL WAS one of the oldest and largest of its kind in Scandinavia. It had long served as the site for the coronation of kings, the consecration of archbishops, and the resting home of saints. Above all, it was a beautiful place of worship. It was ethereal and sublime, adorned with lofty spires, pointed arches, elegant stained glass, and an ornately carved altarpiece.

But there was also something unusual in the cathedral. Reasoning that this was the safest place in town, Rudbeck had chosen it as a repository for his works in progress. Among this vast collection lay one of the most extraordinary theories ever put forth about the ancient past.

Rudbeck had spent the last thirty years of his life on an adventurous hunt for a lost civilization, and he was convinced that he had found it in Sweden. What a marvelous discovery it was! Celts, Trojans, Etruscans, Amazons, and the inhabitants of Atlantis were all one and the same people, who in the dimmest mists of antiquity had emerged from a land of ice in the far north. In fact, many of the great mysteries of history and mythology could be explained by Rudbeck's lost civilization. This was perhaps the most spectacular reassessment of the ancient past ever to be accepted by the learned world. It was also, on that night, at the mercy of the flames.

What follows is the remarkable story of this man and the work he risked everything to protect.

ᐱ

ALTHOUGH ALMOST COMPLETELY unknown today, the name of Olof Rudbeck once cast a spell over his contemporaries. His vision drew enthusiastic applause not only in the twilight of the Swedish empire, but also in the dawning of the European Enlightenment. Rudbeck was greatly admired at the court of Louis XIV, proposed as a member of the Royal Society in London, and celebrated in cafés, salons, and academies across the cosmopolitan Republic of Letters. Avid readers were Leibniz, Montesquieu, and the famous skeptic Pierre Bayle. Even Sir Isaac Newton wrote to request a personal copy of the work.

The name of this "wondrous" book was *Atlantica*. Rolling off an Uppsala press in 1679, it outlined Rudbeck's discoveries in some nine hundred pages of Latin and Old Swedish. Hidden inside was a curiosity cabinet of dazzling speculation, rigorous argumentation, and commanding erudition. The style mirrors Rudbeck's own personality: strong, hurried, and full of charm.

But the project was expensive, and the costs were soon spiraling out of control. Complicating matters further, disgruntled professors formed powerful coalitions to sabotage Rudbeck's efforts. He would be forced to endure everything from petty humiliations to vicious attacks, which included no less than censorship, scrutiny by an Inquisition, and one of the bitterest lawsuits of the day.

Meanwhile, discoveries continued to pour in at an alarming rate. Rudbeck was finding so many "unbelievable things" that he dreamed of publishing a "small addition." By 1702, *Atlantica* had swelled to four and a half colossal volumes, and many scholars believed this work had revolutionized the understanding of the ancient past. Rudbeck was proclaimed the "oracle of the north."

So, when I came across these volumes, it was like stumbling upon an enchanted world. It reminded me of my first encounter with ancient myth, many years ago, when my grandmother gave me a copy of Edith Hamilton's *Mythology*. Rudbeck's *Atlantica* had all the heroic quests, fabulous lands, and endlessly imaginative creatures of Hamilton's book, and it evoked the same sense of wonder and excitement. But, remarkably, it gave the timeless tales an unforgettable transformation.

From Mount Olympus to Valhalla, Rudbeck traced almost all Greek, Norse, and Egyptian traditions back to an original home in the far north. Chasing down clues to this lost golden age, he brought to his work the deductive reasoning of Sherlock Holmes and the daring spirit of Indiana Jones. He excavated what he thought was the acropolis of Atlantis, and sent students on scientific expeditions to the land he believed was the Kingdom of Hades. He retraced the journeys of classical heroes, opened countless burial mounds, and consulted the rich collections of manuscripts, monuments, and artifacts streaming into his country as a result of Swedish victories on the battlefield.

Now, three hundred years later, the story of Rudbeck's adventure appears in English for the first time. It is an epic quest that at every turn shows a bizarre combination of genius and madness. The book takes us back not only to the castles, courts, and peasant villages of the seventeenth century, but also to a world of *lively* imagination. Rudbeck's vision is as stunningly bold as it is beautifully surreal.

Yet it is much more than just a journey through a dreamy landscape. As I came to understand, this story has much to teach us about our own search for enlightenment. It dramatically illustrates how our greatest gifts of mind and spirit can become unexpected perils—and lead us to create our own spectacular monstrosities. At the same time, it is an inspirational tale that affirms the enormous potential for human achievement in the face of staggering obstacles. There is indeed much to learn from entering the strange world of Olof Rudbeck, the last of the Renaissance men and the first of the modern hunters for lost wisdom.

PROMISES

*My dear fellow, life is infinitely stranger than anything which the
mind of man could invent.*

—ARTHUR CONAN DOYLE,
THE HOUND OF THE BASKERVILLES

SOME FIFTY YEARS before the great fire, Olof Rudbeck had
arrived as a young student at Uppsala University. This was
in the cold and dark winter of 1648, just in time for the
enthusiastic celebrations that would soon erupt on the Continent,
marking the signing of the Peace of Westphalia and an end, it was
hoped, to thirty years of the most vicious fighting that Europe had
ever known. War, famine, plague, and plunder had decimated the
populations, spreading misery everywhere the armies marched. Now
the clang of church bells and the clatter of court banquets might replace the roar of cannon and the cries of suffering. Musketeers fired
joyous salvoes into the air, and soaring bonfires were lit to commem-
orate the news. The festivities were especially lively in Sweden, already "drunk with victory and bloated with booty."

Uppsala University was at this time the jewel in the crown of the
Swedish kingdom. Although the university had fallen into disuse a
few years after its establishment in 1477, the state had realized its

enormous potential as a training ground for the new Protestant Reformation and reopened it with royal flair. Young people came from all corners of the realm to learn the theology and acquire the intellectual rigor required to enter the Church. The university also attracted the scions of the great aristocratic houses, sons of the landed and titled families who waged Sweden's wars, administered the empire, and served the Crown in countless other capacities. King Gustavus Adolphus, the famed "Lion of the North," had envisioned just such a role for Uppsala University. He had endowed it with the means to realize it as well, even filling its empty bookshelves with many magnificent collections looted from an almost unbroken string of victories on the battlefield.

Rudbeck was neither a nobleman nor an aspirant to a career in the Church, though he was thrilled all the same to enter the halls of Scandinavia's oldest university. This was understandably an exciting place for a young man. Despite repeated efforts of the authorities, students flocked to the taverns as much as to the lecture halls.

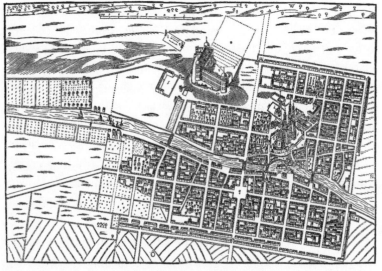

Bird's-eye view of seventeenth-century Uppsala, with its castle, cathedral, and university.

Entertainment options ranged from dice to duels. It was already becoming common for students to carry swords, and sometimes even pistols. New brothels opened to meet the increasing demand, and other institutions emerged to serve the changing times, such as the university prison. Housed in the cellars of the main university building, the prison was rarely unoccupied.

Rudbeck's interests, however, lay elsewhere. Ever since he was a boy, he had enjoyed finding his own way. He sang, he drew, he played the lute, he even made his own toys, including a wooden clock with a bell to strike the hour. Adventurous and independent, Rudbeck yearned to experience the world for himself. In fact, as a ten-year-old, Rudbeck had eagerly tried to follow his older brothers to Uppsala. His father, however, would not allow it, convinced that he was not mature enough to handle the freedom of the university.

Standing tall and giving the impression of no small confidence, Rudbeck was a spirited, highly impressionable youth with short dark hair, broad shoulders, and a barrel chest. He walked, or rather strode, with the air of someone who fearlessly plunged into his latest passion. His imagination, at this time, was fired by the study of anatomy. This was an especially attractive subject for bright, ambitious students. Kings and queens had showered favors on the talented few they chose as royal physicians, and indeed the newly established post of court physician had raised the status of the doctor from its previously undistinguished connotations. Enthusiasm for medicine as an intellectual pursuit peaked when an Englishman named William Harvey published a small Latin treatise in 1628.

Harvey was one of those elite court physicians, serving King James I of England. In his classic *De Motu Cordis et Sanguinis (Dissertation on the Movement of the Heart and Blood)*, Harvey claimed that the heart was a muscle that pumped the blood at regular intervals, or pulses. The vital fluid circulated throughout the body, with the arteries carrying it away from the heart and the veins returning it there. With these propositions, Harvey had revolutionized the study of medicine.

One Oxford doctor and fellow of the Royal Society claimed that these findings were more significant than the discovery of America because they threw centuries of medical belief into uncertainty. Great physicians everywhere now wanted to confirm, refute, or refine Harvey's propositions.

It was in this climate that Olof Rudbeck entered the medical school at Uppsala. His head was full of ideas, his curiosity almost boundless. He could not wait to be turned loose to investigate for himself the mysterious invisible world underneath the skin. But unfortunately the university had very little to offer. Rudbeck's supervisor was too busy for him, preferring instead to spend time in the alchemy lab, trying to change various substances into gold. More challenging still, it was difficult to gain access to the necessary equipment. When acquiring human bodies for observation and dissection was a difficult task even for a professor, what could a student do?

One crisp autumn day in 1650, Rudbeck strolled down to the market, a bustling square jammed with carts, stalls, and stands. There were stacks of cheese, slabs of butter, and fish, gutted and stretched out. Gloves of fine goat-hair and warm wolfskin coats also competed for attention. Rudbeck's eye, however, fell on two women, rough and splattered with blood, as they butchered a calf. There, in the raw dead flesh, Rudbeck saw something peculiar. There was a milklike substance that seemed to emanate from somewhere in the chest, not so delicately split open on the old bench. His curiosity was piqued, and an idea suddenly struck him. With the enthusiasm of someone who had long enjoyed taking things apart and tinkering to see how they worked, Rudbeck asked if he could cut on the carcass.

The women must have been surprised, to say the least, at this young man's request. With their permission granted, Rudbeck borrowed the knife, forced the thick, lifeless aorta to the side, and then separated it from the surrounding red mess of muscle and tissue. He followed that curious milk-like substance along, finding a sort of vessel or duct that carried a colorless liquid. By the time he traced it back to the liver, the dark purplish brown organ undoubtedly destined for dinner fare, he knew he was onto something big.

Rudbeck had discovered nothing less than the lymphatic system. The colorless liquid was lymph, a tissue-cleansing fluid vital to the functioning of the body's immune system. Among other things, it absorbs nutrients, collects fats, and prevents harmful substances from entering the bloodstream. He not only discovered this system but also correctly explained its functions in the body.

This episode clearly shows a resourcefulness that would long be a hallmark of Rudbeck's approach to problem-solving. As William Harvey improved his knowledge of anatomy by investigating the deer bagged by King James and the royal hunting parties, Rudbeck the student relied on the successful meat trade of Uppsala's butchers. Over the next two years, probably working in a dingy makeshift shed by the river, Rudbeck set his dissection table with a veritable smorgasbord of discarded delicacies. He cut, nipped, hacked, and examined, performing hundreds of dissections and vivisections to refine his practical understanding of the body's cleansing mechanisms.

Rudbeck's explanation of the lymphatic system was indeed a major discovery in the annals of modern medicine—the first, in fact, to come from a Swedish scientist. It was also a fulfillment of William Harvey's theories of the circulation of the blood, which were then still fiercely contested. In distant Uppsala, the young Rudbeck, not even twenty years old, had confirmed one of the greatest medical discoveries of the day.

WORD OF THIS remarkable student spread quickly through the Swedish kingdom, and soon reached its colorful queen. Like Greta Garbo, who played her in the film, Queen Christina has intrigued historians just as she fascinated her contemporaries. She was young, barely twenty-six years old, and somewhat shorter than medium height, with thick, curly, dark brown hair often tied with a simple black ribbon. Her voice was soft but deep, and her eyes piercing. Whenever she was displeased, it soon became abundantly clear, the queen's face darkened like a "thunder cloud." Eight years of power had accustomed her to doing exactly as she wished. Controversy, though, was never far away.

Rumors had long circulated that the Swedish queen was a nymphomaniac, a lesbian, a man in disguise, or perhaps a hermaphrodite. After all, when she was born, the midwife first took her for a boy, and even told the king that he had a new son. The hermaphrodite belief was dispelled only when a team of international experts, restoring her grave in the 1920s, decided to take a look. The queen, they confirmed, had indeed been a woman.

Despite all differences of opinion, her admirers and critics agreed on one point: Queen Christina attracted some of the best and brightest of the day. During her short reign, a motley collection of cavaliers, ladies, libertines, and scholars streamed to her court. Perhaps the most famous of these was René Descartes. There was probably no thinker of the day more idolized than this French philosopher.

Indeed, when he arrived in Stockholm, Descartes soon found himself taxed by Queen Christina's enthusiasm for early-morning lessons in the new thought, and equally burdensome demands to compose ballets for entertainment in the evening. The Frenchman, overworked and exhausted, succumbed to an unusually cold winter in Christina's unusually cold castle. He died in February 1650, after shivering through five miserable months at court (though his skull, it turned out, stayed in the country almost two hundred years longer; it had been secretly removed and replaced with a substitute, and was not reunited with his body in France until 1821).

It was now Olof Rudbeck's turn to come to Queen Christina's court. She was much impressed by his anatomical work and sent an invitation for the student to present his discoveries to her in person. On a beautiful spring day in 1652, Rudbeck arrived at the royal castle in Uppsala.

Set majestically on the highest hilltop, the castle overlooked the town barely a stone's cast away from the cathedral. Construction of the castle, begun by King Gustav Vasa in the 1540s, was still unfinished. Only two sides of the desired square had been completed, and the surrounding hillside was overgrown with weeds. On the inside, though, the castle was decorated with treasures including paintings, tapestries, statues, and almost anything else of value that Swedish armies could pack up in chests and carry back to the north.

Like many distinguished guests before him, Rudbeck marched up to the castle, climbed the stone steps, and entered the great hall. As the court looked on, the twenty-one-year-old demonstrated his medical discovery. Queen Christina was dazzled. She never had to tap her fan in impatience, or play distractedly with her spaniels. She just sat transfixed on her crimson velvet cushion with eyes aglow at the spectacle. The courtiers saw a new rising star, and the queen did too. By the end of the day she had offered Rudbeck a royal scholarship to continue his studies at Leiden University. He left the castle, his ears ringing with praise and his head spinning with anticipation.

SWEDEN WAS, at this time, one of the most powerful countries in the world. Despite its small population, thinly scattered throughout the kingdom, Sweden had burst upon the scene in 1630, the year of Rudbeck's birth, with some dazzling victories in the Thirty Years' War. King Gustavus Adolphus's army was praised as the best in the world, and his advanced, modernized bureaucracy was, as one observer put it, the envy of France. By the end of the war in 1648, and Rudbeck's eighteenth birthday, Sweden had emerged with France as the guarantor of Europe's peace.

Swedish territory then encircled the Baltic Sea and its sweet-smelling pine forests, its flat, marshy heaths, and its foggy pebble beaches. The blue and gold Swedish flag was raised in Finland, northern Germany, the modern Baltic states, and as far away as Cabo

Corso on the African Gold Coast. There was even a "New Sweden" confidently planted in America on the Delaware River, including today's Trenton and Philadelphia.

Rudbeck's country had never been more powerful or more influential. Exports boomed, and its merchants, at first mostly Dutch immigrants, dominated some of the most lucrative trades of the day. Sweden was Europe's unrivaled producer of copper and iron, and of the manufactured products that relied on these materials, such as cannon, cannonballs, and lightweight, quick-loading muskets. Lands in its Baltic dominion produced timber, hemp, flax, pitch, and tar, no small advantage in a warlike world just coming to appreciate the advantages of sea power. One Danish historian has compared the Baltic Sea in the seventeenth century to the Persian Gulf in the twentieth: though much of the region was undeveloped and remote, it was the source of scarce raw materials absolutely central to the functioning of the world at the time.

The capital of the kingdom, Stockholm, had grown rich controlling this trade, already boasting a stunning panorama of buildings, bridges, and water that would later earn it the name "Venice of the North." The docks were bustling, too, with men unloading crates into the warehouses along the seafront. Horses drawing carriages clip-clopped down the cobblestone lanes, passing the fine buildings, the noble estates, and the brick churches with copper spires. Down in the center of the capital, tucked away in the Old Town, stood the Stockholm Banco, preparing, in just a few years, to issue the world's first modern paper currency. All told, diligence and decadence went together in creating the period Swedish historians call the "Age of Greatness."

But the small wooden huts clustering in the shadows of the towering mansions were reminders of another side to Sweden's imperial age. For every laced-up, velvet-clad courtier enjoying Italian perfumes, there were many others who toiled under brutal conditions. As many as 90 percent of the population were peasants, squeezing out a tenuous existence on small homesteads, or bound under steep feudal obligations on large manors. Less fortunate still were the many victims of the recent wars. Armless veterans begged in the streets, and legions of orphans roamed in search of food. In desperation, many women became prostitutes, and some people joined the rogues hiding out in forests, preying upon the secluded roadways.

Olof Rudbeck had grown up in this environment of power and poverty. His home was Västerås, then one of the largest towns in the country, and visibly prospering from the "great quantities of copper and iron, digged [*sic*] out of the mines." At the very center stood the cathedral, a restored Gothic structure with a long, tapering spire rising high above its surroundings, and in fact, at that time, the tallest in Sweden. The town also had a castle and even its own curious "wizard" who once, it was said, "made wings and flew, but broke one of his legs."

Västerås also had Sweden's first senior high school, founded by Rudbeck's father, Johannes Rudbeckius, a former field chaplain who had risen to be one of King Gustavus Adolphus's favorite bishops. He was a man of extraordinary energy and presence, with a high forehead, narrow-set eyes, and a long, thin face that ended in a long white beard. Courageous and stubborn, he was not known for tolerating any nonsense. In the words of one observer, he would rather go to the stake than stand down from his principles.

Clashes between the strict father and the somewhat carefree son were bound to occur. Once, as a young boy, Rudbeck received new dress clothes. They were quite a sight, with cuffs on the arms and shiny new buttons in the front. He had never had clothes like this before, as all his previous garments fastened on the sides with hooks, and the sleeves were slashed rather abruptly. Rudbeck was so pleased that he put them on and paraded around in the courtyard, feeling, as he said, as handsome as the pope in Rome. He played on his toy horse, pretending to be a gallant Spanish cavalryman. His father, however, happened to be looking out the window from his study. He marched outside, pulled out his knife, and cut off all the buttons and cuffs. The boy was immediately sent inside "to sit on his bottom."

Since no vanity of any form was permitted in the household, Rudbeck was forced to wear his hair short and cropped around the ears in the seventeenth-century equivalent of a bowl cut. This not only was unfashionable but must have made his head seem unusually elongated. Some of the richer, aristocratic schoolboys took to teasing him with the nickname "Olle Bighead." This was a lasting memory, and he sought solace in biblical reminders about the transitory nature of riches.

The importance of biblical lessons was stressed early and often in Rudbeck's family. Not only by his father, who had mastered Greek, Latin, and Hebrew, some said, as well as his Swedish, but also by his mother, Malin Rudbeckius, born Magdalena Carlsdotter Hijsing. The daughter of a priest, she organized daily lessons for the family. She had read the Bible cover to cover at least seven times, and impressed many with her memory. Whenever anyone cited a passage, she could usually name its exact location, chapter and verse.

Malin Rudbeckius was actually the bishop's second wife; he had married her in 1620 after his first wife died. She was quite young, some twenty-two years younger than her husband, making Rudbeck's mother—eighteen at the time of the wedding—one of the youngest women in Swedish history to be the wife of a bishop. It is hard to believe she gave birth to eleven children in only twelve years. Rudbeck was the ninth in the family, and particularly close, it seems, to his mother. Cheerful and merry, with a good sense of humor, she was the "glittering sunshine" of Olof Rudbeck's childhood.

Some of Rudbeck's most pleasant memories of his youth probably involved the garden. The bishop was an avid horticulturist, enjoying his summer expeditions into the countryside hunting for wildflowers, and handling each delicate petal with an awe worthy of God's creation. Rudbeck's father planted the rosebushes and fruit trees at

Västerås high school, and created Sweden's first teaching garden. It was probably his father's passion that sparked Rudbeck's interest in the world of flowers.

Despite the many differences, there is no doubt that Rudbeck loved and respected his parents. Sadly, both passed away too soon, his father dying in 1646, and his mother following three years later. Rudbeck lost his first guardians, teachers, and champions. Neither parent lived to see their son's triumph, let alone the spectacular discoveries that lay ahead.

ORACLE OF THE NORTH

*Hide not your Talents they for use were made
What's a Sun-Dial in the Shade!*

—BENJAMIN FRANKLIN

IN THE AUTUMN of 1653, Rudbeck seemed destined for a brilliant career in medicine, and thanks to the queen's enthusiasm, he would have the chance to study at Leiden University in the Netherlands. This was the Holland of Rembrandt, the Dutch East Indies Company, and the period that historians call its golden age. At this time the Dutch were the world's foremost merchants, financiers, shippers, and seafarers, as well as its leading anatomists. As Lutheran theologians looked to Wittenberg and Calvinists to Geneva, Leiden was the uncontested center for modern anatomical training.

Once in the town of cobbled lanes and misty canals, Rudbeck allowed his imagination to roam freely. He studied anatomy under the leading authorities, Professors Johannes van Horne and Johannes Antonides van der Linden, admiring the university's relaxed atmosphere. Leiden's medical school was remarkably independent of the clergy, the theology department, and the state. What was unthinkable in Sweden regularly happened in Leiden. In the infamous anatomy theater, *human* bodies were slit open, cut up, and disemboweled before a packed audience.

Rudbeck was soaking up this atmosphere, eager to experience everything that the town had to offer. Even a stroll by the docks could prove instructive. He tended to act on impulse, and became quickly absorbed in new interests. Holland's long history of fighting to reclaim the land from the sea had given its people talents for constructing all sorts of technical devices, from waterworks to windmills. Feats of Dutch engineering, such as sluices, harbor cranes, and timber saws, thoroughly impressed the visiting Swede.

There was another place Rudbeck came to enjoy: Leiden's famous botanical garden, founded in 1587 and full of a bewildering variety of rare and exotic plants brought back from Dutch voyages to the East and West Indies. Rudbeck had never seen many of these flowers before. The tulip, for instance, was the reigning "monarch of flowers." Brought from the frontiers of the Ottoman Empire, its slender stocks exploded into flaming scarlet twirls streaked with the purest white— just one of the seemingly unlimited number of variations that delighted the senses.

In this splendid half-acre retreat, the sweet scents overpowered the stench of the canals, and Rudbeck could hardly contain his excitement. He was learning about new flowers, their ideal growing conditions, and their many uses everywhere from the kitchen to the apothecary. He could also hardly avoid thinking of his father, and how he had lovingly collected flowers for his small teaching garden at Västerås. How Rudbeck must have yearned to share his experience in Leiden among the many beautiful and curious new plants brought back from the other side of the world.

As his stay was winding down, Rudbeck's anatomical discoveries, and a dispute with an esteemed Danish professor who claimed to have discovered the lymphatic system first, had made his name famous throughout Europe. It seemed that everyone wanted a piece of the promising star, and offers of employment poured in from many places. He was offered the position of field surgeon with the Swedish army, and the prestigious post of city physician in Stockholm, at the heart of the empire. Also, a prominent Swedish count wanted to hire Rudbeck to be his personal engineer, while the Dutch tried to persuade him to stay in the Netherlands. Even the French ambassador approached Rudbeck with a tempting offer to serve the king of France. At only twenty-three years of age, the world beckoned for Olof Rudbeck. But he politely declined the kind offers. For now, he could think of nothing he would rather do than return to Sweden and cultivate a botanical garden of his own.

HAVING ARRANGED FOR some eight hundred new seeds and bulbs to be shipped back from the Netherlands, Rudbeck was ready for what he had come to regard as the "most sweet and innocent" of human pursuits. All he needed was a plot of land. And this brought him in touch with an old acquaintance, Mrs. Helena Gustafsdotter Lohrman.

Five years earlier, when Rudbeck first came to Uppsala, he had rented a room from Mrs. Lohrman, the wife of Uppsala's mayor, Thomas Lohrman. Not much is known about her other than that she was one of Rudbeck's early and most significant admirers. When Rudbeck's mother died in 1649, it was Mrs. Lohrman who generously came to his aid. Rudbeck's small family inheritance was divided among the many children, and his share was soon gone. Mrs. Lohrman made it possible for Rudbeck to stay in school. It is likely that in return he tutored the Lohrman children, including their precious daughter, Vendela.

Now that Rudbeck was back in town with his bags of seeds, Mrs. Lohrman offered him a small patch of land on the central Svartbäcksgatan for his garden. There Rudbeck went to work, preparing the beds, scattering the seeds, and, with characteristic vigor, waging war on the weeds. He was also waiting for his professorship, which Queen Christina had earlier offered him.

The problem was, however, that Queen Christina was no longer in a position to make good on her promise. Since Rudbeck's dissection at the castle, Queen Christina had stunned the world, this time even more than usual. She had converted to Catholicism, renounced the Swedish throne, and moved to Rome, where she allegedly rode into town dressed as an Amazon warrior.

With the queen's abdication went the generous patronage, the lively court, and, unfortunately for Rudbeck, the many influential courtiers who had known and admired his talents. And so Rudbeck worked and waited, already showing signs of his almost inexhaustible optimism. He passed the time tending to his plants and looking for new specimens for his ever-expanding garden, which he fondly called his "firstborn son."

Rudbeck's garden was laid out, like many gardens of the day, in a geometrical pattern, with classical Ionic columns adorning the outer wall. A central gate marked its entrance, and immediately ahead sprinkled the cool waters of a small fountain. Regular, straight lanes divided the garden into symmetrical, boxlike flower beds splashed with shades of amber yellow, bloodred, pure white, and soft orange.

Tradition has it that something else was blossoming in Rudbeck's fragrant garden. Rudbeck had known Mrs. Lohrman's daughter, Vendela, for quite a while now, though probably not all that well, as she was only eleven years old when they first met. But now, seven years later, Rudbeck saw a beautiful and refined lady. Mrs. Lohrman had taken up the habit of strolling in the garden, and to Rudbeck's delight, Vendela accompanied her mother more and more frequently. Perhaps it was here along the perfumed pathways, lined with roses, carnations, and lilies all blooming in their seasons that the two fell in love. With the help of Vendela and his garden, Rudbeck was conquering what could very well have been a long, lonely year of uncertainty.

In the late spring of 1655, Rudbeck was finally offered a position in the medical faculty at Uppsala University. It was only part time and

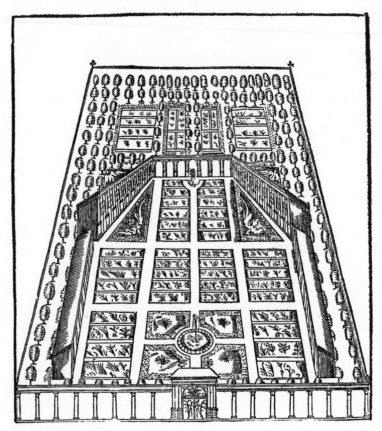

Rudbeck boasted that his botanical garden was the second largest in Europe, surpassed only by Louis XIV's gardens at Versailles.

adjunct, and much humbler than any of the offers he had received in the Netherlands, but he was glad nonetheless. Indeed, on the very day of his appointment, Midsummer Eve, Rudbeck married Vendela Lohrman.

Did Vendela know what she was getting herself into? Did she know that sharing her life with Rudbeck would mean sharing his passions? And that this would in turn mean sharing her house with her husband's stacked paper boxes of seeds, his collection of tobacco pipes, and his indoor gardening ventures, like the cinnamon tree on the ground floor? Did she realize that other rooms in their house would be cluttered with his lutes, paintings, axes, and homemade fireworks?

Almost one year after their wedding, the newlyweds had a terrible scare. Vendela was pregnant with their first child and started experiencing severe pains. Seventeenth-century medicine was, at the best of times, ill equipped to handle unexpected difficulties: primitive anesthetics, crude instruments, and myriad hygienic risks. Women and infants alike died far too often when troubles in childbirth got out of control. For the young couple, too, the situation was critical, and something had to be done.

Although an adjunct professor of medicine, Rudbeck would have had almost no contact with surgery. Nevertheless, he used the skills gained from his many dissections, and performed some sort of surgical maneuver that removed a dangerous obstruction in the birth canal. Older histories called it a Caesarean section, though modern studies have preferred to qualify the position considerably, showing that this was more likely a cutting away of swollen tissue that blocked the opening of the uterus. At any rate, Rudbeck's operation was a success. Both his wife and son survived, and his contemporaries marveled, ranking it a curiosity of the times. Letters came from France, Germany, and the Royal Society in London requesting further details of the procedure. Rudbeck, it seems, was neither eager to answer their specific questions nor keen to stop the escalating rumors of his medical achievements. Their son was aptly named Johannes Caesar Rudbeck.

At this time, too, authorities recognized the young professor's talents, and he rose like a rocket through the ranks of the university hierarchy. He was promoted to assistant professor, then full professor, and by 1661 he had been selected to be rector, the highest position at the university. Although expectations were certainly high, no one had any idea of the outburst of energy soon to be unleashed.

ABOUT TWELVE MILES outside of Paris, Louis XIV was busy turning his father's modest hunting lodge into a palace worthy of the "Sun King." Some thirty thousand workers labored around the clock to complete the complex of gardens, fountains, and ponds, and of course the enormous palace itself. A fusion of classical dignity and Baroque splendor, Versailles was the epicenter of a country greatly influencing culture on the Continent. What was later said about the Revolution was already applicable to this fashionable trendsetter: "When France caught a cold, Europe sneezed."

Scandinavia was certainly not immune to the rays of the Sun King and his court. Young dandies were everywhere opting for a more gilded look, complete with powdered wigs, lace scarves, and silk as colorful as peacocks. The cuffs ruffled more, and the French tricorne was placed on the head, or politely raised. Paint and perfume, gloves

and handkerchiefs, snuff boxes and walking sticks were added for good measure.

Whims of fashion changed all around him, but Olof Rudbeck kept to his old ways. He preferred a simple black coat, white collar, and knee-length breeches. This attire would have been the height of fashion around 1650, but, as with his long hair, which now flowed naturally onto his shoulders without benefit of a powdered wig, Rudbeck looked increasingly outdated and drew more and more attention for his old-fashioned manner.

He probably appeared a bit eccentric, though in a charming sort of way. His eyes gleamed with hints of mischievousness and flashed with his exuberant love of life. His face was somewhat elongated; his cheeks were rosy. Thin, butterfly-wing whiskers perched above his mouth. His voice was a deep baritone of phenomenal strength, and his laughter often filled the room with mirth.

Happily, Rudbeck had taken up his position as rector of Uppsala

Uppsala's skyline was characterized by the royal castle, the cathedral, and also, after the early 1660s, Rudbeck's anatomy theater.

University. Over the next few years, vitality and exuberance would permeate almost everything he touched. After his pioneering work with the lymphatic system, Rudbeck went on to build an impressive anatomy theater. He actively participated in its construction, from drawing the designs to hammering in the nails, and the building was praised for its architectural wonders. Not least of these was the way in which he managed the light so that it focused on the dissection table at the center, yet avoided casting shadows that would obscure the view from anywhere in the octagonal auditorium. For special occasions, Rudbeck brought out his collection of skeletons, mummies, and even specimens of human skin.

The anatomy theater was actually only one of the prominent landmarks that the city owed to Rudbeck's efforts. Another was a special institution designed to attract young Swedish aristocrats who might otherwise be tempted to study abroad. This was an elite academy that exercised the body as well as the mind. Built by Rudbeck in 1664–65, this Collegium Illustre had in only a couple of years enrolled fifty-five students who fenced, danced, and rode with skill and flair. Fluent in French, they worked zealously to perfect the gentlemanly arts. This program survived until the late nineteenth century, when the building was torn down and its prime real estate used to house the university administration.

Some contemporaries believed Rudbeck had been born under a lucky star. From the anatomy theater to the botanical garden to the elite exercise academy, visitors could not fail to see his legacy all around town. There was also an apothecary laboratory, a community house to provide free food and shelter to the poor, and a workshop that harnessed the town river to power several machines simultaneously. When his term as rector expired, a new position of curator was created, and Rudbeck was named one of its first officers (along with two others). The multitalented professor had indeed exerted a profound influence over his beloved town and university.

But all that was about to change. By the end of the 1660s, the

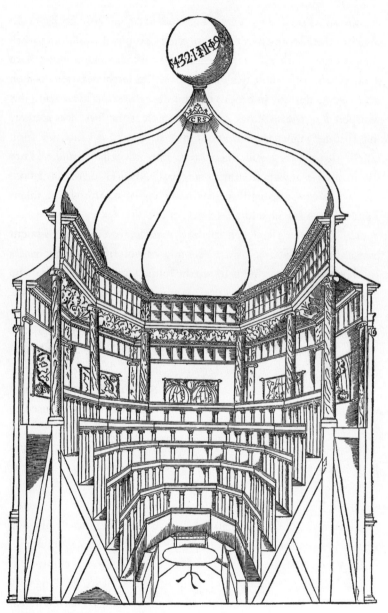

Rudbeck built the anatomy theater in the middle of Uppsala, just opposite the cathedral and atop the main university building.

economy had started to falter. The Swedish copper coin took a nose-dive in value, and income from university properties went into startling decline. This meant that salaries at the university were often delayed, and in some cases even unpaid. Professors started to look back in anger at the ambitious builder of the previous decades. They whispered in the shadows, grumbled in the corridors, and increasingly brought their discontent out into the open.

All these issues, still unresolved, were soon to explode. They would also be transferred onto a new battleground, where they would rage with even greater ferocity. In the midst of the chaos, Olaus Verelius, a colleague and an expert on the Vikings, came with a request: he wanted Rudbeck to draw a couple of maps of ancient Sweden to accompany his forthcoming edition of a Norse saga. As Rudbeck set out to help his friend, he found something that dramatically changed his life.

3

REMARKABLE
CORRESPONDENCES

Just amusing myself by indulging in fantastic dreams. Toys!
Yes, I suppose that's what it is—toys!

—FYODOR DOSTOYEVSKI, *CRIME AND PUNISHMENT*

T WAS THE *Hervararsaga* that Olaus Verelius brought to his
friend. Set in the dim and misty past, this was a fantastic
tale of a sword named Tyrfing. Hammered in the hidden
forges of two talented dwarves, this was the "keenest of all blades,"
never failing to render its wielder victorious while shining all the time
with the radiance of the sun. Tyrfing was something of a Norse
Excalibur, a magical sword fit for a Viking King Arthur. There was,
however, one important qualification: this sword carried a nasty
curse. Once drawn, it had to take a human life, and then return to its
scabbard still warm and red. Generation after generation suffered
from the bitter truth that this irresistible sword with the golden hilt
brought untold violence and misery.

In the late 1660s, many unreservedly ranked this *Hervararsaga*
as one of the oldest and most impressive texts illuminating Sweden's distant past. What a thrill it must have been to pore over this

treasured manuscript and prepare its first-ever publication. And to adorn it with the most up-to-date and valuable scholarly accessories, Verelius asked Olof Rudbeck to make a map of the many places mentioned in the saga.

This may seem like a strange favor to ask of a medical doctor. But Rudbeck had earned a reputation for producing high-quality maps. He excelled at sketching the mountains, hills, and rivers of the countryside, and then reducing them to a series of lines and dots on a flat surface. Measuring with a great concern for precision and calculating with a single-minded patience, cartography was virtually an extension of Rudbeck's skill in technical areas. His curiosity and his own love for discovery, moreover, helped him understand the value of a good, accurate map. Many officials requested Olof Rudbeck's services, including no less than Carl Gustaf Wrangel, one of Sweden's most feared generals during the Thirty Years' War.

But this time, when Rudbeck accepted the offer, no one could have known what this curious little manuscript would mean for Uppsala's distinguished professor.

"It was like a dream," he later recalled. Behind the story of the cursed sword, the deadly runic magic, and the wild, howling berserks whipped into a furious rage, Olof Rudbeck saw many strange parallels between the Norse world and what he remembered from classical Greek traditions. All through the manuscript, in fact, were many "remarkable correspondences." Kings, queens, customs, and places— far too many features in this late Viking saga struck with a peculiar resonance.

What exactly it was that first captured Rudbeck's attention and launched him on what would be a lifelong quest may never be known. His earliest notes on the search do not survive, and the first draft of his work was later destroyed. The list of possibilities is extensive. For instance, as Rudbeck combed the saga looking for material for his map, he would have encountered some extraordinary information. The very first line in the manuscript noted a beautiful kingdom that once flourished in the north of Sweden, called Glasisvellir. This may not at first sound even remotely classical, but when translated from the Old Norse *glaes,* "amber," and *vellir,* "rolling landscape," it would be something altogether different.

The Glasisvellir were the "Glittering Plains"—a name that would have evoked the brilliant and shining Elysian Fields of classical mythology. According to the oldest of the ancient Greek accounts, the Elysian Fields were the great plains at the end of the world where the mild, cooling breezes blew, and its inhabitants lived what the ancient poet Homer called "a dream of ease." Now, too, in this old manuscript of the *Hervararsaga,* there were provocative images of a place in the far north that seemed to have more in common with those joyous fields than just their name.

As in the classical Elysian Fields, the fortunate residents of the Norse Glittering Plains enjoyed a happy existence, living to a great age and effectively banishing sickness from the realm. They were also, like their classical depictions, keen sportsmen who enjoyed tossing a goatskin back and forth, that is, when they were not reveling in the dances, songs, and feasts along the soft meadows and meandering riverbanks. Indeed, the Norse wrestled on the Glittering Plains, just as the classical warriors fought for fun in the Elysian Fields.

Located beyond Gandvik, literally "the Bay of Sorcery," the Glittering Plains flourished in a mythical landscape that included yet other features that sounded familiar from classical mythology. There were the violent neighbors of Jotunheim, "the land of giants," who recalled the Greek stories of the large, fierce creatures that waged war on Zeus and the Olympian gods. In Norse mythology, as Rudbeck would soon learn if he did not know already, the giants also fought relentlessly with Odin and the Aesir gods. Further, the king of the Glittering Plains was introduced in an evocative way. "A mighty man and wise," King Gudmund held out against the forces of chaos and barbarism, ruling over a kingdom whose inhabitants reached such an advanced age that outsiders believed that "in his realm must lie the

Land of the Undying, the region where sickness and old age depart from every man who enters it, and where no one can die."

Wisdom, strength, longevity—all these factors made the northerners in the Glittering Plains seem like a blessed people, and their home a fabled "Land of the Undying." Could this golden age kingdom really have existed, and could it have possibly been related to the Elysian Fields of classical mythology? For that matter, could this utopian civilization of the far north have had anything to do with the land of the Hyperboreans, another blessed people of classical mythology who were said, as their name suggests, to live somewhere "beyond the north wind"?

Whatever it was that first captured Rudbeck's attention, it virtually sounded a call to action. Ideas swirled in his head, and "for some peace of mind," he said, he had to "put pen to paper."

ONE DAY RUDBECK showed his notes to his friend Verelius, the eccentric but undisputed authority on Scandinavian runes and Norse sagas. Recently appointed to a brand-new post as Sweden's first and for a long time its only "Professor of the Antiquities of the Fatherland," Verelius was charged with the responsibility of seeking out old manuscripts, gathering them together, and promoting anything "that can serve to enlighten the deeds of the ancient past." In this respect, he had found his scholarly niche. He lectured widely on Swedish history—its runes, its Viking sagas, and many other aspects of the pagan past. Despite the fiery patriotism that heated up his accounts, Verelius's lectures have been described as some of the most pioneering and erudite given at Uppsala University in his time. Unfortunately, though, as he lamented, this was usually only to the benefit of three or perhaps four students who made it to the early-morning lecture in the otherwise empty hall.

Rudbeck's notes were hastily written, as he put it himself, "not polished, or even once read all the way through." But Verelius was greatly pleased, and he praised Rudbeck's "many excellent conclusions and exemplary deductions." In a letter written much later, shortly after Christmas 1673, Verelius described his own reaction to Rudbeck's work. He had been particularly impressed with the rich proposals for bringing order to the chaos of Swedish history. These outlines could in fact build a foundation for a true chronology of ancient Sweden, something he admitted "up until now we have never hoped to establish with any certainty." Rudbeck, he added, "has taken it much further than I had ever expected."

As he also cheerfully noted, Rudbeck had succeeded in "correcting" many errors that often prevailed in the image of the Swedes abroad. This was a reference to the medieval Danish historian Saxo Grammaticus, whose colorful early-thirteenth-century account of the far north showcased the heroics of Sweden's archenemy, the Danes (and by the way, Saxo's history includes our oldest account of the misfortunes of Prince Amled, elaborated centuries later in Shakespeare's tragedy *Hamlet, Prince of Denmark*). Composed in a lofty Latin that even drew praise from no less a stylist than Erasmus of Rotterdam, Saxo's work dismissed many parts of Swedish history with the haughty disdain of a man at the center of a powerful Danish kingdom looking down at the backward periphery.

To Verelius's mind, the implications of Rudbeck's work were vast: if he was correct, he would have uncovered some major problems in Saxo's influential history. The Swedes could finally expose some errors enshrined in the standard histories, sickening "lies" that had long offended Swedish sensibilities.

Pleased with the prospects of such a work, Verelius asked Rudbeck to speak with another authority, Professor Johannes (Johan) Loccenius. This was a stern, scholarly man, a former Royal Historiographer and a renowned expert in Swedish antiquities. Called over from Germany in the middle of the century, Loccenius had emerged as one of Uppsala's prized scholars. He lectured regularly on ancient authorities such as Livy, Tacitus, and Cicero, and he seemed to be a man who, in modern parlance, "lived completely for science." After Loccenius took up the history of his new homeland with a burning passion, his ambitious histories earned him praise for producing Sweden's "first truly critical work." A tireless scholar who trudged through the material slowly and cautiously, building his way to reasonable conclusions, Loccenius had earned his reputation as one of the greatest living experts on ancient Scandinavia.

When this scholar first saw Rudbeck's notes, he was also visibly delighted. The seventy-year-old Loccenius burst into tears of joy and expressed his wonder: "How many times have I and other historians read [these texts] and never realized that they referred to Sweden." As he put it, Rudbeck was working on an unparalleled project; in fact, it was unlike anything Sweden had ever seen before.

RICH IN IMPLICATIONS, Rudbeck's "remarkable correspondences" were especially thrilling in the vibrant atmosphere of the late seventeenth century. Like its rival, Denmark, Sweden was then in the throes of a "Norse renaissance." Patriotic scholars working in the universities of Copenhagen and Uppsala were experiencing an enthusiastic, somewhat romantic revival of interest in the old Vikings. Drinking horns, magical spells written in strange runic scripts, and dragon-headed prows adorning oak longships, the fact and fantasy of the Viking Age (roughly A.D. 800–1050), had long been sealed off into a virtually lost world.

A number of Scandinavian antiquarians in the sixteenth and seventeenth centuries, including Arngrimur Jónsson, Christiern Pedersen, and Brynjólfur Sveinsson, began rediscovering this Norse heritage. Forgotten and unheralded though they are today, it is largely through their efforts that so much of our material about the Viking world has survived. They hunted down the old manuscripts in the original language wherever they might be found, gathered them together into collections, and sought to add these to the accumulated treasury of history. Given the merits of the cherished rediscovered sagas, these Scandinavian antiquarians "brooded over them like the dragon on his gold."

Such enthusiasm for all things Norse flourished in the aftermath of the classical Renaissance, the dramatic rebirth of interest in ancient Rome and Greece that began centuries before in the Italian city-states. After spreading across the Alps, this revival had splintered into a cluster of movements that, for better or worse, came for a long time to shape the ways historians viewed the past. One thing the many Renaissance thinkers had in common, though, was a firm belief in the great importance of antiquity. Some went so far as to celebrate the classical past as the source of almost all our knowledge.

But as northern thinkers delved deeper into the Greek and Latin texts, they came across curious references to their own past. The plains, forests, and wastelands at the edge of the classical world swarmed with hordes of northern tribes—Celts, Cimbrians, Sarmatians, and countless others. They were not always well known, and were often subject to glorification, vilification, mystification, or just plain error. Yet all these peoples, however represented and interpreted, were, to the classical mind, simply barbarians.

The word *barbarian* did not, of course, have a pleasant ring, deriving originally from the observation that the nonclassical outsiders spoke a different language—one that sounded to ancient Greeks like incomprehensible gibberish, which they mimicked as "bar-bar-bar." The name stuck, expanding to a general term of scorn. The barbarian world seemed primitive and insignificant next to the monumental achievements of the Greco-Roman civilization, with its baths, aqueducts, amphitheaters, and thriving cities, not to mention its rich cultural legacy.

Of all the outlandish barbarians mentioned in the texts, Swedish humanists in the sixteenth and seventeenth centuries came to focus on one tribe in particular: the ancient Goths. Long a terror on the frontiers of the Roman Empire, the Goths had swept south through the Balkans and humiliated the legions that powered the relentless Roman fighting machine. If that were not shocking enough, the Goths had stormed the gates of Rome in A.D. 410 and sacked the Eternal City itself. The Romans, who had conquered a vast empire reaching from the Scottish moors to the Sahara Desert, were now themselves forced to pay ransom. Trying their best to intimidate the rough invaders at their gates, Roman officials warned of a fierce resistance from one million imperial citizens. Unfazed, the Gothic king Alaric replied, "The thicker the hay, the more easily it is mowed."

Reading about this martial people, Swedish humanists believed that the Goths had come originally from somewhere in central or southern Sweden. Most prominent among the new champions of the Gothic past were two brothers, Johannes and Olaus Magnus, the last Catholic archbishops in the country. In their wide-ranging works, both had tapped into a long and deep medieval tradition that linked the Goths to the north.

But even if the vision of a heroic Gothic past extended back for centuries, it would be the Protestant Reformation that truly rekindled the Gothic fire. Sweden had regained its independence from Denmark in 1523, and had broken away from the Catholic Church in the 1530s. Both changes had fueled the great burst of enthusiasm about the Goths, whom they claimed as their own ancestors. The humanists started also to shake off the Greco-Roman prejudice, revived along with the classical texts themselves. They celebrated other, more redeeming qualities in the seemingly uncouth and barbaric illiterates—qualities such as valor, honesty, and simplicity. The large tomes of the Magnus brothers and their followers marked the beginning of a gradual yet monumental shift from shame to a renewed pride in their wild, untamed ancestors who, they claimed, had overthrown the Roman Empire.

And as many northern countries broke away from the Catholic Church in the sixteenth century, it seemed that Rome had once again been stormed. The Goths, this time wearing the modern guise of sober, black-clad Protestants, had punished the empire a second time for its unbridled decadence. And after 1630, history again seemed to repeat itself. During the Thirty Years' War, King Gustavus Adolphus's Swedes were modern Goths carrying the Protestant banner, indeed perhaps saving the Protestant cause from what then looked like certain destruction at the hands of the determined Holy Roman Empire of the Hapsburgs.

The Swedish king played the part well, too. With his broad shoulders, his rotund figure, his golden beard groomed to a point, the musket ball still lodged deep in his neck, Gustavus Adolphus looked and acted like a modern Goth. At the royal coronation, he had literally dressed up as the Gothic king Berik. He gave speeches challenging the Swedes to uphold the old Gothic virtues, admonishing the noblemen, for instance, "to bring renewed luster to the Gothic fame of their forefathers." His march from victory to victory indeed made Europe think it was seeing the rejuvenation of the barbarians. Sweden's sudden rise to great power had made possible—and even demanded—a greater, more dramatic past.

INTO THIS GLORIFIED vision of history were swept the ornately copied pieces of parchment found in hamlets of Iceland and Norway. Exciting tales of tall, fierce Vikings launching many adventurous raids seemed to fit quite seamlessly into this larger Gothic framework of Swedish history. Many of the original manuscripts would in fact end up in Uppsala, through purchases, gifts, and other, more sordid means. In 1658, for instance, the Swedish army looted Danish libraries and estates, carrying off many priceless manuscripts, in a way strangely reminiscent of the old Vikings that they would soon be celebrating.

The saga that would start our saga, however, did not come by conquest or piracy. The manuscript of the *Hervararsaga* was carried over by a young, talented Icelandic student named Jonas Rugman, or, as Rudbeck affectionately called him, "Icelandic Jonas." Rugman had come to Uppsala by accident. Leaving his native Iceland, he was planning to continue his studies at Copenhagen University. But a terrible storm blew his ship off course, forcing the crew to seek shelter in the Swedish west coast harbor of Gothenburg. Given the tense state of affairs between Denmark and Sweden and the fact that hostilities had once again flared up into open conflict, the Danish crew of the ship found themselves taken captive. Rugman was now unable to make his way to Copenhagen. Instead he decided to try his fortunes in this new country, and eventually ended up at Uppsala, where he started to work with Olaus Verelius.

A native speaker of Icelandic, the closest of all Scandinavian languages to Old Norse, Rugman was a "gift sent from heaven" for Verelius and the circle of Viking enthusiasts at Uppsala. Besides invaluable knowledge of the old language and its culture, Rugman had something else in his possession: a chest full of old Icelandic manuscripts! Most of these had never been seen before anywhere outside the small villages and homesteads of Iceland.

Icelandic Jonas's treasure chest of sagas was indeed an invaluable trove of material about a still undetermined ancient past, and Verelius was one of the first in the world to lay eyes again on these old stories. Among these was a copy of *Rolf and Gautrek's Saga,* a beautiful tale loosely focused on an old Swedish king named Gautrek. After losing his wife, the king suffers a tremendous grief, finding his only solace in sitting on her burial mound and flying his favorite hawk. There was also the rollicking *Herraud and Bose's Saga,* which deals with the long friendship between an odd pair: Herraud, the son of a Swedish king, and Bose, a tough peasant. Many other sagas, too, were in Rugman's case, though he had left a handful behind, pawned in a tailor's shop to cover the costs of his expensive taste.

Grateful for the privilege of seeing these sagas, Verelius paid for the food, housing, and expenses of Jonas Rugman for the first year and a half of the young man's stay in Uppsala. This was perhaps only fair, given the incalculable benefit the impoverished student had provided. Brand-new stories were just waiting to be read, translated, and culled for original insights into Scandinavia's heritage. They were full of figures only dimly perceived before, if known at all. Rugman's sagas made it painfully obvious how little the Swedish past was really understood.

As RUDBECK LOOKED through the manuscript of the *Hervararsaga* closely and drew his map of Sweden, a spectacular new world was indeed opening before his eyes. The *Hervararsaga* offered a fresh account of the distant past of Europe's newest great power, and its tantalizing suggestions would send Rudbeck to the heights of enthusiasm. Yet as breathtaking as the vistas were, it was not simply a matter of chasing down books and following leads.

This is because Rudbeck was already committed to an ambitious program of teaching at the university. Besides lecturing on anatomy and botany, Rudbeck would take students on strolls in his garden, emphasizing the importance of firsthand knowledge of the properties of plants. He had also pledged to give informal instruction in other technical subjects, including architecture and shipbuilding, just two of the many classes he taught at his factory down by the river. Some of the kingdom's most prominent future technicians and engineers would indeed be trained by Rudbeck. His absolute favorite course, however, was pyrotechnics; he loved to send up his own homemade fireworks to light up the Uppsala night sky.

Perhaps an even more serious challenge than his teaching commitments, though, was the array of other projects fighting for his attention. Since Rudbeck had built the anatomy theater, for instance, he was expected to actually use it. Some professors were already heard mumbling about this great expense, complaining that Rudbeck, in characteristic fashion, had built the theater way out of proportion to what was actually needed. At a time when the number of students in the medical school was at best ninety and at worst only three, Rudbeck had built a theater of approximately two hundred seats.

The academy could of course fill this capacity by opening its doors and selling admission tickets to public dissections, as did on occasion happen, but some had already started to notice the glaring lack of dissections taking place there. In fact, no more than two or three dissections were ever held under Rudbeck's leadership in that expensive theater.

His botanical garden was another concern, though for a slightly different reason. It required regular care and constant vigilance, planting, watering, and cultivating, as well as maintaining the small buildings Rudbeck had constructed on its site. Given the expense, this scientific luxury was often dangerously close to being axed from the university budget. Many professors did in fact want to close it, and Rudbeck had to defend it many times. The common professors did not value this particular garden, Rudbeck once sarcastically explained, because it did not give them any delicious "cabbage, carrots, or turnips."

Besides that, Rudbeck was trying to keep another one of his typically ambitious projects up and running: the waterworks system. With one man, one horse, one pump, and an elaborate network of underground pipes, Rudbeck had devised a rather ingenious scheme to bring water from the river to many places around town. For the time it ran during the 1660s and early 1670s, many people in Uppsala enjoyed having water carried right to their doorsteps. Beneficiaries included the royal castle, the bishop's estate, and, according to Rudbeck's design, even the house of Olaus Verelius. The waterworks also served his botanical garden and even the Community House, so that even the most underprivileged in the university town, quite radically, shared the luxury of fresh water with Sweden's royalty and their guests at the castle.

The theater, the garden, the waterworks, the Community House—
so many projects, so many interests, so many considerations for a
man of Rudbeck's passions. A great deal indeed depended on the investment of Rudbeck's time and energy. Additionally, as a high-
ranking official at Uppsala University, he was obliged to attend
countless meetings in the council chamber. And now, as old stories
from Norse manuscripts caught his fancy, the dilemmas of being a
Renaissance man were all too clear.

4

A CARTESIAN WITCH HUNT

I have a theory that scientists and philosophers are sublimated romanticists who channel their passions in another direction.

—CHARLIE CHAPLIN, *MY AUTOBIOGRAPHY*

FTER MAKING ITS way through several continental centers of learning, a dreaded outbreak started to appear in Uppsala in the 1660s. The cause of concern was a new "suspect philosophy" known as Cartesianism—a highly controversial school of thought that led to some of the fiercest clashes that ever raged in the turbulent academic world of the "scientific revolution."

Drawing its name from the Latin form of René Descartes' name, Renatus Cartesius, the Cartesian doctrine threatened to upset many cherished beliefs. Fundamentally this was a deterministic system that envisioned the universe as a machine. In this pure world of matter and motion, animals were soulless and unthinking automata. Human beings worked like machines as well, statues equipped with the power of reason. Like other types of matter, humans, animals, and all forms of life were whirling about in motion in a larger universe which was conceived of as a giant vortex, and which in turn consisted of an infinite number of other vortices. From the whirls of the tiniest particles to the largest planetary sweeps, Descartes had brought the heavens and earth together under the same single set of laws, with no center, no limits, and, many said, no place for God.

As if that were not troubling enough, such radical notions took place in the context of Descartes' exciting new method, which excelled in overturning traditions. His entire philosophical edifice was built on what he called a "method of doubt." After abandoning all previous knowledge, dismissing it as empty, "vain and useless," and then casting it "wholly away," the philosopher put his method to use challenging everything else — that is, until he found something that simply could not be doubted. The result was one of the famous lines in philosophy: "I think, therefore I am" (and at the same time, one of the most punned upon: from the college T-shirt "I drink, therefore I am," to the skeptic's quip about modern gullibility, "I am, therefore I think").

But Descartes' concept was the kernel of his larger system, providing an unassailable foundation from which he would construct his broad vision of the world. At its heart, Cartesianism was a rational, deterministic philosophy that built on this method of doubt, emphasizing the strict necessity of proof, and proceeding through the investigation of cause and effect to reach "clear and distinct" propositions. Not surprisingly, this methodical approach appealed greatly to natural philosophers, who were inclined to logical and mathematical thinking.

No surprise, either, that this doctrine excited emotions in one of the most passionate centuries in modern history. Despite fierce denials by Cartesians, many theologians suspected that Cartesian thought ultimately challenged sacred scripture and the very basis of religious faith. When the Cartesian natural philosophers responded that they could use reason "to prove God," this also seemed repulsive, and secretly subversive.

Watching this radical vision of a machine-universe, best understood by using a method of doubt and apparently leading only to cryptic creeds, the Uppsala theology department had good reason to be alarmed. At stake, too, was its long-established authority at the university, where it had enjoyed a frankly privileged position. The department had long exerted a great influence over everything from selecting staff to examining materials for publication to teaching the theology classes that were mandatory for all degree candidates.

In many ways the Cartesian philosopher was a real threat to this established order—and the battle over this heretical metaphysics was waged as if it were a life-and-death struggle.

WITH THE HIGHLY esteemed theologian Lars Stigzelius leading the charge, the theologians went after individuals who were suspected of harboring Cartesian sympathies. Well trained in logical discourse himself, Stigzelius was teaching Aristotelian logic at the university when Olof Rudbeck was a boy playing the gallant Spanish knight on his hobbyhorse. Stigzelius began by complaining of the *imbecillitas animi,* or feebleness of mind, that had recently struck the academy.

The problem emanated, the theologians said, from the medical faculty, particularly some of the young professors, who were almost certainly the first Swedes to import Cartesian thought. Many Uppsala doctors had studied at Leiden University, a hotbed for the dangerous philosophy. The leading medical authorities, Olof Rudbeck and Petrus Hoffvenius, had both studied there, and they were now accused of being the first Cartesians in Sweden, that is, after René Descartes himself.

One of the first occasions for this inevitable showdown, and the incident that first brought Rudbeck into the proceedings, came quite early. The jovial "Don Juan of doctors," and good friend to Rudbeck, Petrus Hoffvenius issued a dissertation in the spring of 1665 with a blatantly Cartesian veneer. The theologians rallied, and requested that the troublesome medical doctor receive a scolding.

Claiming that he could not bear the arrogance of Hoffvenius's accusers, Olof Rudbeck came to the medical professor's defense. It was a peculiar situation, he said, to see scholars so vehemently opposed to

Hoffvenius's treatise when in fact very few of them had ever read the work, or would even have understood it had they tried. "They had not even looked at the index of topics on the title page," Rudbeck observed.

Disturbed at the turn events were taking in this attack on Hoffvenius, and the implications for the university at large, Rudbeck could not restrain himself. He blurted out, "If this is the way a faculty or a professor will be treated, no honest man will ever be able to write anything for the public good," then continued, "I recognize no one's right to censure my work before he shows himself to be more skilled in those matters than I am, and as long as I am recognized by both the King and scholars abroad as knowing something in physics, I will not tolerate a professor or faculty to censor my work."

Inside these strong words was a thinly veiled pledge of resistance against anyone who would try to bully Uppsala's playful genius.

Adding a coda that made him sound like a Swedish Galileo, Rudbeck affirmed in no uncertain terms that the business of doctors was to cure not the soul but the body: *Non curare animam, sed corpus.* Rudbeck was, as usual, speaking his mind, clamoring for greater independence for science in Sweden's oldest university.

Hoffvenius and Rudbeck simply would not back down, nor would the theologians, and the whole affair was about to blow up. As Hoffvenius continued to complain that the theologians acted with a *libido dominandi,* "a passion for dominating," Rudbeck was even more provocative: "If a faculty member shall be allowed to censor another one, then it would be best for the academy to hire little boys as professors." That way, they could make sure they would hire the best sort of people to perform the childish tasks of censorship, as well as those most suited to laboring in a university subjected to an iron grip.

"I would rather advise Hoffvenius," Rudbeck said, "to tear up the disputation in pieces, or burn it completely and never write anything at all, than allow it to be censored word for word." Yet however well Rudbeck made his point, and however much he took up the struggle, he was the only one to speak publicly in Hoffvenius's defense, and so this first battle of the Cartesian affair must be seen as a defeat for the doctors. Hoffvenius's work was not allowed to be published, and he had to promise, on pain of penalty, not to teach Cartesian thought again at the university. As for Rudbeck, many professors would not forget his outburst or, for that matter, what he did next.

While the embittered Hoffvenius tried to resign from his position, Olof Rudbeck decided to have some fun at his enemies' expense. He wrote a short work titled *De principiis rerum naturalium* (*On the Principles of Natural Things*). Behind this impressive scholarly sounding title, Rudbeck penned a hilarious parody of his enemies' view of the physical world. He coyly pretended to see the light in the darkness of his soul, merrily poking fun at his opponents' cherished Aristotelian principles of nature while all the time staying carefully within the prescribed orthodox framework. Some laughed at the humor and others were silently amused, but a great number were offended or even outraged at this jest.

Stigzelius and the theology faculty decided not to let this "obnoxious prank" pass. This time, though, they did not choose the strategy of beginning the usual official proceedings against what one called "such a formidable opponent." For Rudbeck was indeed outspoken, dreadfully stubborn, and quite unpredictable in his antics. Their strategy was instead to go behind his back in a rather calculated way, and take their complaint straight to the highest echelons of Uppsala University.

AS THE THEOLOGIANS sought to silence Olof Rudbeck, the academic atmosphere was threatening to take another turn for the worse. A certain fiery-tempered professor just recently hired at the university, Professor of Law Håkan Fegraeus, was very angry with Rudbeck. Among other things, he had never gotten over the fact that

Rudbeck had forcefully though unsuccessfully supported his own friend Carl Lundius as a rival candidate for Fegraeus's professorship.

So, when the university's financial difficulties became severe in late 1667, and the economic crunch meant that he had not received even a small part of his promised salary, Fegraeus was quick to blame Rudbeck for his plight. A few months later, during the beginning of the winter term of 1668, word reached Rudbeck that this desperate professor was now walking the streets of Uppsala carrying a pistol in his pocket. He displayed it openly and made no secret of his intentions.

Now, Rudbeck had a vivid imagination, but such threats of violence were certainly not to be dismissed as idle talk or early warning signs of delusional paranoia, as some have claimed. One notorious incident the year before had shown how easily tensions at the university could erupt into an outbreak of violence: frustrated students donned masks and went on a rampage of destruction, vandalizing much property, including the houses of some professors. Rudbeck's brother Petrus was one victim; his front gate was broken off the hinges and tossed into the icy waters of the river Fyris.

More-daring students even stormed the royal palace, leading to a shooting and the serious injury of a couple of guards stationed there. The Swedish government dispatched a small troop of military forces, comprising one lieutenant and thirty-six mercenaries, to restore order and maintain the peace. Many students were expelled from the university, some were sent to the academy prison, and four even received the death penalty. A few months later, though, the government fortunately commuted their sentences; the hooligans were instead expelled from the university and sent on a three-year exile from the Swedish kingdom.

By the spring of 1668, Rudbeck felt it necessary to tell the chancellor of Uppsala University, Magnus Gabriel de la Gardie, about this threat to his life. Horrified at the news, the chancellor acted immediately. He called for an investigation, and many meetings in the university council tried to sort through the layers of charges and countercharges. In the end, Professor Fegraeus was forced to apologize, and a few years later he would be encouraged to take another position elsewhere. A real messy situation, this was also a fair indicator of the high levels of tension prevailing at the time.

Feeling more comfort with the stalker chastened and the danger apparently subsiding, Rudbeck had also been tipped off that the theologians intended to complain to the chancellor. His brother Petrus had heard the rumors from one of his colleagues in the theology department and, realizing the seriousness of the situation, warned Rudbeck, giving him the opportunity to address the matter first.

In a letter to the chancellor of the university in early September 1668, Rudbeck affirmed that he had neither directly nor indirectly, publicly nor privately, proclaimed anything whatsoever that would conflict with "religion, good morals, or the common good." Nowhere did he admit Cartesian sympathies or any wrongdoing, focusing instead on his efforts to avoid "shady transactions." Very carefully he drew a distinction: he did not agree with the Cartesians when it came to religious matters. As for the theologians' accusations, Rudbeck asked to hear their specific allegations. "If they think I am guilty, then let them charge me, so I can defend myself."

This proved a good defense, and things went reasonably well for Rudbeck. In addition to his self-proclaimed innocence and his well-argued case, there was another, probably more influential factor in Rudbeck's escape. The theology professor Lars Stigzelius saw how things were going and avoided pushing the matter too far. He decided not to press formal charges, surely realizing that such an appeal to higher authority would set a dangerous precedent that might end with the theologians losing the very control of the university that they were fighting so hard to maintain. Deferring judgment to government officials, or even to outside committees of priests, would hardly be a desired outcome to the current situation. Wisely, he would choose caution and moderation.

Rudbeck had emerged from the Cartesian controversy relatively untouched. By no means, however, would this be the last time he would face opposition. As for his enemies in the theology department, this affair only seemed to strengthen their resolve.

ANGER, RIVAL AMBITIONS, and not a little jealousy at Rudbeck's easy talents added to the simmering resentments, and continued to keep the university split apart. In late 1668 the old opponents raised the stakes, and blamed Rudbeck for mismanaging the university.

His work with the Community House came particularly under fire. Located right in the heart of Uppsala, in the basement of the Gustavianum, the main university building, this was an experimental institution that provided free food and housing for students who otherwise would not have had the opportunity to attend the university.

Forty places were reserved solely for the poor, particularly orphans and children of widows, while another twenty places were given on the basis of academic merit or musical talent. Rudbeck had not been its original founder, as the institution had first started operating in 1594. But after the Community House had fallen on hard times and had been completely abandoned by the 1630s, it was Olof Rudbeck who had been the foremost champion of restarting it. Given his forceful and outspoken support, Rudbeck would also be the person whose fate was most closely linked to its fortunes.

Rudbeck not only succeeded in convincing Uppsala to reopen this Community House in the early 1660s, but typically he decided to improve on the model as well. He opted for expansion, increasing the number of students who would receive free food and housing, and then even extending the number of days of this provision all the way to fifty weeks a year! During the prosperous years, all costs for every student were waived, so as not to cause undue pain for the very poor who could not pay the minimal fee required by the regulations of the original Community House.

Understandably, given its ambitious aims and Rudbeck's efforts to take them even further, this institution often ran at a loss. In many cases it was a *great* loss—much greater than anyone had expected. When criticized, Rudbeck tried to explain this away as a result of inadequate original estimates, in addition to unforeseen factors that were beyond anyone's control. The war that broke out between the Dutch and the English in the early 1660s had, for instance, significantly driven up the price of food, especially staples like salt and fish. Others believed the whole thing was a miserable fiasco. Sensing the general will in the chamber, Rudbeck felt that " 'the powers that be' [were] once again trying to take everything from us."

Knowledgeable insiders were indeed predicting that the Community House would soon suffer a premature death. Besides its economic woes, which were at the center of the debate, Professor Stigzelius attacked it for failing to attract any good students, and bringing instead only a "group of the unlearned." Rudbeck strongly objected to such fears of flooding the university with illiterates, and countered with a passionate defense that touted the merits of the program. Successes of the Community House, he was pleased to say, were considerable. No less than twenty-one orphans, eight sons of tradesmen, and, remarkably, even seven children of peasants had been able to obtain degrees in this way from the university.

Yet the dreadful economic circumstances persisted, and forced the council to address its future. Rudbeck argued strongly in favor of sustaining the Community House, though by now he was championing a lost cause. Only two other professors joined him, one of them being Olaus Verelius. The Community House was slated to be abolished, gradually reduced in its services until it disappeared completely in 1676.

Such was the story of this odd early experiment with social welfare, well over one hundred years before utopian communities would spring up in Britain, the United States, and elsewhere. It is interesting to note, however, that about 150 years before Marx and Engels

started contemplating the plight of the poor and persuading some
people to call themselves communists, there was already a Swedish
Communitist receiving free food and housing in Uppsala.

Meanwhile, unfortunately for Rudbeck, the university's income
from its properties continued to shrink, falling to about half its
bloated early 1660s value. This unpleasant experience gave rise to
many grueling decision-making dilemmas, made more taxing as the
university had no emergency reserve funds. Many buildings were in
need of repair, and stayed that way. Professor Claes Arrhenius, for
one, was complaining about how the faculty and students were forced
to suffer in this dusty chaos and, worse still, "destroy their clothes."

With a sense of impending doom, the university urgently called
for the creation of a special committee of eight professors to investigate the overall situation at Uppsala University. Arrhenius, a young,
ambitious historian, was one professor who scrambled to join this
committee.

When he was not appointed, he complained angrily in the council
meeting that he had been "passed over as usual." Although Rudbeck
had nothing to do with the election of members, Arrhenius's stinging
remark was, among other things, a reference to Rudbeck's style of
leadership: his cavalier tendency to cut straight through the bureau-
cratic red tape and bypass the cumbersome official procedures so
highly regarded by Arrhenius. At this point Rudbeck could hardly
control his fury. He confronted Arrhenius, and demanded to know
when, exactly, he had been passed over.

What remaining rules of procedure that were still being respected
gave way to a shouting match—a vigorous quarrel that lasted until
the chorus of voices was drowned out by Rudbeck's determined baritone forcing his question again to Arrhenius. No answer. Relentless
as ever, Rudbeck asked the question three or four more times. Finally,
he burst out, "I hear once again such nonsense that you have been ig-
nored, and when I ask you how, you will not answer me. I shall sing
you a different tune. . . . I have been to Stockholm two times without

asking a single penny. You went one time to Ekholm [a village outside Uppsala] and took ten *daler* compensation."

This was undoubtedly true, as Rudbeck had made many trips on behalf of the university and had never asked for any compensation, while others seemed to take great efforts to note every possible expenditure. Later, though, Arrhenius would write a long, fawning letter going into ridiculous detail to exonerate himself from Rudbeck's accusation. He would also explain his silence at that moment in the meeting by claiming that he had not heard the question.

But Rudbeck's behavior was now working against him. Arrhenius complained that he had been "threatened" when Rudbeck promised to "sing [him] a different tune." Professors rallied to Arrhenius's side, asking what right Rudbeck had to treat a colleague in that way. At the very next meeting, too, the council appointed Arrhenius to the new committee. Rudbeck's outspoken opposition, not to mention his unpredictable outbursts, was making him a dangerous man. And if the new committee had anything to say, he would be an endangered man as well.

THEIR PERFECT OPPORTUNITY would come the very next month. In late June 1670, the university's chancellor, Magnus Gabriel de la Gardie, was planning a visit to Uppsala to celebrate an official occasion. Hours before his arrival, Stigzelius hustled together enough members of the council to hold a secret meeting. After they carefully drafted a list of grievances, Stigzelius rushed them to the chancellor the very day he arrived in town. Rudbeck's old nemesis was no longer professor of theology—in February of that year, Lars Stigzelius had been consecrated the new archbishop of Sweden.

Briefed about the situation, De la Gardie opened the meeting of the council the next day. The success of the professors' ambush is made all too clear by the minutes of the meeting. After hearing some complaints, the chancellor spoke out in an unmistakable reference to

Rudbeck: "It is beautiful that one builds; however, it is best if the re-sources allow for what one builds." In other words, *ratio est, pecunia deest:* "reason is there, money is not."

If we listen to these forceful detractors, the turmoil of the 1660s happened as a result of Rudbeck's activities alone. There was little understanding, or willingness to consider, any subtle nuances of the matter. How, for instance, the confident and flourishing 1650s had raised expectations beyond realistic capacities; how authorities had swelled the ranks of the university with many new positions — Queen Christina tending to make her appointments to the university first, and inquiring about available funds afterwards, if at all. Other leaders, such as the university chancellor, had also seemed unconcerned about mundane matters like budgets when there was an opportunity for expansion.

Competing with the waves of professors hired with little secure means of adequately funding the positions, Uppsala University's treasurer Bo Chruzelii was busy pursuing his own line of recklessness. Sloppy accounting and embezzlement of funds had combined, by the time of his death in 1653, to put the university in a potentially hazardous situation that would not easily bear all the extra appointments. So, when the crash came, it was completely unexpected, and the university was totally unprepared.

Now, in the summer of 1670, it was obvious what the problems were, or rather who the problem was. It was also painfully clear that no one would come to Rudbeck's support. Some colleagues tried to wiggle out of any association, while others sat in silence. To Rudbeck's dismay, even the chancellor appeared to be under their influence. The talented professor who had offered "blood and sweat" for his university now stood completely alone, both in his defense and in his defeat.

The very next week, July 4, 1670, Rudbeck showed up at the council meeting with a long letter. Despite protests from the council members, Rudbeck obtained permission to read it. Breaking down the charges point by point, he answered every accusation with a detailed account that had not been possible before. The anatomy theater, the botanical garden, the exercise house, the Community House—Rudbeck showed that he had in fact never carried out a single project that did not have the authorization of the council, the chancellor, or the Crown.

The professors were also reminded of what many had conveniently forgotten. In many of those projects, Rudbeck had donated his time, his talent, and indeed much of the materials for their completion. The university had not needed to hire an architect or an on-site manager for the anatomy theater, for instance, because Rudbeck had drafted the designs himself and then led the construction free of charge. The accusation of mismanagement was like a thrust to the heart. Virtually the same pattern applied to many other large projects as well as many other discrete contributions: the donations of musical instruments, the business trips to Stockholm, the seven hundred letters he had written—all of this he had done for the university he loved so dearly. In everything, Rudbeck had neither requested nor received a single Swedish öre.

After delivering this thundering statement, Olof Rudbeck demanded to be released from his administrative duties.

5

FOLLOW THE FISH!

Discovery consists of seeing what everybody has seen and thinking what nobody has thought.

—ALBERT SZENT-GYÖRGYI

SHOCKED AND DEEPLY HURT, Rudbeck was also angry at the way the professors had behaved. All his hard work had been brushed aside, haughtily dismissed, and answered with little more than "one thousand curses," hurled from the very center of the university that he had so energetically served. With his reputation stung and his pride wounded, Rudbeck retreated, as one said, like Achilles into his tent.

Resolved to leave the council to its deserved fate, Rudbeck threw himself into the search for the new world envisioned on the old maps. He worked day and night, chasing many "beautiful things." One of the first discoveries would not only enlarge his vision of the past, but also transform it beyond all recognition. Rudbeck had reached the astonishing conclusion that Sweden must have been the original cradle of civilization.

It all started when he was out investigating the old burial mounds and runic stones in the countryside. He brought along a very special instrument that would soon accompany him everywhere he went, and would enable him to invent an extraordinary dating method. To understand Rudbeck's theory, it is important to understand this method—one of the truly innovative, even pioneering results of his mad adventure.

Rudbeck had observed that the surface of the earth, whenever it remained undisturbed, was covered by a layer of fertile black soil (Latin *humus,* or colloquial Swedish *matjord*). This layer could never be found underground, but rather developed gradually as a result of decayed leaves, vegetation, dust, and other "contamination" deposited by snow, rain, or wind. Rudbeck explained that "no rain or snow is so pure as to be without soil, which I myself as well as other natural philosophers have observed and found out."

This is not only an early awareness of the problem of air pollution and one of the first on record in the modern world, but it also offers a wonderful insight into how ordinary soil can help date objects from the distant past.

First, though, however perceptive this observation seemed, it had to be tested. To verify his hypothesis, Rudbeck placed a container in his garden at the beginning of winter. Several months later, after the snow had melted and the rain had evaporated, there was indeed a thin layer of dirt at the bottom of his vessel. If left untouched over a period of time, Rudbeck further concluded, this soil would, like the specimens he had found, continue to develop everywhere with "distinctions in color, thickness, and layer." And if these distinctions, presumably a function of time, could be measured, perhaps they would provide clues to the age of any surrounding monuments.

So Rudbeck hunted down artifacts, stones, buildings, any significant structures, and then put his new device, a skillfully crafted measuring stick, to the test, trying to translate the nearby layers of soil into a more precise number of years. He searched the most distant places he could reach, far away from cultivated land, since regular working of the soil upset his method. He ventured out to remote mountains, cliffs, and crags, where it was "impossible for any human to live" and where he could reach only "with the greatest effort." Everywhere he examined the soil, and measured the fine distinctions in its layers.

All the while, too, Rudbeck was gradually refining his method. Comparing the data of constructions whose age he knew with those whose age he could reasonably deduce, Rudbeck proceeded to test his method thousands of times. The knowledge of elderly town residents was a valuable complement, Rudbeck thought, to his own rigorous approach. One nearly one-hundred-year-old man, Ingelbrecht Swensson, for instance, offered friendly assistance, pointing Rudbeck in the direction of likely places to find humus that had not been

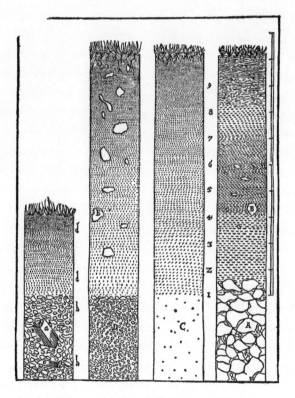

Rudbeck's archaeological dating method assumed that the soil offers a key to discovering the age of nearby structures. His measuring stick is depicted on the right side.

disturbed for a very long time. Varying his samples as much as possible, Rudbeck measured the distinctions, and again marveled at how gradually the humus actually developed.

Equipped with his measuring stick, Rudbeck hurried to an alluring site outside of the university town: the famous giant burial mounds of Old Uppsala. With the largest one standing twelve meters high and spanning fifty-five meters at the base, these monuments, most certainly tombs of dead kings, dominated the surrounding countryside. Objects of curiosity and romance for centuries, they are still today seen as royal resting places; in one theory enjoying wide currency, these mounds are the tombs of three pagan warrior kings, Aun (Onela), Egil, and Adils, mentioned in the Anglo-Saxon epic *Beowulf.*

By the end of a lengthy process, after some reported 16,000(!) tests, Rudbeck had found a ratio between the depth of the accumulated humus and the time that had passed. Thanks to the Great Flood, some four thousand years ago, which had swept away all existing humus and, as it were, reset the parameters of history, Rudbeck established his formula: one-fifth of a finger corresponded to one hundred years. Each tenth of a quarter on his measuring stick corresponded to five hundred years.

Later, when he announced this discovery to the world, Rudbeck would add specific instructions for the reader who wished to make his own measuring stick and put it to use reading the layers of the soil. For optimal results, Rudbeck advised choosing a dry day, long after any rain, and looking for surfaces of "red, gray, or white sand, or clay," which provide much better contrasts to the black humus. One should learn, also, to tell it by touch: humus differed from the other soil, as it felt "like velvet," a "fine cloth" compared with the coarse and hardy normal fare. Indeed, after applying Rudbeck's dating method, natural philosophers on the Continent testified to its success in unraveling the secrets from inside the "black coat" that covered the earth.

As a result of his indefatigable efforts, Rudbeck came to the startling realization that there was "no more certain" way at our disposal to date the events in the past. Historians may make mistakes, and even deliberately mislead, but the dirt showed "clearer than the sun" how old an artifact actually was. Field archaeologists all over the world still rely on studying distinctions in layers of soil to reach an approximate age of surrounding objects, though geologists are commonly credited with inventing this method of stratigraphy. Yet, almost two hundred years before, Rudbeck, too, had measured the layers of the soil to date the ruins, runes, and relics dotting the Swedish countryside.

What's more, this truly pioneering method confirmed that the history of Sweden stretched back to 2300 B.C.—some fifteen hundred years before the first Olympic games (776 B.C.). Founded supposedly by the mighty Heracles in honor of the god Zeus, this celebration of the games was traditionally one of the oldest dates in the accepted chronology of ancient history. Even more striking, Rudbeck's dating method also showed that a civilization had flourished in Sweden well over one thousand years before the Trojan War!

The implications were immense. In an age still under the spell of the Renaissance, many humanists greatly admired the achievements of classical antiquity and praised its merits for the modern world. Ancient wisdom was found almost everywhere, encapsulated in pithy maxims, hidden in veiled allegories about the gods, and displayed in memorable portraits of great heroes. All of this legacy served to provide perfect models for attaining eloquence and excellence, master keys for unlocking the secret "treasure chest of wisdom." Now Rudbeck was proudly proclaiming the discovery in the far north of a civilization that threatened to upset established traditions.

His claim meant that all the leading figures of the grand epics the *Iliad* and the *Odyssey*—Achilles, Odysseus, Ajax, and Agamemnon, as well as Hector, Paris, and Aeneas—must have lived significantly more recently than the warriors buried in Old Uppsala. Since Homer's accounts of the Trojan War were the earliest such narratives in European history—so early, indeed, that they were sometimes treated as history and at other times as mythology—this meant that Sweden had been populated well before those famous heroes rushed into the Trojan War, to sing along with Homer, like the "unnumbered flies that swarm round the cowsheds in the spring, when pails are full of milk." In fact, given standard historical chronologies of the day, this meant that Sweden was the oldest known civilization in Europe—and possibly in the world.

At this time Rudbeck's true colors shone through: his preference for reading what early natural philosophers often called "the Great Book of Nature"; his reliance on observation and his own experience over the evidence derived from authority, just as when he made his discovery of the lymphatic glands. No less important, Rudbeck was showing his independent spirit, his maverick willingness to go his own way, even when it meant putting more trust in the dirt than in the greatest and most celebrated chronologies of the ancient past.

SUCH RADICAL—indeed revolutionary—conclusions urged Rudbeck to probe into the history of Sweden, seeking an explanation for its great age. Reasoning like the Cartesian that many suspected he was, Rudbeck began at the beginning, hoping to find something fundamental that he could not doubt. As described in the seventh chapter of the Book of Genesis: "On that day, all the springs of the great deep burst forth, and the floodgates of the heavens were opened. And rain fell on the earth forty days and forty nights."

Given this destruction, Rudbeck reasoned that all evidence of the earliest period of world history had been lost. The oldest period that any historian could possibly reconstruct, according to Rudbeck, was the time immediately after the Great Flood, the postdiluvian world, when Noah; his wife; their three sons, Japheth, Shem, and Ham; and their wives dared to leave the massive ark, and started to rebuild human civilization. This momentous event not only appeared on almost all standard chronologies of the day, usually calculated as *anno mundi* ("the year of the world") 1656, or 2400 B.C., but it also became the undoubtable foundation to his own theory.

Then Rudbeck asked himself two crucial questions: How did the earth get repopulated, and why did the descendants of Noah settle in Sweden? His answer was as logical as it was grounded in biblical evidence.

The key to these questions lay in what sources of food were available to the survivors of the ark. No cows, pigs, lambs, chickens, or other land-dwelling animals, Rudbeck reasoned, would have possibly survived on an earth flooded for 150 (or 190, counting the first forty of rain) days. Animals of the air would also have died, since they needed food as well as places to rest from flight, both of which would have been underwater.

It was not necessary to be a botanist to understand that such a state would have eliminated most vegetation, too. This could be inferred, Rudbeck pointed out, by observing the effects of spring floods in Uppsala. These leave so much sand and gravel in their wake that they end up choking any surviving vegetation. Only a few trees such as willows and sallow flourish in such surroundings, and if a simple spring flood causes so much damage, imagine a flood on an enormous scale. In short, no animals, birds, or vegetation would have lived. But fish, on the other hand, were a different matter.

Creatures of the water would have been better positioned to survive this cataclysm. Nowhere in the sacred text were fish specifically ruled out as destroyed, and reason also suggested that they would have survived, flourishing in their natural environment. In this way, fish provided a central element in Rudbeck's vision of the past, and a key to a new understanding of the earliest events in history.

Given the passage of time since the waters of the Flood subsided in 2400 B.C., and the population of the world in Rudbeck's day, 1670, simple mathematical calculations showed that fish were absolutely necessary in order to repopulate the earth. There was simply no other way for the world's population to reach the present level in such a short period without this huge and steady supply of food. Rudbeck compiled many tables to work this out, calculating the first eight humans, the number of children recorded in the genealogies, and the rate at which the population must have grown, mathematically, for the descendants of Noah to fulfill the command "be fruitful and multiply." Rudbeck was more convinced than ever about the role of the fish in rebuilding civilization.

Looking at ancient peoples, Rudbeck asked: Did they not settle near the water? The Greeks colonized around the Mediterranean, as Plato would say, "like frogs around a pond." The Chaldeans encircled the Persian Gulf, the Chinese gathered around the East Indian Ocean, and the Scythians colonized the Black Sea area. The eminent Harvard historian Frank Manuel noted that Isaac Newton had proposed an early theory of the riverbed origins of civilization in his *Chronology of the Ancient Kingdoms Amended* (1728). Newton was indeed early, but Rudbeck suggested a similar theory almost fifty years before.

Relentlessly following the reasoning, Rudbeck further pursued this line of thought. Water not only provided the most secure food supply for early humans, and promoted the growth of old civilizations, but helped in other ways as well. Long before the invention of the compass or the systematic use of stars for traveling, rivers offered the best orientation for early explorers, as well as the most reliable source of food on their perilous journeys. Again Rudbeck looked to ancient texts to see if this rationale corresponded with the accounts of the earliest history.

Beginning with our oldest surviving historian, he turned to Herodotus, "the father of history," as Cicero called him. This fifth-century-B.C. historian told the story of how an ancient barbarian tribe, the Cimmerians, fled from the even more barbaric Scythians, making the escape by following along the coasts. Julius Caesar similarly wrote about how the ancient Gauls preferred to march along the rivers, particularly when they were lost in foreign lands. Going back into the realm of myth, and one of the oldest journeys on record, Jason and the Argonauts, too, progressed in their search for the Golden Fleece by following the rivers.

To persuade remaining skeptics, Rudbeck invited them to read the travel reports of explorers in the New World. Even in the modern age, with the mastery of the compass and the ability to read the stars, Spanish, Portuguese, English, Dutch, and Swedish travelers made progress inland by following the course of rivers.

Many places of course had fish in abundance, but according to Rudbeck, there was no place that could rival the north. Here the rivers teemed with fish and the land overflowed with abundance. Herring, salmon, pike, cod, mountain cod, whales, whitefish, and so on, all this variety and wealth was made all the more vital when the animals, birds, and vegetation died in the Flood (and the pairs saved on the ark were too few to prevent starvation, let alone suffice to repopulate the earth). This natural asset was still very much tangible in his own day, Rudbeck ventured, pointing out how wealthy Dutch, Norwegian, and English fishermen had become on their trade. It was impossible to count how many distant lands and peoples were still fed by the reservoirs of fish found in northern waters.

The significance of Rudbeck's finding was not lost on his contemporaries. In an oration delivered at the University of Kiel in the 1680s, one professor painted a picture of Sweden in a way highly reminiscent of Rudbeck's vision of a marvelous land that had once served as the cradle of civilization:

> Sweden is rich in metals, overflows with herds and flocks, and in all places crowded with forests. . . . Which waters in the world gush forth so many kinds of fish one after the other and in greater abundance than those which flow in Sweden?

Nature has taught the hearts of people, the professor said, to turn like a magnet in a compass to this original homeland in the north. Such a notion would live on for quite a long time, indeed well after many parts of Rudbeck's story had been abandoned or forgotten.

As Rudbeck was beginning to see, survival in the earliest times was a matter of following the fish north to Sweden. With this vision of the ancient past, founded on the sacred history, his archaeological dating method, his wide experiences in natural history, and his own logical deduction, Rudbeck concluded that "it simply could not have happened otherwise."

And so the search was on. The remains of the world's oldest civilization lay just out in the countryside—its dirt, its stones, and its fish had yielded the most astounding and unbelievable conclusions, and who knew what else might be found there. Olof Rudbeck was at the beginning of what would be an extraordinary adventure. Ultimately, too, he was taking the first steps in another quest, a personal mission to gain redemption after the day he had been so publicly humiliated and thoroughly discredited.

Meanwhile, Olaus Verelius and Johannes Loccenius were overjoyed with the potential of this project. Both experts fired off letters of support to a dashing count who was then not only chancellor of Uppsala University but also chancellor of the Swedish Empire. Hoping to interest this gentleman in the quest, everyone waited in heightened expectation.

6

GAZING AT THE FACE OF THOR

Not only I, but the whole world, seemed filled with delight. The animals, the houses, even the weather itself reflected the universal joy and serenity. . . .

—LUCIUS APULEIUS, *THE GOLDEN ASS*

*T*HE MAN THEY HAD in mind was Magnus Gabriel de la Gardie, and he sat in a peculiar position. Called "the most beautiful man in the world," he was a true cavalier who dazzled the court with his wit and charm. As the Chancellor of the Realm, controlling ambassadors, resident diplomats, and the machinery of foreign policy, De la Gardie effectively stood at the summit of authority at a time when Sweden had reached the zenith of its power.

Behind all the thundering pomp lay a colossal fortune. The count owned about one thousand farms and a couple of hundred estates spread all over Sweden and the Baltic region. Some of these properties were sizable indeed. His castle straddling the beautiful Lake Vänern in west Sweden, Läckö, for instance, had 248 rooms, and 176 servants caring for his every whim. That is, when he happened to be there, and not at one of his other castles. There were four others alone just in Stockholm and on its outskirts. Ranging from stony medieval fortresses to sprawling baroque spectacles, at least two dozen castles then belonged to Magnus Gabriel de la Gardie.

Both Verelius and Loccenius knew that the count could, if he wanted, be of great assistance to Olof Rudbeck. He had the power, the wealth, and the status that they lacked—and, more than that, he was known to spend lavishly on parties as well as projects. One observer, an Italian ambassador writing a few months after the Uppsala scholars, noted De la Gardie's restless pursuits:

> He is the worst economist, and greatest waster in the world, maintains numerous staff, runs a big table and pays out large sums for his furniture, his gardens, and his enterprises.

According to court rumors, the count had no fewer than forty or fifty different building projects all in progress at the same time on his estates. Whether he was constructing churches, adding wings to hospitals, or embellishing his favorite gardens with the latest fashions, whatever he touched tended to take on immense proportions. The count seemed to be building everywhere, almost all the time, and with very little sense of restraint. On the banks of the river at Lidköping, he was even building his own city.

At that point in the early 1670s, De la Gardie clearly seemed at the top of the world, and it is easy to understand that he looked untouchable. But then again, it had seemed that way once before. In the middle of the 1640s, De la Gardie had returned to Sweden from his studies on the Continent speaking French like a "Frenchman" and a master of the latest Parisian fashions. Everyone admired his gift of sparkling conversation, and he lacked, as one Frenchman put it, "none of the qualities which should win him friends."

Just back from his grand tour, De la Gardie caught the eye of young Queen Christina, and she took quite a liking to the dashing gentleman. In fact, he became her obvious favorite. Generously disposed to those she liked, and apparently seeing him as a kindred soul, the queen showered him with gifts, titles, and honors on an unprecedented scale. She paid his personal debts, which had already reached the enormous sum of twenty thousand *riksdaler*. Courtiers looked on at the gallant spectacle that surrounded Sweden's uncrowned prince of the court.

But then the count received some startling news. It came in a letter from Her Majesty at the end of 1653 informing him, "I am from henceforth incapable to have any other apprehension for you than that of pity, which nevertheless can nothing avail you, since yourself hath made useless the thoughts of bounty which I had for you." She added her blunt determination to break all contact with such a worthless and weak soul.

Did the queen's angry letter mask a deep affection, perhaps spurned love, or did it merely reflect more mundane power shifts at court? Christina was starting to favor a newly arrived French doctor, Pierre Bourdelot, who had cured her of an ailment and, she thought, saved her life. At this point, De la Gardie watched jealously as he lost ground to the upstart physician, and his own behavior precipitated the whole confusing affair. The last face-to-face encounter between the queen and her courtier, in late November 1653, had indeed been awkward.

Evidently feeling his influence slipping away at court, De la Gardie contrived a reason to address the matter with the queen. He claimed to have heard word of her disapproval of him, and when the queen asked about his sources, he stalled, very reluctantly mentioning names. When the queen checked out De la Gardie's alleged sources, the whole thing backfired. There was nothing "grand, beautiful, or noble in his actions," she fumed. In light of the embarrassing scene that followed, many trace the count's fall not to some unreturned love, but rather to De la Gardie's own insecurities about his position. At any rate, whatever the ultimate causes, the results were all too clear.

The letter was the first in a long line of losses. Titles, honors, and privileges started to disappear, generally announced at irregular, unpredictable intervals, with understandably a more crushing effect. Then the count saw his cool ostracization thaw into an icy official banishment that turned the former twentysomething superstar into a thirty-one-year-old apparent has-been. Nothing, the queen said, would change her mind. And she meant it, much to the displeasure of De la Gardie, his friends, and his mother, who came to plead with the queen. Even Christina's future successor, Charles, could not convince her of De la Gardie's merits.

Nothing worked, that is, until Queen Christina left the Swedish throne. Once she moved to Rome, and brought the famous Vasa dynasty to a close, the Pfaltz family captured the throne under Christina's cousin, Charles X Gustav. Among other things, the new king had strong family ties to De la Gardie, not to mention having been swayed by his undeniable charm. Now, with De la Gardie's cousin and brother-in-law Charles X Gustav in the saddle, Sweden was preparing for the count's triumphant return. After the king's coronation in 1654, offices slowly started to come his way again, and he enjoyed them with his usual flair, though his real break came six years later.

At the death by pneumonia of King Charles X in 1660, Magnus Gabriel de la Gardie experienced a quick, sudden elevation that once again landed him at the top. He was named Chancellor of the Realm, with the power to authorize everything that should be executed in the king's name. The count was made responsible for all foreign policy and a considerable part of domestic policy; he would in fact lead the government until the future king—then only four years old—came of age.

Such experiences with the stresses of power, not to mention the wild uncertainties of fortune, had undoubtedly exaggerated the count's already impulsive behavior. He could bounce unpredictably from one idea to another, one project to another, one favorite to another. He appeared whimsical and wavering. Even at the height of his authority, De la Gardie was racked by terrible self-doubt.

Additionally, as the threats of international war and economic stagnation loomed, De la Gardie would find himself increasingly and publicly challenged. He also found himself resorting to old tactics. When things did not go his way, he would often get up in the middle of a debate and go home. Advocates well versed in the principles of power politics strongly advised him against such rash actions, as did his own sister, Maria Sofia, who correctly saw the risks of fleeing to the countryside in the heat of a debate.

By the early 1670s, the vicissitudes of fortune and the volatilities of the passions reigning at the center of power had confirmed his worst fears. He felt vulnerable once again. Worries consumed him, and made him especially prone to fits of anxiety. As many of his allies learned, far too often it seemed that De la Gardie nervously yielded under challenge. He seemed too unreliable and much too mauled by second-guessing phantoms. Shunning confrontation and indulging a tendency to fret, this gentleman was hardly a modern paladin.

Such was the man that Uppsala's scholars hoped to attract to Rudbeck's search. And indeed De la Gardie seemed overjoyed with the news from the academy. He could not have been more enthusiastic about Rudbeck's quest. The question, though, was how long the attraction would last.

ESTEEM FROM THIS powerful man and the learned historians must have been exhilarating, but it could hardly compare with the excitement sparked by the maps and the manuscripts. Armed, too, with his new archaeological dating method, Rudbeck made progress on his search with lightning speed. The secrets of the distant past could now be teased from the nearest burial mound, and faint signs of this forgotten world rendered more clearly than ever before. With an instinct as sharp and exact as any compass he had made, Rudbeck wondered if he stood on the verge of unlocking the secrets to some of the greatest mysteries of all time. And he was delirious with joy.

But what difficulties lay ahead — centuries of error and ignorance had covered the trail with "tall, terrifyingly impenetrable overgrowth." To clear this path, he would need a combination of historical knowledge, language skills, and an uncanny ability for uncovering clues and deciphering them correctly. Distant, often obscure, and almost always ambiguous, the evidence would need the rigor of the scientific method. Yet it would also need a bold, almost reckless ability to see the world in a new way. Success in this quest, as he was just starting to see, would require a delicate balancing act indeed.

There were already nagging questions about the people buried in the giant mounds of Old Uppsala. If their civilization was really so old, and he had repeatedly confirmed this, why hadn't the ancients written more about them? Why hadn't they, for that matter, written more about themselves, leaving a large body of literature like the Greeks and the Romans? Surely such a sophisticated civilization could not have escaped the notice of every single ancient observer.

These were serious matters that needed to be addressed. As he tried to figure out why the ancient Scandinavians had not written more about their civilization, other than the "beautifully carved runes" adorning the stones, Rudbeck would venture into one of his many provocative discussions about the nature of history.

The lack of a written record, he conjectured, actually made perfect sense. Civilizations experiencing golden ages were not likely to write; presumably they were too busy enjoying peace, prosperity, and the good life. History as we know it comes only with more difficult times. Whether wars, invasions, or civil strife, conflict on a grand scale is needed to give rise to history, and to inspire stirring narratives. With no struggle, there was no history, he suggested. In the process, Rudbeck was anticipating some fertile musings about the "philosophy of history" that flourished among fashionable Romantic thinkers of the nineteenth century. One of these leading figures, the German philosopher Georg Wilhelm Friedrich Hegel, put the idea more famously: "The periods of good fortune form [history's] emptiest pages."

Feeling that he had solved the problem of the silent golden age, Rudbeck did not, unfortunately, develop this thought, or the idea of struggle, further. If he had, his commentary would probably have made an interesting read. For the role of struggle in history would have a long life, not least with Hegel and one of his readers, Karl Marx, who elaborated the notion and made it a cornerstone of his understanding of the entire historical process. All history, Marx would later say, was about struggle: "The history of all hitherto existing society is the history of class struggles." The centrality of conflict would indeed last a long time in standard historiography—that is, until the rise of analytical schools that would show other ways to craft the past that did not rely on clash-driven narratives.

As for the first and more immediate problem—the lack of references to Scandinavian civilization in ancient texts—there was a possible solution. Many Greek and Latin writers had recorded impressions about the Hyperboreans, and a number of Swedish thinkers had started to wonder if this enigmatic nation might have been located in the far north of Sweden. Olaus Verelius, for one, had already given much thought to the matter, and considered the possibility almost a certainty. So did his teacher, the poet and philosopher Georg Stiernhielm, as did his teacher Johan Bureus at the beginning of the seventeenth century. Even before that, some medieval continental thinkers, including Adam of Bremen and Albertus Krantzius, had placed the Hyperboreans on maps of Sweden.

Despite all the lively speculation, however, no one had been able to prove or disprove that the Hyperboreans had actually lived in Sweden. Both Bureus and Stiernhielm had devoted years to the study, but both, unfortunately, died before they could realize their ambitions. The vast majority of their reflections about this ancient people had in fact never been published, and existed only in the form of manuscripts.

Given this state of affairs, Verelius would prove to be highly useful to Rudbeck's search. He knew the traditions about the Hyperboreans, having discussed them regularly in his commentaries to the sagas. He had access to the unpublished works of his teacher, Stiernhielm, which he almost certainly loaned to Rudbeck. By the early 1670s, too, Verelius was regularly reading Rudbeck's own notes, gladly offering advice and guidance.

Verelius was, in many ways, helping Rudbeck navigate through the sea of speculation that placed the original home of the Hyperboreans everywhere from Celtic Britain to the Netherlands to Siberia (and in modern times, Oxford University's professor of Greek E. R. Dodds proposed China). The Hyperboreans were placed all over the "north," anywhere that could conceivably be understood as "beyond the north wind"—that is, when authorities did not dismiss them outright as myth, as most would do today.

The more Rudbeck read about the people, however, the more familiar the Hyperboreans sounded. Ancient travelers venturing into their lands described them as tall and healthy, and enjoying great fame for their wisdom, righteousness, and justice. They worshiped outdoors, in sacred groves. With flutes and lyres, laurel-wreathed Hyperboreans danced and sang praises to their chief deity, Apollo, the archer god with his silver bow who came down to visit them every nineteen years. Everything Rudbeck heard and read sounded like a portrait of his northerners, a people who were building burial mounds long before the beginnings of classical civilization.

With the help of Verelius and his manuscripts, Rudbeck would try to be the one who could finally find the Hyperboreans, and show that they had once lived in Sweden. The paths he blazed would be far from conventional.

READING WIDELY IN ancient Greek accounts, Rudbeck felt that he had stumbled upon a fundamental error that had long caused confusion, and had kept the Hyperboreans enveloped in a gilded mist. He explained, "It often happens that when one people hears the name of another people, and cannot determine its meaning, they willingly interpret it according to their own language."

Ancient Greeks had, in other words, heard the name of the Hyperboreans and, not knowing its original meaning, had interpreted it as if it were a word in their own language: *hyper* meaning "beyond" and *borea* referring to Boreas, the north wind. This etymology made sense, at least in Greek, and sounded poetic, but Rudbeck wondered how a foreign people, Hyperboreans, with their own distinct language, could have a name that might meaningfully be reduced to Greek etymologies. Such an interpretation was bound to make mistakes, and create what Rudbeck called "strange animals."

In his mind, the word *Hyperborean* was clearly Swedish, and he had found evidence in the village of Ekholm, outside Uppsala.

There stood a stone with two intertwining dragons, and carved on the back of one of them was the word *Yfwerborne* (pronounced ew-ver-BOR-nuh). The Greek word for the Hyperboreans is Ὑπερβόρεοι, pronounced hew-per-BOR-eh-oi. Their similarities can be seen below:

Swedish	Y	fwer	Bor	ne
Greek	Ὑ	περ	βόρε	οι

The main difference between these two words, as Rudbeck saw it, was the second syllable, with an *f* sound in Swedish and a *p* (π) sound in Greek. This could, however, easily be explained by the dynamics of the consonant shift that show how easily *f* and *p* change over time and across borders. Rudbeck cited many examples of this phenomenon: from the word for father, Swedish *fader* and Greek *pater* (πατήρ), to

the word for fire, Swedish *fyr* and Greek *pyr* (πῦρ). (As for the suf-
fixes, *ne* and *oi,* these were just standard plural endings.) In other
words, the Swedish runic inscription *Yfwerborne* was basically a direct
match to the Greek *Yπερβόρεoι.*

With his burning interest in antiquities, Rudbeck quickly realized
that this was not a stray find. Surviving examples of the Swedish
Hyperboreans were turning up in many places. There was, for instance, a preservation of this memory in an old song he knew, a tune
that ended every refrain with the thunderous words, "The *Yfwerborne*
Swedes who conquered every land."

The breakthrough discovery about this people, however, came when
Rudbeck pored over the old Norse sagas and eddas. In an old manuscript of the Icelandic poet Snorri Sturluson's *Edda,* actually one of the
oldest copies in existence, Rudbeck found a reference to a figure that
was described in typically Hyperborean terms: "beautiful in appearance, big and powerful." The name of this northerner was, interestingly,
Bore. He was the founder of a family that would be praised to the skies.
According to Norse mythology, Bore was the first god who appeared on
earth, and his son Bor would be the father of Odin, "the greatest and
most glorious that we know." In other words, this Bore — whoever he
was — was remembered as the ancestor of Odin, his wife Frigg, and, as
the *Edda* made clear, many of the leading Aesir gods who would rule
"heavens and earth." The manuscript would also credit the children of
Bor for going on to do many splendid deeds, from creating the first
human beings to constructing Midgard, the fortress of the earth.

Inside this passage were many "riddles" that Rudbeck felt needed
clarification, and indeed he would spend most of his life trying to
separate the history from the mythology. For now, though, the claim
that Bor's children ruled over the "heavens and earth" could be seen
as a poetic celebration of ancient kings, much like the praises that
Egyptian priests heaped on the pharaohs for commanding the sun to
rise and the Nile to flood. The more Rudbeck read the stories of the

children of Bor, the more he thought that these tales preserved distant memories of an advanced people who were building civilization in the north. Their deeds were so illustrious that they had been remembered over time as the achievements of gods.

So far the legacy of the Hyperboreans was revealed by the fallen warriors in the burial mounds, the figures commemorated on the standing stones, the *Yfwerborne* celebrated in the tavern song, and the mythic "children of Bor" honored in the old Norse manuscripts. A glance at a map of Sweden showed many other surviving memories as well. The names Bore and Bor had lived on in many places around the kingdom: Boresland in the north (Terra Borealis), Borsfiord (Mare Borealis), Borö (Bore's Island), Bore's siön (Bore's Sea), Boreswik (Bore's Bay), Borristelle (Bore's Place), and so on.

All of this added up to Rudbeck's new understanding of the word *Hyperborean.* The ancient Greeks had spelled the word correctly, though they had made a mistake in interpreting its origin and its meaning. The term did not stem from Greek words meaning "beyond the north wind," but instead, coming from the Swedish *Yfwerborne,* the word derived from one of two possibilities. Either it referred to the founding king Bore and his illustrious descendants, the Boreades, or, alternatively, it came from the Swedish words *y fwer,* "high," and *borne,* "born," referring to the "highborn" or elite Boreades who surrounded the king. Either way, these were the true Hyperboreans of classical legend.

To find out more, Rudbeck would attempt to use every form of evidence that might conceivably shed light on this enigmatic people and their proposed home in Sweden. His search would, in the process, lead him to make a final break with traditional historians, whose work at that time consisted primarily in the interpreting and commenting on written accounts. In a sense, the deeper Rudbeck pressed into the old traditions, the more necessary it was to find new ways to understand what he saw as their true meaning. Sometimes the results were innovative; at other times they were odd at best.

RUDBECK WAS DETERMINED to show what the lyric poet Pindar would call "the wondrous way" to the blessed Hyperboreans. What if, however, this legendary people had never really existed, other than as the inhabitants of an imagined utopia, a dreamland for classical Greece? After all, it is striking to see how many ancients had their doubts. The oldest historian, Herodotus, for example, expressed his skepticism about the existence of the Hyperboreans:

> I will not tell the tale of Abaris, who was supposed to have been a Hyperborean, and carried his arrow all round the world without eating a bite. Let me just add, however, that, if Hyperboreans exist "beyond the north-wind" there must also be Hypernotians "beyond the south."

Other authorities from the geographer Strabo to the natural historian Pliny joined him in their hesitancy, though Rudbeck remained unfazed.

No wonder, he thought, that many intelligent people had questioned whether or not the Hyperboreans had existed. Knowledge of the north had somehow disappeared over time, leaving an unfortunate accumulation of errors that had confused the ancients. For example, many sources had stated that the Hyperborean isle was "not smaller than Sicily." Yet, if you look at ancient maps, including those from the most famous and influential geographer, Ptolemy, Sweden would not even satisfy this minimal requirement. Antiquity's greatest geographers had shrunk Sweden so much that it actually looked smaller than Sicily, mistaking the far southern tip of the peninsula, Skåne, for the entire country.

Ptolemy's original error, Rudbeck conceded, was made worse by a certain lazy ignorance on the part of his successors. Instead of inves-

tigating the matter for themselves, many scholars had simply copied
Ptolemy's view and, in the process, his mistakes. As this happened for
centuries, error built upon error, leaving the mistake firmly in-
grained, and the discovery of the true identity of the Hyperboreans
indefinitely postponed.

History was like mapmaking, Rudbeck suggested: a geographer
could not make a map by uncritically following the statements of others, or by relying solely on the experiences of other people. Rudbeck
showed the futility with a story:

> One time, I called over a number of students here at
> Uppsala from each province of Sweden, and asked them
> where such-and-such place lay in such-and-such
> province. When one said west, the other said southwest,
> one two miles, the other four miles.

With this method, it would be difficult to find anything. Because
the students sometimes took different paths to the destinations, and
some were better than others at measuring distance, the result was
chaos. Even when he took advantage of actual maps of the regions,
Rudbeck still could not make any sense out of the conflicting reports
about the distant provinces as long as he sat hundreds of miles away,
in a comfortable study in Uppsala. "How would Ptolemy, who sat
down in Egypt and drew his maps as best he could using many writings of ancients and others, do any better?" he asked.

Once Rudbeck gained more confidence in peeling away the layers of
errors, he would try to overcome the other objections by showing how
much of the Hyperborean legacy still existed in Sweden. In this task,
Rudbeck's ingenuity and resourcefulness had few limits. When the ancients described the Hyperboreans as tall and healthy, Rudbeck knew
how to find out. He wrote, "I have diligently examined all the large burial mounds, where skulls and whole skeletons have been found." The
size of the skeletons was sometimes enormous. "The largest ones

Rudbeck used many original manuscripts of Norse sagas in his search for Atlantis. This image, for example, comes from Snorri Sturluson's Edda.

have been five to six *aln* [ten to twelve feet!], although there were not many of them, but I have found countless skeletons four *aln* long [eight feet] or thereabouts."

Too bad Rudbeck did not elaborate more on this rather odd passage. Hurrying to keep up with the rapid flow of his ideas, Rudbeck just noted how these skeletons showed the great height that the ancients attributed to the Hyperboreans, and then moved on to discuss other exciting finds. Legends of northern giants were well preserved in many places, not least in the Norse sagas.

The opening of Snorri's *Edda*, the *Gylfaginning*, "the tricking of Gylfi," told the memorable story of Thor and his companions' journey to the land of the giants. When they entered the region called Utgard, somewhere in the far northeast, they saw a castle so enormous that they had to "bend their heads back to touch their spines before they could see up over." The door alone was too large for Thor to open, leaving the gods, ungracefully, to squeeze their way into the giant stronghold in "between the bars" and slip into the great hall.

Besides fanciful and imaginative stories that held some kernels of truth, Rudbeck found evidence of the tall Hyperboreans in many other places. One time he assembled a number of Uppsala students and measured them. Dividing them into categories, according to their home provinces in the kingdom, Rudbeck dutifully measured and correlated his results. The tallest students indeed came from the north. He believed that height increased broadly the farther north one went, reaching a climax at about the 68th degree of latitude before dropping off significantly with the nomadic Saami in the farthest north.

Another prominent characteristic that had almost invariably appeared in the ancient discussions was that the giant Hyperboreans enjoyed a reputation for great health. Drawing on his experiences as a physician, Rudbeck was convinced that these stories reflected a truth he had often observed in his medical practice: the Swedes rarely succumbed to typhus fever, leprosy, the plague, and other nightmare contagions that struck so frequently on the Continent. Swedish health, he added, was not due to any inborn racial advantage, but stemmed instead from fundamental differences in the environment.

The legendary Hyperborean health was, in other words, explained by Sweden's cold, brisk weather, which hardened the body's resistance to disease, and a well-rounded diet also enhanced immunity. Apples, carrots, walnuts, and chestnuts formed a large part of the Swedish diet, Rudbeck noted, especially compared with other countries. Even more, his countrymen regularly consumed many kinds of meat like ox, pork, ham, and "countless fish and birds," and this went, remarkably, also for the Swedish peasant. An entire day of food in Italy, he suspected, would equal only a hearty "Swedish breakfast."

Such a fortunate combination of climate and diet was one reason why so many had marveled at the northerners' resiliency, from the geographer Strabo, writing at the height of the Roman Empire, to

Adam of Bremen, writing one thousand years later in the Holy Roman Empire. The Norse texts were also full of references to immortal realms of the north—not of course literally immortal, Rudbeck added, but rather references to the fact that the people lived such happy and healthy lives, overcoming sickness. In Rudbeck's mind, Hyperborean tendencies and traditions had lived on in the stories of the legendary lands of the Undying, like that of King Gudmund in the *Hervararsaga*.

To show how this Hyperborean trait was a Swedish characteristic, Rudbeck asked his brother Nicholas for some help. As bishop of their hometown, Västerås, Nicholas Rudbeck granted access to the records of baptism for some twelve parishes between the years 1600 and 1673.

No fewer than 230 people had lived past the age of ninety in these years. There were some rather memorable examples, which Rudbeck of course relished. One old man named Israel in a small village supposedly had lived to the age of 156, and another one, Tor Ulfsson, was said to have lived to 260! He would then have lived, Rudbeck noted, to see his great-great-great-great-great-grandchildren, some "six, seven, or eight generations."

During the course of his investigations, Rudbeck met many villagers whose wisdom intrigued him, when others would have scoffed. In a village outside Uppsala, Rudbeck learned to read runic staffs from a "wise peasant named Anders." A runic staff was a roughly three-foot-long wooden staff that bore intricately carved runes, the ancient written language of Scandinavia. It was essentially a calendar that could work for every single year. Once you had a code, a symbol for a particular year, you could use that symbol to read the "heavenly clock," and date the seasonal events. Uppsala's distinguished professor would sit down and take lessons from the humblest of peasants.

One of Rudbeck's most memorable experiences came years later, when one illiterate man taught him to use medieval runic staffs to predict celestial phenomena. Rudbeck the astronomer walked away amazed at how his colleagues of the scientific revolution were just

The runic staff helped the Swedish peasant in everything from setting the dates of movable feasts to predicting "the characteristics of the coming year."

learning to grasp the understanding of the stars shown by his special teacher, one "wise gray-haired peasant."

Reflecting on these unexpected encounters ignited a chain of thoughts that would enable him to gain a deeper appreciation of ancient history. He had come to the stunning realization that the ancient wisdom of the Hyperboreans had indeed survived! It lived on in Sweden, though more in some places than in others.

This wisdom was not to be sought near seacoasts or borders with other countries, which often undergo rapid change through trade, war, and a host of other interactions. Nor could it be found in royal and princely courts, so subject to changing fashions, which made language "taste like a well-flavored and cinnamon-sweetened porridge." Nor, for that matter, should one seek out the oldest wisdom among the well-traveled and the learned, who have often drunk up traditions in their wide variety of experiences, with the many new, outside influences slipping in unsuspected, causing a historian to go astray. One should go instead far into the countryside, and deep into the distant parts of the kingdom, into the humblest villages. There the bearded peasant offered a mirror onto antiquity, where the past was most preserved and far from tapped out as a historical resource. Pondering the experience years later, Rudbeck described a sense of appreciation:

> When I see ... Anders Tomeson, who is a man over 115 years old who is still able to go by foot to Uppsala, and has a rosy face, white hair, and a long beard which covers his chest, shining as the snow, I think that then I have seen the original image of our old gods and kings. . . .

Then, after a digression on the history of beards, including a lament on how the long beards had unfortunately gone out of fashion in most places in Europe by about 1600, replaced instead by the thin, "catlike whiskers," Rudbeck added his wish "that to the end of the world, our peasants would want to hold the image of the old gods in their body and their honorable beards." For there was pleasure and knowledge in close contact with the peasant. Sometimes, indeed, it seemed like gazing at the face of Thor.

In this state of affairs, even common expressions, children's games, and drinking songs were immensely valuable sources in the quest to reveal a world otherwise lost. Rudbeck was indeed to become one of the first modern collectors of folk customs. All the more remarkable, this was

A peasant with a long beard conjured up, in Rudbeck's mind, an image of Old Norse gods.

during a century dominated by an aristocratic elite that dismissed peasants as socially and intellectually inferior. It was also well over one hundred years before Romantic collectors such as the Grimm brothers would work to save classic tales from certain disappearance.

There was, in short, not a single quality of the Hyperboreans that Rudbeck, with the talents of a Renaissance man and the exceptional ability to put his expertise to use in innovative ways, could not place in the far north. And the ease with which he made the discoveries only convinced him of their truth and whetted his appetite for more. From now on, the lure of the anatomy theater would pale beside the attraction of the past—for his knife would be more productive dissecting our misunderstandings about the ancient world.

The Quest for the Golden Fleece

He has a genius equal to anything; but like all other genius requires the most delicate management to keep it from running into eccentricities.

—John Adams, describing his grandson George Washington Adams

During the summer of 1674, a sophisticated Italian diplomat named Lorenzo Magalotti came to visit Sweden. Well connected and observant, the thirty-six-year-old Florentine noted the smallest details, leaving a vivid portrait of his experiences. His aim was to describe the host country with such clarity and precision that it would be unnecessary to add the phrase "this is Sweden."

As part of his stay, Magalotti made a brief trip out to Rudbeck's Uppsala. He saw the anatomy theater, visited the botanical garden, and heard about Professor Rudbeck, "a learned man in all areas." Entering the main university building, Magalotti admired the council chamber with its benches "decorated in scarlet red cloth all around, and at the far end a canopy of red velvet." He also glanced into the room of another important institution housed there: the College of

Antiquities. This was a prestigious antiquarian society, founded by Magnus Gabriel de la Gardie to counter the "incuriosity" that plagued the past. Arguably Sweden's first scientific academy, the College of Antiquities would loom large in Olof Rudbeck's life.

Established in 1667, the college's mandate was to preserve and promote all manuscripts, documents, and other matters that shed light on the ancient Swedish heritage. Special emphasis was placed on the study of language, "the foundation and most lofty pillar to all sound knowledge of the ancient Swedish writings and laws in the kingdom." Of central importance, too, were the Norse manuscripts. Collections purchased, bestowed, or captured over the years were turned over to the society, and annual expeditions to Norway and Iceland were planned to discover additional material. Membership in this elite society certainly brought many privileges, not least the promise of funding for all future scholarly work.

With these aims, spirits had been high in late January 1668 as the College of Antiquities moved into its newly refurbished room in the Gustavianum for its historic first meeting. Seven full members had been selected, many of them leading scholars of Uppsala. The president was the poet and philosopher Georg Stiernhielm. The historian Johan Loccenius and the classical philologist Johan Schefferus were also selected as members, as was Olaus Verelius, professor of the antiquities of the fatherland. One person not invited to join, however, was Olof Rudbeck, who at this time had not yet been consumed by Swedish antiquities.

Even though it was only a few months old, the hopeful academy was already beginning to struggle. Rhetoric proved easier than adequate funding, and soon there was a noticeable gulf between scholarly ambitions and true financial health. The choice of leadership did not help all that much, either. The president of the college, the seventy-year-old Georg Stiernhielm, much preferred to stay at home in Stockholm than journey to Uppsala for the meetings. Not counting the inaugural ceremonies, Stiernhielm was not present at more than one or two meetings over the entire course of his term before his death in 1672.

Given the lackluster leadership threatening to paralyze the institution, a young scholar named Johan Hadorph was more than eager to fill the void. The same age as Rudbeck, Hadorph was a short, stocky, dark-haired man who was passionate about the past. He had begun his studies at Uppsala University at the age of eleven, and continued until he reached his thirtieth birthday—an unusually long time by any standards. Energetic and resourceful, Hadorph was the youngest member of the academy, and one of its most promising. His achievements were already considerable.

In addition to being one of the leading experts on the study of runes (the symbols carved on stone and wood found across Scandinavia), Hadorph had managed to persuade De la Gardie to push through an unprecedented law that deserves to be better known in the annals of historic preservation. Under his proposal, castles, fortresses, abbeys, manor houses, indeed any significant ruin or relic, including heaps of stone, would be protected against potential looters. Enacted in December 1666, with governors, bishops, and local officers authorized to enforce its stipulations and some two thousand *daler silvermynt* granted in funding, this was nothing less than Sweden's first state law passed to care for its monuments—and perhaps the first of its kind in the world.

With his diligence and stamina, not to mention his endless stream of creative ideas, Hadorph was undeniably one of the most valuable members of the College of Antiquities. Yet he had his own ideas about how the fledgling society should develop, and he was not afraid to act on them, even if it meant bypassing the elderly absentee president. By simple force of will and the tacit acceptance of his colleagues, Hadorph had steadily gained in power and influence, until it seemed that he virtually controlled the college.

Helping Hadorph obtain his prominence was a professor of history and one of Rudbeck's old enemies, Claes Arrhenius. Elected in the second wave of nominations in 1670, Arrhenius had developed a close friendship and collaboration with Hadorph. One thing that bound the two antiquarians together was a vision of the college as the principal and most suitable interpreter of the Swedish past. Another thing they shared was a marked resistance to Olof Rudbeck's rival antiquarian project. His conclusions were already being dismissed with easy and ruthless skepticism. All of it was pure nonsense, or, as Arrhenius once put it, "a cloud castle of hypotheses."

Even Magalotti, who knew several members of the College of Antiquities, seemed to share this initial reaction, though tempered with nonchalance and bemusement. The Florentine gave one of our earliest known international verdicts on Rudbeck's quest, and it is not favorable:

> If this book can be a success, then I refer to the blind reverence for such a highly regarded and learned man. But I cannot however avoid making the observation that the Swedes are gullible in the highest degree, perhaps even more than the Germans.

So Rudbeck's renegade pursuit was already raising eyebrows among expert antiquarians in the college, and rumors of De la Gardie's enthusiasm were causing concerns. But at the same time there was a strong tendency to underestimate what this passionate physician was capable of accomplishing.

IT WAS BECOMING increasingly clear, at least to Olof Rudbeck, that the Scandinavian past had been known among the ancients. He was working with the "greatest energy" to find surviving memories of this lost world in ancient texts, in peasant villages, and anywhere else they might be found. Soon he came across a story that truly caught his imagination.

This was the voyage of Jason and the Argonauts in search of the Golden Fleece, the skin of a flying ram that had been sacrificed to the gods and was hanging in an oak grove somewhere among the barbarians. Surviving accounts of the journey tell how Jason and his band of heroes, named after their well-crafted ship the *Argo,* sailed from the Mediterranean into the Black Sea. According to Greek tradition, this was nothing less than the oldest sailing venture of all classical mythology. Some even thought that their mighty ship, the fifty-oared *Argo,* was the first large sailing vessel to ride "the wine-dark sea."

When Rudbeck read the accounts, however, he became convinced that the Argonauts had, in their quest, sailed to Sweden. And his efforts to learn about this adventure would lead to what one seventeenth-century English gentleman called the "Heroik undertaking of incomparable Rudbeck," indeed a "second Argonautick Expedition."

A complex figure of classical mythology, Jason did not always show the proper behavior of a hero, and in some portraits he acted like a heartless scoundrel. His adventurous life had begun in great turmoil. As a newborn baby, son of King Aeson of Iolcus in northern Greece, Jason had been smuggled out of his hometown when his ambitious half-uncle Pelias seized the throne. This usurper imprisoned Jason's father, the rightful king, and then proceeded to carry out a campaign of slaughter, putting to death any of Aeson's relatives whom he could capture. Amid this bloodbath, the infant Jason was hurried out to the lonely mountain wilds around Mount Pelion.

There Jason would be raised by the half-man, half-horse centaur Chiron, a wise barbarian who incidentally would teach many future heroes, including the champion Achilles and the Trojan prince Aeneas. After years of training in the arts of life, Jason made his return to the city of Iolcus. With "locks of glorious hair . . . rippling down in gleaming streams unshorn upon his back," and sporting a distinctive leopard skin, the young stranger was a sight to behold as he strolled in the town's marketplace.

But it was not the hair or the leopard skin that caught his uncle's attention. "Terror seized him when his glancing eye fell on the clear sign of the single sandal on the man's right foot." An ancient oracle had warned Pelias long ago to beware the stranger with the single sandal. Sure enough, there was an unrecognized man with one shoe, as the other had stuck in the mud immediately before his arrival when Jason helped an old woman across a river. That old woman, it turned out, had been the goddess Hera in disguise, and she was so impressed by Jason's courtesy that she made him one of the few mortals ever to receive her patronage.

Recalling the warning and fearing its dire consequences, King Pelias saw an opportunity to get rid of this potential threat to his power. He agreed to allow Jason to succeed him on the throne, claiming that his old age was better suited to retirement than kingship. The catch, however, was that Jason would have to travel to the distant shores of Colchis, located on "the unfriendly sea," to retrieve the famous Golden Fleece. This trophy was needed, the king said, to put a stop to the nasty famine that raged in the town of Iolcus. Pelias was effectively sending Jason on a wild-goose chase.

Despite his suspicions about his uncle's motivations, Jason eagerly took up the challenge. He recruited some of the best adventurers in Greece, legendary leaders who figure prominently in the oldest classical stories. The hot-tempered warrior Heracles, the talented harpist Orpheus, and, in some accounts, the beautiful hunter maiden Atalanta, all agreed to come along. Spurred on by the helpful prodding of Jason's new patron goddess, Hera, the "flower of sailor-men" joined in this quest for the fleece of "gleaming gold."

Understandably, many scholars were skeptical about this tale, believing it only a matter of myth or fiction. Over the course of their travels, the crew encountered fire-breathing bulls, men springing up from sown dragon teeth, and of course the giant dragon who guarded the prized Golden Fleece. When the *Argo* had sailed past the Hellespont into the Black Sea, it seemed that its heroes had entered a world of fantasy and marvels on the fringes of civilization. Yet when

Rudbeck reread the oldest, most authoritative accounts of the myth, he became convinced that the voyage contained kernels of historical fact.

The deep streams, stormy lakes, and crashing rocks all along the way to the ends of the earth, where the shadowy mists prevailed, were not myth, but a somewhat accurate depiction of an actual voyage into the Arctic north.

THE FIRST TASK was to establish that there were genuine historical elements underlying the many fantastic adventures. In this regard, Rudbeck belonged to a solid historiographical tradition. The majority of ancient authors and some modern scholars had believed that the quest, in some form, had actually occurred.

Rudbeck, too, sensed the realistic undertones of the story. The ports of call, the amounts of time that passed between their stops, and the overall course of the expedition did not seem particularly strange for an ancient Mediterranean voyage. As Rudbeck's notes showed, with his calculations still preserved in the archives of the Swedish National Library, the Argonauts made their way from the home port of Iolcus along the Magnesian coast with stops on the islands of Lemnos and Samothrace, as they headed toward the famed city of Troy. This was in line with the ancient way of sailing, which favored, as one modern expert put it, a strategy of "coastal navigation and island-hopping" to facing the open sea.

The Argonauts passed the difficult straits of the Hellespont (today called Bosporus) that bridged Europe and Asia; they then entered the Black Sea. Next, "hugging the right side of the coast," they sailed on, overcoming challenges, until they reached the city of Colchis, situated in today's Georgia. In this land of towering peaks and sweeping plains, the Argonauts accomplished their mission. They gained the renowned Golden Fleece, largely with the aid of the king's daughter, the sorceress Medea, who had fallen madly in love with the *Argo*'s captain, Jason.

What interested Rudbeck most, however, was the journey *after* the Argonauts had snatched the Golden Fleece and escaped with the king's daughter, her "maiden's heart racked by love-cares."

As they left Colchis with the king in hot pursuit, the Argonauts were blown off course. The events that followed were never agreed upon in the ancient tales of the myth, or in the many later efforts to penetrate this mystery. In fact, wildly different suggestions have been put forward for the exact path of their disoriented return home by those who have looked for some historical basis for the voyage.

Some have claimed that Jason came out of the Black Sea into the Caspian Sea, and then into the Indian Ocean, beating a return to the Mediterranean via Lake Tritonis in the Egyptian territories. Others see the *Argo* continuing along the shores of the Black Sea until it reaches the outlet on the Danube, then following the river down until it empties into the river Po in northern Italy. From here they entered familiar waters either on the Adriatic or the Rhone. Another favorite option was that the Argonauts simply returned the same way that they came, retracing their steps through the Hellespont back to their home in northern Greece. A look at the perils they saw and experienced afterwards, however, made Rudbeck offer a different proposal.

They did not return the same way they came, Rudbeck claimed, because that contradicted the words of the blind seer Phineus, who predicted a different route. He had been right with his predictions regarding just about everything else, and there was nothing in the text to show that he had been wrong in this case. For another thing, as Rudbeck might also have added, the westward sailing required to return home clashed with the natural system of winds and currents— so this route was hardly a likely possibility at a time when they were desperate to escape from the king's fleet.

As for deciding among the other possible return routes, Rudbeck immediately recognized that the widely differing options were mainly a function of the plethora of surviving accounts of the adventure. Besides the short references in Herodotus's histories and elsewhere, the most influential versions were the fifth-century-B.C. lyric poet Pindar, particularly his fourth Pythian ode. Encyclopedists from Apollodorus to Diodorus Siculus also recounted the tale in summary form. Even more comprehensive was the third-century-B.C. Apollonius of Rhodes, who gave a stirring treatment in his epic *Argonautica*. Latin authors came in force as well, with Ovid's eloquent *Metamorphoses* and the first-century Roman Valerius Flaccus's somewhat artificial though never finished *Argonautica*. The fact that these authorities often contradicted each other made the story even more entangled and difficult to unravel.

All things being equal, Rudbeck believed that the oldest texts were most likely to capture the truth. Coming nearest in time to the events they purported to describe, the primary accounts had had the least opportunity for errors, envy, and other distortions to intervene. The case of the Argonauts was a classic example of this principle, and Rudbeck proposed going back to the very beginning, before the popular, though late, Hellenistic and Roman versions to the oldest source available.

With only a few exceptions, classical scholars at the time deemed the so-called *Argonautica Orphica* vastly older than all other accounts of the quest. According to the standard interpretation, this short, fourteen-hundred-line poem was viewed as part of the secret traditions of the ancient Orphic cult, written by an initiate into those mysteries, probably even by the leader, the legendary guru-shaman Orpheus himself. Although this poem is known today as a much later work, unlikely to be placed earlier than the fourth century A.D. and probably coming even later, Rudbeck was in good company when he traced it back to the mystic leader Orpheus, whose "beautiful music charmed the stubborn rocks upon the mountains and the course of rivers."

Relying mainly on the *Argonautica Orphica,* believed then even to predate Homer's *Iliad* and *Odyssey*, Rudbeck retraced the steps of the Argonauts' voyage. Moving north from the Black Sea, they would have passed the swampy marshes and sailed on some rivers through the forests of southern Russia. "Orpheus does not mention the names of the rivers," Rudbeck acknowledged, and neither did any surviving account. Nevertheless, the terrain of the narrative fit perfectly with the area north of the Black Sea. It was "pure vanity," Rudbeck thought, to seek the rivers, portages, and immense forests or other topographical features along the Danube, the Caspian, or anywhere other than this likely choice.

The desire to know if Jason and the Argonauts had in fact reached the Arctic north led to yet another remarkable chapter in Rudbeck's adventure. For the crux of this theory rested on the assumption that the Argonauts would have sailed from the Mediterranean to the Black Sea, and then into the Baltic Sea by navigating on the Russian rivers. This would mean that the heroes would have followed the river Tanais, today called the Don, all the way to its sources, where they must have disembarked and pulled their ship over a stretch of land (from Lake Fronovo to the Lovat River) until they reached the mighty Volga. From here they would have passed along other Russian rivers and waterways (the Volshova River, Lake Ladoga) until finally they came out in the "northern sea," or the Baltic. At this point Jason and the crew would have sailed to the edge of Rudbeck's lost world.

This proposed journey would have been daunting but, according to Rudbeck, not far-fetched. Actually this path had been used many times, he said, by Viking raiders in the Norse sagas that he was reading (and that his printing press would soon start publishing, in many cases for the very first time). Besides, the Vikings had a much more difficult challenge than the Argonauts, that is, pulling a small fleet as opposed to only one vessel. The tradition of dragging a ship was very important in that region, still a common feature of daily life for many Russian peasants, Rudbeck added, with plenty of examples of this practice.

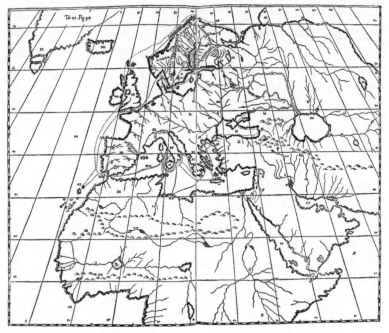

The dotted lines show possible routes of Jason and the Argonauts after they had retrieved the Golden Fleece. Rudbeck believed that the voyagers had sailed from the Black Sea to Sweden, following along the Russian rivers.

So, in short, Rudbeck asked himself: If the Vikings had taken this route to the south, could the Argonauts not have taken it to the north? With three boats that he intended to use for his own postal service and commercial passenger transport system (the first in Sweden), and with the help of some faithful volunteers, Rudbeck set out to test the possibility of the heroic voyagers' visit to the ancient golden age under the North Star.

RUDBECK AND HIS men would have to perform this feat, dragging the ship along at top speeds, in accordance with the time constraints recorded in the epic. One of the great authorities, the seventeenth-century historian Georgius Hornius, had calculated that Jason and his fellow Argonauts would have to have covered a distance of some four hundred Greek *stades,* or some forty-five (American) miles, and completed the task in only twelve days. This made for an exhausting but, Rudbeck ventured, imminently possible advance of just under four miles per day.

The boats were fifty-foot yachts built in Rudbeck's shipyard, and normally they would have been used to transport passengers, for a small fee of two *mark silvermynt,* between Uppsala and Stockholm. Every Monday, Wednesday, and Friday during the prime sailing season, Rudbeck's ships departed from the harbors of the capital city and the university town at precisely 8:00 and 11:00 a.m. Space was even provided for passengers who wished to smoke tobacco, though Rudbeck insisted that this be done in a special, restricted area on deck, "in the fresh air."

The first of the ships, constructed "about the size of the Argo," was carried from Rudbeck's shipyard down to the water, a distance of some 2,400 feet. This attempt was not very successful. It took a full eighty men, straining with all their might, to transport the fifty-footer, and the pace was excruciatingly slow, far too slow to cover the distance in the specified time. The exhausted volunteers must have been relieved when the day was over — Rudbeck did not exactly have a reputation for being the easiest man to work for. As demanding of others as he was of himself, Rudbeck had little patience for the work ethic of the contemporary boatsman, who preferred, he huffed, to stretch out on deck in the warm sun, porridge ladle in one hand and pipe in the other.

Undeterred by the disappointing first effort, Rudbeck tried again, this time dragging the boat over poles. Much more successfully, they moved at approximately three times the speed of the men who had tried to carry the ship. Then, in another attempt, Rudbeck had the crew smear grease on the well-rounded logs and drag the ship to the harbor—moving at the fastest time yet, and requiring the work of only fifty men! Allowing for eating, sleeping, and resting, and assuming ten hours of labor a day, "so long as it is believed that they could have worked," Rudbeck concluded, Jason and the Argonauts could easily have covered the required distance in the twelve-day period.

This rather quixotic episode was an early attempt at what we now call experimental archaeology, the effort to test a hypothesis by recreating its conditions, put to such dramatic effect in our time by the late Norwegian explorer Thor Heyerdahl. Until his death in 2002, Heyerdahl made many pioneering voyages to show how the ancients could have accomplished some very difficult deeds that he had suggested, namely sailing the oceans in rafts made of papyrus and balsa. His *Kon-Tiki*, most famously, crossed from Callao, Peru, a full 4,300 nautical miles to the Polynesian island of Tuamotu in the South Pacific.

Although a controversial method, still met with derision in some academic circles, this can be an effective way to learn about the past. And Rudbeck was one of the first to put it to use, albeit in a rudimentary fashion, and far from drifting 101 days on a balsa raft in the Pacific. The principle, however, was not completely alien. Rudbeck wanted to see if what he believed could in fact have been possible.

As his experiment with the passenger boat in his yacht service showed, the Argonauts *could* have dragged the ship the required distance in the given time, and thus overcome what he saw as the main obstacle to the voyage actually reaching the north. Interestingly, too, the names of the places that the Argonauts saw after they emerged from their ship-dragging hike through the unknown forests sounded strikingly familiar. Orpheus, for instance, sang about Leulo—and right in the very spot where the Argonauts would have come out in Rudbeck's proposed course was the Swedish town called Luleå (pronounced loo-le-oh). Orpheus described the town of Pacto, and Rudbeck connected it with the Swedish town Piteå, while Orpheus's Casby showed up in the Swedish Kassaby, or perhaps the smaller village Kasby. Rudbeck marveled at how well it all fell into place; if Orpheus

had not lived almost "three thousand years ago," he would have concluded that the poet had read a book about Swedish geography.

The quest for the Golden Fleece was yet another spectacular confirmation that such Swedish place-names had in fact existed in the
most ancient times accessible to historians. Just as his archaeological
dating method had shown to his satisfaction that the great antiquity
of Sweden far preceded the Trojan War, here were Swedish towns already flourishing in the Arctic north in the earliest recorded sailing
voyage, and observed at least one generation before that epic conflict.
After all, when the *Argo* first rowed away on its mission, the future
Trojan War hero Achilles was still a baby. He had been carried down
by his guardians, the centaurs Chiron and his wife, who galloped
down to see the Argonauts off, with Chiron's "great forehoof waving
them on their way."

As for the temptation to see Jason's voyage as "only a poem or a
dream," Rudbeck was ready with a response:

> I would rather believe the dreams of this harper than
> the great mathematician Ptolemy, who, for all his math-
> ematical art, was not able to find Sweden's mountains,
> provinces, darkness, and Ice Sea, nor even its length, but
> made it a small island thirty Swedish miles long.

"So I would rather keep to the true dreamers than the untruthful
writers."

And for this dreamer in the middle of the 1670s, still wounded by
the previous humiliations and insults, it was fairly clear that his
beloved Sweden had also had a glorious past, one that was much better known among the ancients than had ever been imagined before.

RUDBECK'S DESCENT INTO the world of mythology was in many
ways an addictive and fanciful escape. Following Jason and the

Argonauts in search of the Golden Fleece was helping Rudbeck forget about his enemies, all their hateful accusations, and also some painful misfortunes at home.

Vendela had given birth to seven children, but alas not all had survived. In the past year, their oldest son, Johannes Caesar, had died at age sixteen. This tragic loss followed the death of their two-year-old daughter Magdalena, six years earlier. Unfortunately, within a couple of years, the family would also bury their toddler Karl. Although child mortality was high in the seventeenth century, and few parents at that time escaped its trauma, the death of a child was not necessarily any less heartbreaking than it is today. Olof and Vendela Rudbeck coped as best they could.

The other children in the household happily seemed to be healthy and prospering. The precocious fourteen-year-old Olof junior, tall, thin, and multifaceted in his abilities, was taking more after his father every day. Johanna Kristina, the oldest daughter, was showing her talents as well, especially in painting, drawing, and singing. Their son Gustaf, however, was more of a problem child. Less willing than the other children to please his parents, he was earning a reputation as a downright troublemaker. The youngest surviving child was their adorable six-year-old daughter, Vendela, who, like her older sister, was impressing others with her beautiful voice. Rudbeck must have been proud of his talented children, and pleased with the interest they had begun to show in his activities.

Reading the preliminary notes as soon as Rudbeck wrote them, Olaus Verelius was ecstatic. However, he also sensed the inherent risks and came again with a request. Verelius strongly encouraged Rudbeck to begin printing the book at once; he did not wish to see such an extraordinary work collapse under the weight of its own success. Rudbeck, too, knew the dangers of delay.

After presenting his discovery of the lymphatic system at Queen Christina's court, Rudbeck had dragged his feet in writing up this great medical achievement. By the time he finally did, in the summer of 1653, another physician, Professor Thomas Bartholin at Copenhagen University, had managed to publish his account first, sparking the priority dispute of the early 1650s.

Not wanting to see his historical work suffer the same fate, Rudbeck took Verelius's advice, and planned to publish as soon as possible. He would take his manuscript, as soon as it was ready, to the Uppsala University press, located in a little red building in the court around the Gustavianum. For the last twenty years this press had been in these cramped quarters. The offices were in one room, with another holding enormous stacks of paper, and a third serving as an attic or storehouse. The man in the middle of the mess was the printer Henrik Curio.

Apparently a learned man, the forty-four-year-old Curio spoke Latin, Italian, Spanish, French, English, Dutch, and Swedish, in addition to his native German. According to Rudbeck, he could also read Hebrew and Greek, a combination of ancient and modern languages that was certainly valuable in the growing international book trade of the seventeenth century. It was Rudbeck, in fact, who in 1661, after almost two years of attempts, had persuaded Curio to leave his work in a successful Stockholm printing house and open up shop at Uppsala University—a decision for which Rudbeck would later feel responsible, and eventually guilty.

Although the two men were different in many ways—Rudbeck alert, obsessive, and unrelenting, while Curio was more aloof and lackadaisical in his pursuits—they had become good friends over the years. Their relationship had grown closer after 1671, when Curio married Rudbeck's cousin Disa. With these ties of family and friendship, it was important to Rudbeck that Curio would be the printer of his work.

But Curio was no angel. Since the early 1670s he had often been described as a slacker. His irregular habits, the critics complained, were undeniably affecting the quality of his work. He was careless, was a bit of a drunk, and did no proofreading whatsoever. The products were terrible and getting worse. Such negligence was also, people thought, bringing the press into chaos, and the university into disrepute. Soon "no one will be able to read [the books] at all." Even observers uninvolved in the matter said his work was "unusually lousy."

Complaints were getting louder, with demands for official inquiries and inventories of the press. Some professors were heard calling for Curio's resignation. Overjoyed by his successes in finding the Hyperboreans and in his quest for the Golden Fleece, however, Rudbeck clearly did not realize how serious a threat was posed to Henrik Curio.

For the more Rudbeck looked, the more evidence he found of ancient Sweden, and the more his imagination helped him overcome the many difficulties that arose. Once he was on the trail of ancient heroes, it was apparent to Rudbeck that Jason and the Argonauts were not the only classical figures who had reached the far north.

ACCORDING TO ANCIENT MYTHS, many heroes had made the long, arduous journey to a land of "shadowy mists." Retracing the path of these classical wanderers and examining what they had seen along the way, Rudbeck became convinced that these journeys to the kingdom of Hades were in fact trips to ancient Sweden.

The main clues for this startling, indeed mind-boggling, conclusion came from the oldest surviving descriptions of the dreaded Underworld. In Homer's *Odyssey,* the Greek warrior Odysseus made the daring voyage. The crafty king of Ithaca described what he saw as he approached its distant shores:

> *By night, our ship ran onward toward the Ocean's bourne,*
> *the realm and region of the Men of the Winter,*
> *hidden in mist and cloud. Never the flaming*
> *eye of Helios lights on those men*

at morning, when he climbs the sky of stars,
nor in descending earthward out of heaven;
ruinous night being rove over those wretches.

Few would disagree that the "Helios [that] lights on those men at morning, when he climbs the sky of stars" refers to the Sun. *Helios* (ἥλιος) was literally the Greek word for "sun," with the "flaming eye" one of its common representations. The Greek root *helio-* is seen in our language, too, in the heliocentric theory, which places the sun at the center of our solar system, and helium, the element named after its discovery on the sun. So when the *Odyssey* notes that "Never the flaming eye of Helios lights on those men," Rudbeck believed that the poet's words needed very little commentary. This was not fantasy, but rather a clear description of actual phenomena that take place in the far north, above the Arctic Circle.

For three long months at that high latitude, Sweden indeed looked like what Homer called the "sunless Underworld." Scandinavians living near and around the Arctic have long adjusted to the harsh environment. As Rudbeck saw it, they skated and skied, rode sleighs and pulled sledges, and even held markets on the thick winter ice. Cold weather provided natural refrigeration that kept fish fresh for four, five, and sometimes six months with no need of salt. The same ice also created spectacular vistas, hanging down from roofs of houses and heated cabins "like tallow candles or lances, with different colors and in various positions, as though the pipes of an organ were placed vertically next to the walls."

As for the "mist and cloud" predominating at the entrance to the Underworld, this was another well-known feature of Rudbeck's far northern location. Frost, snow, and mist created a dreadful concoction that inspired Homer's Hades, or what he called "the realm and region of the Men of the Winter." Pools and lakes emerged on the high ground, and the cold weather in turn hardened them into ice.

When additional water came from nearby caves and channels, the traveler saw "the waters throw up a steamy mist into the heights and in their descent form inverted pyramids of ice at the sea."

One of the big objections to Rudbeck's emerging theory of Hades was of course the fact that classical mythology presented the Underworld as the abode of the dead. But under the sway of his imagination, Rudbeck cast this problem aside without much ado. Indeed, his reading of the ancient myths made him question that part of the tale. As Odysseus himself showed, the Underworld was not literally a home of the dead. Not only did he and his crew sail there, but, even more remarkably, they returned! Many other ancient heroes sailed to the Underworld—Hercules, Perseus, Theseus, Orpheus, and so on—and they, too, returned from the voyage. With so many arrivals and departures, the halls of Hades did not exist in the classical imagination as only a place for departed souls.

In fact, Rudbeck believed that Homer had made it absolutely clear that the kingdom of the Underworld was located not only aboveground, but also in the far north. When Odysseus arrived at the abyss, for instance, some of the shades showed surprise at how far he had traveled. But it was not a surprise, as Odysseus's guide, the beautiful witch Circe, had given him unmistakable sailing instructions for reaching this kingdom at the world's end:

> *Odysseus, master of land ways and sea ways,*
> *feel no dismay because you lack a pilot;*
> *only set your mast and haul your canvas*
> *to the fresh blowing North.*

Then she added, just "sit down and steer, and hold the wind."

What clearer words, Rudbeck thought, on the need to sail north to reach the Underworld, "the gloom at the world's end." There Homer's "region of winter" seemed to correspond well with the deep, dark winters known to prevail in the Arctic. The poet had also given another possible name for "the Men of the Winter": the Cimmerii, or Cimmerians. This name survives in many modern translations of the *Odyssey*. To Rudbeck, though, the name raised even more questions, for if you pull out a map of the north, you will find this name of the Cimmerii, remarkably, almost verbatim.

More exactly the name was *Kimmi* or *Kimmerii,* and it was found all over the north. There was a region called Kimme-Lapmarck, located on a peninsula called Kimmer-näs. There was also the Kemi River, which flowed through northern Finland, not to mention Kimmi town and Nort-Kimm and Kimmi marsh, bordering on the White Sea. So many other examples were also close at hand. By Rudbeck's derivation, the Kimmi or Kimmerii drew their name literally from the Old Swedish for "darkness"—no surprise, as Homer's Cimmerii were said to live in perpetual darkness somewhere near the entrance to the Underworld.

But why had the ancient mariner pointed his rudder north? Because he needed to know the future, and according to Rudbeck, there was no better place to consult seers, soothsayers, and sorcerers than northern Sweden.

Indeed, many branches of fortune-telling and superstition thrived particularly well in the small villages around the Arctic Circle. Some of the dwellers excelled in predicting the future, reading everything from the flights of birds to the movements of vapors rising from the distant mountains. Some knew spells to enchant victims, and to summon the good, favorable winds for distressed ship captains. There were others who claimed to be adept in shape-changing, and there were even some who could "put out the stars, melt the mountains, solidify springs," and perform striking feats of wind magic. With its soothsayers and magicians, the northernmost lands were still, as one observer put it, "as learned in witchcraft as if it had had Zoroaster the Persian for its instructor in this damnable science."

On his visit to Sweden, Magalotti had also noted how deeply rooted witchcraft was during the 1670s: "Never does one hear anything else spoken about in the northern provinces, Boshuslän, Dalarne, and Lappland, than witchcraft."

There was not enough ink and paper, Rudbeck said, to record all the stories about this art of magic, prophecy, and dream interpretation that flourished in the bubbling witches' pot he was finding in the far north. Most spectacularly, Rudbeck believed that he had found a connection between the seer Odysseus sought in the Underworld and a traditional authority among the indigenous peoples of the Arctic. Tiresias, the blind seer who foretold Odysseus's future, was a Saami shaman, a Tyreas, who went into ecstatic trances and claimed to tell the future.

Odysseus's perilous voyage to the Underworld was not simply a good story told for entertainment as the minstrel strummed the harp and the wine went around the warrior's halls of Bronze Age Greece. The very details of Odysseus's journey could be seen in the far north of Sweden. The Cimmerians, the darkness, the mists, the seer Tiresias, and the reputation for wisdom were all there, around the Arctic Circle. Before long, Rudbeck would also have proposals for other missing elements. The name of Charon, the boatman who ferried souls to the Underworld, was derived from *baron,* a funeral barge used among the indigenous peoples in the largely unexplored regions of the far north. Cerberus, too, the three-headed guard dog of Hades, was originally Garm, the fierce hound of Hel remembered in the Old Norse sagas, and probably, Rudbeck thought, a survival of an ancient bodyguard force stationed at the entrance to the kingdom.

So, full of excitement, Rudbeck was amazed at how closely Homer's vision of Hades fit his proposed Arctic home. He made plans to send some of his mathematical students on a scientific expedition to survey the mountains and rivers of what he now claimed was the original kingdom of Hades. As thrilling as it was tantalizing,

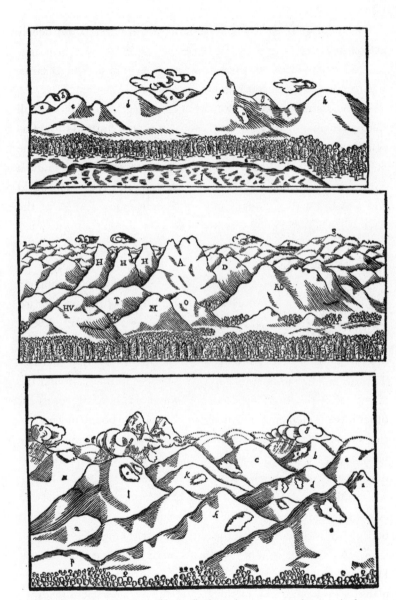

Hyperborean Mountains surveyed by Rudbeck's students in an expedition to the far north of Sweden.

every clue suggested a new understanding about the forgotten golden age of the north.

Rudbeck pledged to continue writing "as long as God gives me health, and the moon continues to become full." What he found next would lead into the tangled web of one of the greatest and most enduring enigmas of all time—and cause his sharpest critics to think it was really a result of moonstruck lunacy.

8

MOUNTAINS DON'T DANCE

Your theory is crazy. The question is, is it crazy enough?

—NIELS BOHR, DANISH PHYSICIST AND NOBEL PRIZE LAUREATE

SOMEWHERE BEYOND the "Pillars of Hercules" lay the fabled island of Atlantis, home of an advanced civilization that once exerted a profound influence over the known world. After rising to a peak of power, refinement, and grace, this virtual paradise soon succumbed to vice and folly. Then, in a single "day and night of misfortune," earthquakes shook the island to its foundation, and sent the formerly unrivaled civilization to the bottom of the sea.

This was the story according to the ancient Greek philosopher Plato, whose fourth-century-B.C. dialogues *Timaeus* and *Critias* unleashed this fantastic vision onto the world. After a series of marathon discussions about the nature of justice, a wealthy old man named Critias was reminded of the story of Atlantis, which he had heard as a child. His grandfather, also named Critias, had heard it from his father, who in turn had gotten it from the distinguished Athenian Solon. This politician-poet had allegedly come across the old tradition on his journey to Egypt in about 600 B.C., when he met some priests who lived in the town of Sais on the Nile delta.

"O Solon, Solon, you Greeks are always children," one of the elder priests dismissed the traveler, marveling at how little the Athenians remembered the past. The Egyptian records, by contrast, he was told, preserved the bewildering tale, fully developed in hieroglyphics carved on stone pillars in the temple. When Solon returned to his native Athens, he hoped to give the island of Atlantis its own full-length epic poem, one that he thought would surpass the masterpieces of Homer.

Having heard the tale as a ten-year-old boy, Critias did not think a single detail had escaped him over the years. The image of Atlantis, he said, had been "stamped firmly on my mind like the encaustic designs of an indelible painting." With this assertion, Critias proceeded to tell the remarkable story of the world's greatest lost civilization: its rise to power, its immense glory, and then its violent destruction, which left only a "barrier of impassable mud"—a formidable obstacle that still blocked access to this golden age, supposedly vanished since 9400 B.C.

Plato certainly knew how to capture the imagination. But could it really have happened? Could there have been such an idyllic civilization that was once destroyed by an earthquake and swallowed by the sea?

It is easy to dismiss the whole narrative as the product of an active imagination, and indeed you would be in good company. For just as the story of Atlantis is at least as old as Plato, debate about its existence has been lively since his own student, Aristotle, openly voiced his doubts. After all, with Aristotle's mastery of ancient knowledge, which prompted the Roman natural philosopher Pliny to label him "a man of supreme eminence in every branch of science," it is striking that he had not even heard of Atlantis before Plato outlined it in his famous dialogues.

Surely such a tale would not have escaped the attention of every previous chronicler. Not even the colorful historian Herodotus mentioned Atlantis. Like Solon, he had also visited Egypt, had spoken at length with the priests, and had a flair for the sensational and the mysterious. For Aristotle and the many critics who followed after him, Atlantis had of course never existed. Plato had conjured the whole thing out of his head, and then, as if to cover up for an embarrassing lack of corroborating evidence, conveniently made it all disappear.

Yet Plato repeatedly assures us that, however strange it may sound, the story of Atlantis is absolutely true. None of his other portraits of idealized societies, including the utopian community outlined in *The Republic,* shares the same pretensions to factual accuracy.

Plato's plan, according to the first-century biographer Plutarch, was to create nothing less than a grand and stirring masterpiece. Solon had been unable to complete his epic poem, preoccupied perhaps by renewed tensions of Athenian political life, or, as Plutarch suggested, restrained by a fear of failure in the ambitious enterprise of trying to surpass Homer. As if claiming his family inheritance, Plato sought to build on this "fine but undeveloped site." He marshaled his creative talents and then released them on lost Atlantis. It was to be constructed with a magnificence "such as no story or myth or poetic creation had ever received before."

Unfortunately, however, Plato died before he could fully realize these aims, or perhaps abandoned the project when he struggled to find the fitting climax—and this leaves the oldest known account of Atlantis to end literally in the middle of a sentence.

Sure enough, over the last two thousand years, scientists, adventurers, visionaries, mystics, eccentrics, and lunatics have raced to fill in the missing details of this unfinished dialogue. Redrawn maps place the supposedly submerged civilization almost everywhere, and many come complete with elaborate theories painstakingly or at least passionately argued. From the Atlantic to the Pacific, from the Mediterranean to the Caribbean, few places have not been named as possible locations for the legendary island of Atlantis.

But few, it seems, were as unlikely a candidate and few would inspire as much enthusiasm, for a time, as the theory put forward by Uppsala's professor of medicine, Olof Rudbeck.

"BY GOD's GRACE, I have recently found such antiquities for our country and its great praise in the oldest Greek and Latin texts that it is unbelievable," Rudbeck wrote to Chancellor de la Gardie at the end of December 1674, promising, though, to save the full details until he saw De la Gardie in person.

It must have been quite a conversation when Rudbeck told the count about his latest discovery. For that matter, it must have been quite an experience when the idea first struck him. The lost world of Atlantis, Rudbeck was growing convinced, had actually been in Sweden! Its capital was in fact just outside the university, in a place called Old Uppsala.

All learned Swedes knew this town as one of the earliest inhabited sites in the country. Popular belief, medieval sources, and Rudbeck's own archaeological investigations had all confirmed its great age. Now, reading Plato's dialogues *Timaeus* and *Critias* closely, Rudbeck must have felt a strange sense of déjà vu. Here in the philosopher's tale was a place beyond the Pillars of Hercules, that is, at the ends of the world, with a reputed center of culture, just as he had envisioned in the land of the Hyperboreans. And upon inspection it sounded increasingly like what he knew about Old Uppsala.

Blessed with many attractions, this town would indeed have been a most appropriate place for the kingdom builders. Just as Plato regarded it as the "fairest of all plains," Old Uppsala was well known as a fertile, rich region, and at one time it had been the most populated area in Sweden. Its pleasant meadows and adjacent farmlands also enhanced the appeal of this ancient center.

According to Plato, this plain stretched some 3,000 stadia in length (about 550 kilometers) and 2,000 stadia in width (365 kilometers) reaching from the capital city to the "great sea." Each of these points, Rudbeck ventured with typical boldness, could be found in Sweden. Although he concluded that Atlantis was in fact 5,000 stadia in length, the first measurement (3,000 stades) approximated the size of the kingdom, calculated from the capital at Old Uppsala to Torne in the Arctic north (the other 2,000 stadia ran south from Old Uppsala to Skåne). The width of 2,000 stadia estimated the distance across the center of the realm and did in fact end at a great sea, the North Sea in the west. The rocky, mountainous terrain encircling Atlantis also fit well, Rudbeck proposed, pointing to the Scanderna chain in the west and north, from which came the name *Scandinavia*. Enclosing the region of Old Uppsala, too, were many famous burial mounds—could these be the "sacred hills" of Atlantis?

When Rudbeck went out to the proposed capital city for the first time to investigate, he was amazed to find more than coincidental correspondences. Accompanying him that initial day, most likely in the summer of 1674, were four sons of the powerful nobleman Gustaf Kurck, who also marked out and measured the dimensions of the old capital. Eight other Uppsala students, who came along on the expedition, confirmed the length, breadth, and width of the capital, the dimensions laid out almost precisely as Plato had written two thousand years before. They had measured, remeasured, and, to his astonishment, found that the dimensions corresponded "not only with stadia but also with feet and steps." The team concluded with another round of measurements using Rudbeck's "mathematical instruments." "Because neither I nor they," he added, "could ever before believe this to be true."

Leaving aside for the moment the many difficulties Rudbeck would face (and soon for the most part confront), there was actually good reason for his bursting enthusiasm. He had combed the pages of Plato's dialogues, especially the more detailed *Critias,* looking for precise information about the physical location of the city: "At a distance of about fifty stades, there stood a mountain that was low on all sides."

In addition, the philosopher noted other distinguishing features at the heart of the capital: the royal palace, the great temple, and a cluster of amenities, including gardens and exercise grounds. Nearby were also the three main harbors, and two rivers for transporting timber to the capital.

Beginning with the landmark least likely to change, Plato's low mountain was immediately located. "This hill is none other than the one you see in Old Uppsala," Rudbeck said, pointing out the distance, meticulously marked out and reproduced in a map of Atlantis he drew with the help of his students, who were somewhat overwhelmed at the easy genius of their unpredictable teacher. "Make a circle," Rudbeck said, and trace its lines through the markers *n* and *p*; inside this circumference were to be found all the sites of the lost capital city.

To the north, just as Plato said, were the two rivers for shipping timber and grain. Known to any local peasant were Junkils aan, which still carried wood and grain from outlying regions, and Tensta aan, now limited only to smaller craft. So, if this latter stream did at times widen and narrow, causing occasional divergences from Plato's specified width, Rudbeck was not overly worried. This was because, since the time when Atlantis had flourished, other streams, the Ekeby and Edshammar, had encroached on its waterways, and made it less passable for ships (as did the construction of an old mill). Besides that, Rudbeck was sure that the water levels had once been much higher.

They certainly had! As geologists later discovered, impenetrably thick glaciers had once covered the land around Old Uppsala and central Sweden, as they had most of northern Europe. When the glaciers began to thaw at the end of the last ice age, the water rose significantly, leaving the great plain still underwater as late as 4000 B.C. Rudbeck could not have known about this phenomenon, for glacial recession was as unfamiliar to scholars of his day as woolly mammoths, saber-toothed tigers, or heavy-jawed Neanderthals. But evidence of high water was spotted, Rudbeck was convinced, deep in the layers of the humus, and the story of a drowning Atlantis did seem consistent with observable facts. Figure B on his map shows where the level of water in 1670s Old Uppsala fitted Plato's descriptions more closely. The gently flowing streams were, in his view, the last remnants of the commercial rivers that had been so important to the economy of Atlantis.

Over the course of the 1670s, Rudbeck would make the four-kilometer carriage ride out to Old Uppsala many times to explore the terrain of Atlantis and search for any surviving remains. Sometimes he would bring along fellow professors of Uppsala, and at other times his gifted mathematical and engineering students, who were assisting with the land surveying. Much to his surprise, he found that Plato had captured the Swedish landscape rather well. "Not a single point," Rudbeck said, "seems to be missing."

Indeed, another readily identifiable landmark turned up, and this was certainly one of the rarest and most difficult finds for Atlantis hunters over the centuries: the track where the Atlanteans staged races and held equestrian contests.

When Plato put it at the center of the capital, Rudbeck knew a likely spot to start looking. He had heard that there had once been a course at Old Uppsala that had in fact still been used as late as the sixteenth century. Races had stopped at this old track only when King Charles IX, the father of Gustavus Adolphus, built a new, more modern one near the royal palace in Uppsala.

Although Rudbeck had looked over the proposed site on many occasions and his investigations had not yet unearthed any evidence, he knew some elderly gentlemen who did remember races being held there. One ninety-eight-year-old retired commander, who had served five Swedish kings at Uppsala Castle, confirmed the accuracy of the location, as did Gostaf Larsson, a grandfather of Rudbeck's wife, Vendela. A closer look at the dimensions also showed a striking

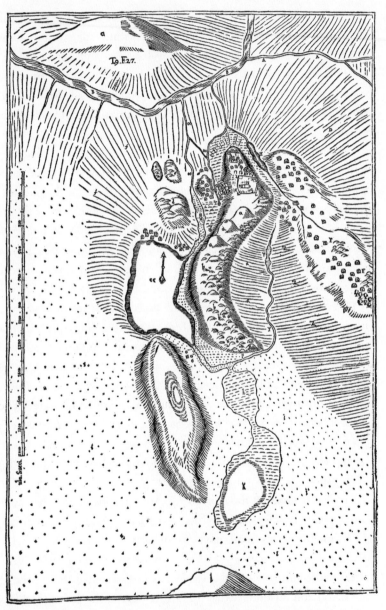

Map of Old Uppsala, the ancient site that Rudbeck identified as the capital of Atlantis. Plato's mountain, rivers, sacred grove, racetrack, and royal burial mounds were quickly found, as were many other things over the next thirty years of Rudbeck's quest.

resemblance to the track of Atlantis, right down to the width, which ran to one stadium, or some six hundred feet, and into the edge of the swampy area that stabled the horses.

This was indeed a stunning coincidence, and Rudbeck made plans to pursue this promising lead. But, even more fantastic, Rudbeck announced another discovery: he had found the old pagan temple of Atlantis.

According to Plato's fable, the temple was an imposing open structure dedicated to the god Poseidon and his Atlantean lover Cleito. Located near the sacred grove and the sacred springs, this temple was "encircled with a wall of gold." Inside stood golden statues, including the sea god riding a chariot with six winged chargers, "his own figure so tall as to touch the ridge of the roof, and round about him a hundred Nereids [sea nymphs] on dolphins." Outside were many gold images of Atlantis's extensive royal family.

Set against this lavish scenery, the kingdom of Atlantis hosted a monumental ceremony every five or six years. Each of the ten provinces that made up the federated power of Atlantis came together at this temple to evaluate their laws, "the precepts of Poseidon" that had long ago been inscribed upon a pillar of orchical-cum, a controversial mysterious metal that "sparkled like fire." The festival began with a ritual bull hunt using only "staves and nooses":

> And whatsoever bull they captured they led up to the pillar and cut its throat over the top of the pillar, raining down blood on the inscription. And inscribed upon the pillar, besides the laws, was an oath which invoked mighty curses upon them that disobeyed.

After consecrating the limbs, the Atlanteans then took one gout of the blood and mixed it with wine. As the rest of the pure blood was poured over the sacrificial fire, the leaders "swore to give judgment according to the laws upon the pillar and to punish whosoever had committed any previous transgression," adding the further promise not to "transgress any of the writings willingly, nor govern nor submit to any governor's edict save in accordance with their father's laws." The wine-and-blood mixture was then drunk, with the cup offered as a gift to the temple.

Such clues were critical, since there was clearly no pagan temple of Atlantis standing in the middle of Old Uppsala. So imagine Rudbeck's pleasure to read a fascinating description of Old Uppsala during the late eleventh century. The observer was a medieval monk, Adam of Bremen, who had come to Sweden while preparing his church history of the north. In his chronicle was an account of a "well-known temple" at Old Uppsala that could only catch Rudbeck's attention:

> It is situated on level ground, surrounded by mountains.
> A large tree with spreading branches stands near the
> temple. There is also a spring nearby where the hea-
> thens make human sacrifices. A golden chain com-
> pletely surrounds the temple, and its roof, too, is
> covered with gold.

Statues of three gods, Adam continued, stood inside the temple. On one side was Wotan, brandishing armor and weapons befitting this god of war; on the other side, Frey, a fertility god with a giant phallus. In between the two stood the god Thor, holding a scepter for his control over the primal elements, governing "the air with its thunder, lightning, wind, rain, and fair weather." A glance at this temple and the many offerings, the monk also noted, showed how eagerly the Swedes tended to worship their ancient heroes.

"Every nine years a great ceremony is held at Uppsala. People bring sacrifices from all the Swedish provinces." "Animals and humans," Adam of Bremen continued, "are sacrificed, and their bodies are hung in the trees of a sacred grove that is adjacent to the temple."

Held in the highest honor, this grove was made "sacred through the death and putrefaction of the many victims that have hung there." The sacrifices, the monk said, had been personally witnessed by a seventy-two-year-old man he had met. "The heathens chant many different prayers and incantations during these rituals, but they are so vile that I will say nothing further about them."

There were others Rudbeck found, however, who would gladly expound on all the "impurities and abominations" that had once been practiced in Old Uppsala. One of the most vivid accounts came from the sixteenth-century Swedish humanist Olaus Magnus, who was Sweden's last Catholic archbishop (though never consecrated). Looking back from the vantage point of the Swedish Reformation, Magnus used his historical background and his wonderful imagination to paint a gruesome portrait of the last days when the pagan religion flourished at Rudbeck's selected site:

> Now the man whom chance had presented for immola-
> tion would be plunged alive into the spring of water
> which gushed out by the sacrificial precinct. If he
> quickly breathed his last, the priests proclaimed that the
> votive offering had been auspicious, soon carried him
> off from there into a nearby grove, which they believed
> sacred, and hung him up, asserting that he had been
> transported into the assembly of the gods. . . .

For such an event, the "whole mass of the people would attend" and "wish [the victim] utmost joy." This was after all "considered to be an offering most favorable for the kingdom," taking place within the "rich magnificence" of the old temple, so sumptuously decorated that it was impossible to see any "inner walls, paneled ceilings, or pillars that did not glitter with gold."

For Rudbeck, the monk and the bishop had preserved descriptions of an age-old rite that had survived in Sweden since the early days of the Atlantean empire. Clearly, though, there were many differences between the accounts of the temple of Atlantis and the pagan temple of Old Uppsala: Plato had said that the Atlanteans met every five or six years, and Adam of Bremen said the worshipers met every nine years; Plato noted that the Atlanteans worshipped Poseidon, and Adam of Bremen said that Norse gods were the objects of veneration; Plato specified the sacrifice of bulls, and the others mentioned "humans and animals." But none of these or other differences seriously troubled Olof Rudbeck.

Such contradictions and disagreements were not so much obstacles to a hunter of the truth as they were guides of potentially great significance. He illustrated the point using a story from everyday experience.

Suppose a group of people take a trip. Would each individual in the party, Rudbeck asked, describe the same circumstances with the same words? His answer was a confident "no way." Yet instead of simply concluding that the journey had never taken place, the differences in the various accounts could, if properly used, point the way to a greater knowledge and understanding of the event. If the example of the travelers failed to make an impression, Rudbeck had a more memorable one: the Four Evangelists, Matthew, Mark, Luke, and John, all wrote the truth, though they were nevertheless not always in agreement "in all words and all circumstances."

The same thing, he thought, was the case with Atlantis. Small differences in detail, such as Plato's saying that the assembly was held every five or six years and Adam's saying that it was held every nine years, did not irreparably harm the case. The fact that such differences existed, occurring over such a span of time, could potentially increase the value of the testimonies and add more credibility to the events they described. Taking the idea even further, Rudbeck believed such contradictions were preferable to the alternative. Had Plato and Adam of Bremen agreed in every single detail, then historians would have had to approach their accounts with more caution, for such an overwhelming agreement does not often occur naturally. Far more often, one account has been borrowed, copied, stolen, or just plain derived from—or influenced by—another.

Navigating through the chaos and uncertainty, in other words, was the surest way to find certainty. The historian's task was to follow the trail wherever it might lead, uncovering the underlying kernels of truth among the diversity of conflicting evidence.

So, in the case of the temple, Rudbeck started trying to sort through the claims for the essential factual core. Plato had described the temple as lying near a mountain with an ornate wall of gold, and Adam of Bremen also mentioned the nearby mountain and the overlapping "golden chain." Both noted the nearby springs, the sacred grove, and the rich offerings brought to the temple from the provinces. Sacrifices were performed in both accounts, and the victims were kept in the groves and springs. As for the particular differences, it was not inconceivable that those aspects could change over time, depending on the desires, needs, and priorities in each age.

Examination of the manuscripts of the Norse sagas did in fact turn up a closer resemblance between the sacrifices held in Atlantis and at Old Uppsala than Adam of Bremen could have known. In addition to the gruesome human sacrifices, the practice of offering bulls to the gods had also been carried out on Rudbeck's chosen site, with the tradition "surviving" well into the Middle Ages. Snorri Sturlusons's *Heimskringla,* or *History of the Northern Kings,* put it very clearly: "There was a custom in Sweden to rear a bull which would be sacrificed to Odin."

The Viking sagas also helped clarify the reasons why the Atlanteans tied the bulls in the sacred grove, a situation that Plato never explained. The binding of the bulls, Rudbeck concluded, was carried out to make them "half-crazy" and ensure more of a challenge in the ritual hunt.

And the fact that no such golden chain or wall now existed in this location did not mean that none had existed there before. Many sources had reported the elaborate golden decorations, and it was a well-known fact that this temple had been plundered of its riches in the Middle Ages, after the introduction of Christianity and the gradual demise of the pagan religion. Yet, centuries after this disappearance, Rudbeck was making the shocking revelation that some remains of the great temple of Atlantis had actually survived. Astonishingly, according to Rudbeck, they were visible in plain sight.

Standing in the middle of the plain near the sacred grove and sacred spring was a very old structure, one of the first Christian churches in Sweden and the seat of the first archbishopric in the kingdom. Built over the course of many years in the middle of the twelfth century, Old Uppsala Church still stands today as one of Sweden's oldest sites. And Rudbeck believed not only that this church was built on the grounds of the demolished pagan temple, but that its construction had incorporated many of the temple's materials. Bits and pieces of Atlantis were, in other words, to be found in the walls of the old church.

Many times over the next few years, Rudbeck and some fellow enthusiasts would come to Old Uppsala and chip away at the old walls, "so loose in places that [chunks of Atlantis] could be taken out with the fingers." On one outing with a classics professor, Anders Norcopensis, and the vice-librarian, Professor Wallerius, the scholarly ensemble searched "every nook and cranny." They found much evidence in the walls of gold, silver, and copper having been combined with the limestone, presumably by talented Atlantean goldsmiths. Next time, when Rudbeck was back with one of his students, the engraver Petrus Törnewall, they found a large, crooked, rusty nail containing scattered specks of pure gold.

This may not sound like a lot, but the traces of gold in the rusty old nails would be more than enough to keep Rudbeck pressing on at Old Uppsala. And when he started looking near the sacred grove, he found an "unspeakable amount of jawbones, teeth, and feet of horses, pigs, oxen, and dogs burned and unburned." This finding, Rudbeck said, "gave us good reason to search further."

❧

WHILE RUDBECK HAPPILY wrote in December 1674 that he planned to begin printing his book in less than two months, he would soon learn that the celebrations were a bit premature. For in the meantime, his loyal printer Henrik Curio had been sacked.

The process of removing this alleged slacker had begun at the end of 1674, with the official inquiries and inventories turning into a full-fledged trial. Some of Uppsala's most distinguished theologians, Rudbeck's old adversary Lars Stigzelius among others, were leading the prosecution. They were joined by prominent members of the College of Antiquities, Johan Schefferus and Johan Hadorph, who were quite upset by the slow progress and the poor results at the press. Representing the defense was a young man named Ingo Rudbeck, Olof's cousin and at that time a student training to become a lawyer.

Finally aware and genuinely concerned that the situation had moved beyond mere warnings and rumors of dismissal, Rudbeck wrote a long letter to De la Gardie pleading on behalf of his printer and friend. Curio had managed to publish many excellent works from Uppsala's scholars. Johan Schefferus, Johan Loccenius, and Olaus Verelius had all seen their works produced with success by the printer, despite the slim financial resources and rather unenviable working conditions.

When Curio had arrived at the Uppsala press, for instance, he had found that the previous book printer, Johannes Pauli, had illegally sold the equipment. The journeymen apprentices were "ready to kill each other," with one stealing the movable block letters and floating them on the black market. Curio encountered a host of other unexpected obstacles, including Professor Johan Hadorph, who was keeping his cows in a nearby university building. So if the books were now deemed of poor quality, an embarrassment, then the university should share much of the blame for not providing better facilities. Then Rudbeck admitted his own responsibility for the state of affairs.

Not only was he the one who had persuaded Curio to come to Uppsala, but he had also promised an attractive salary and a workable printing budget, neither of which the university actually saw fit to grant. In fact, the issue of the unpaid salary would blow up in its own right into a nasty side quarrel between Rudbeck and some Uppsala professors on the university council who simply denied that he had the right to make such an offer. The salary never materialized, and now Curio was unceremoniously turned out with few prospects in the current economic conditions.

Rudbeck's concern seems so strong that, at times, one can only wonder if he rushed up the plans to publish his book as part of an immediate and desperate attempt to save his friend. He knew how much De la Gardie had come to value his quest. Should anything threaten its well-being, such as the trouble with Curio, then perhaps the chancellor would intervene and protect the future of the historic search for Atlantis.

At any rate, Rudbeck's letters were to no avail, and neither were the efforts of his cousin Ingo. The defense was inexperienced, but even so, the merits of the case seemed decidedly in the favor of the prosecution. By the conclusion of the trial, speedily ended in January 1675, Curio had been officially dismissed from his duties, and ordered to return the entire press to the university in the same way that he had received it, in addition to paying a three-hundred-*riksdaler* fine. In a related case, brought on by the antiquarian Hadorph and one prominent theologian, Curio was sentenced to fourteen days in prison (for falsely accusing the prosecution of tampering with its key evidence).

"They wanted his throat," Verelius said of Curio's accusers. The printer had lost easily, and the prospects of a successful appeal were small. Given the strength of the prosecution, it is not hard to imagine the Swedish supreme court simply affirming this verdict. What Rudbeck decided to do next was, to say the least, surprising.

In an age when legal rights depended largely on one's position in society, Rudbeck first removed himself from the protection of university law. By virtue of his shipping company, he signed himself instead under the less privileged jurisdiction of the town law. Then Rudbeck persuaded Curio to sue him personally, that is, for failing to keep the terms of their agreement. And Rudbeck, now under Uppsala town law, would in turn sue the university for breaking its contractual obligations.

It was a very clever move that seemed to solve many problems at once, stealing the thunder from the prosecution and shifting the thrust of the debate onto an issue in which Rudbeck's and Curio's chances of victory were at least not hopeless. Most important, Rudbeck's juggling of jurisdictions would buy some valuable time, and allow Curio to remain at his post as long as the court cases were pending. By then, Rudbeck's discovery of Atlantis would almost certainly be printed, and Curio would perhaps even enjoy a happy retirement.

Postponing an inevitable defeat, Rudbeck had found a brilliant solution to their predicament. But, typically, it showed an outrageous disregard for his fellow professors who wanted a more conscientious printer, and, unfortunately for Rudbeck, stirred a hornet's nest of resentment.

The university had not faced such a brazen challenge to its authority in recent memory, and it had certainly *never* been sued by one of its own professors. Even Count de la Gardie, Rudbeck's most trusted supporter, was furious. As chancellor of the university, the count sent a letter full of uncommon passion and anger, denouncing Rudbeck's complete lack of judgment, and threatening, ominously, that he would not tolerate such unabashed disrespect. The count's words were so strong that Rudbeck's many enemies reveled, and the effects on Rudbeck were unmistakable:

> All my troubles, worries, sicknesses and sorrows that I have had since my childhood up to this day, and all the ill will my enemies wish me, have never moved my heart to hate, or caused sickness, or tears to break out, [because]

by virtue of God's Grace I have been able to consider all
that vanity, and meet it with the heart's patience and a
glad face; but the letter I received from Your Excellency's
graceful and always comforting hands now from Läckö
was more difficult for me than all that. . . .

Rudbeck tried to apologize, claiming that he had been completely
oblivious of the uproar he had created. He had no idea how serious
his offense was, or how passionately the university would react. He
was only, he said, trying to support his friend, and do what he thought
was right.

He affirmed again how he felt partly responsible for Curio's misfortunes, and could not pay the fines himself—not, that is, "without
bringing my wife and children into ruin." This letter also shows one
of the first signs of Rudbeck's changing disposition, from the strong,
self-confident, and enthusiastic achiever to what some historians
have called a tendency to hypochondria and paranoia—a tendency
that had perhaps been there all along, only concealed underneath his
cheery and vivacious personality.

"Now that I am in my last days, and have so sickly a constitution,"
Rudbeck cried out, "I fear that God the Highest will not wait much
longer before He takes me away from here." This was no mere melo-
dramatic pose or appeal to pity, both of which he had certainly mastered. He really seemed to feel that he was falling into worse health,
and, often during times of crisis, that he was on the verge of death.

Further, he would see enemies everywhere, gossiping, spreading
malicious rumors, and plotting to bring him down, just as they had
done before in front of the university, and seemed to be doing again
with their attack on his friend Henrik Curio. They must also, he sur-
mised, be behind De la Gardie's unexpected anger. Rudbeck's feelings
of persecution and fear of imminent death were easily magnified by his
inventive mind. All these anxieties only added to the pressing sense of
hurry that was driving his lifelong quest for the lost civilization.

Twelve Trumpets,
Four Kettledrums, and
a Bag of Gold

Now that I was free, and my own master, I supposed that I could do anything, achieve anything. I had only to take one leap, and I could rise and fly through the air.

—Jean-Jacques Rousseau, *Confessions*

RUDBECK'S COMBINATION OF talent, charm, and groveling would win back the favor of Magnus Gabriel de la Gardie with stunning speed. For the count had a weak spot for avoiding unpleasant conflict and an even weaker spot for the clever professor. The count, it seemed, had an almost unlimited tolerance for Rudbeck's shenanigans.

De la Gardie was certainly in a very different position than were the professors who had to deal with Rudbeck on a day-to-day basis. Given his political influence, economic power, and social status, De la Gardie had the luxury of admiring Rudbeck's extraordinary gifts. He could afford to look away when his favorite professor slipped up, acting in some rash if not also irresponsible ways.

Many scholars at Uppsala, by contrast, did not appreciate Rudbeck's complete disregard for the rules, deeply resenting his lawsuit, his support of the sloppy printer, his flirtations with Cartesian thought, and of course the decreases in salaries that were so closely linked to his carefree building spree. Still others were probably just threatened by Rudbeck's abilities, which, together with his lack of humility, sometimes made him look like an annoying, reckless show-off who did as he pleased. And when he got into trouble, as he was bound to do, De la Gardie would come to the rescue.

So, once again, despite Rudbeck's scandalous behavior in suing the university, De la Gardie listened, forgave, and forgot. Rudbeck's offense was overshadowed, in the count's mind at least, this time by his latest spectacular discovery. The count was thrilled with the hunt for Atlantis, and did not wish to see Rudbeck hindered in any way, least of all by something as trivial as a lack of funds.

A longtime patron of Swedish antiquities, De la Gardie promised financial assistance to help cover Rudbeck's printing costs. He sent over stacks of paper, right away, for the first printing of the images to accompany the texts, which, as Rudbeck planned, would be extravagant.

Detailed maps of Atlantis were to show the capital, the temple, and the racetrack. Representations of the layers of humus around the old burial mounds were also being cut, pictorially confirming the great age of Sweden. Rudbeck's ambitions would soon be growing here as well, preparing not just images, but *life-size* reproductions of the objects he had found and which were housed in his makeshift curiosity cabinet, a seventeenth-century predecessor to the private museum.

Nails, rings, ax heads, swords, drums, and castration knives would all be lauded as artifacts of Atlantis. Some of his gifted mathematical students, including the experienced College of Antiquities draftsman Petrus Törnewall, were hard at work helping prepare the woodcuts and copper engravings that De la Gardie was so generously funding.

The count was once again, as Rudbeck said, "his greatest admirer," offering timely advice, support, and encouragement. He also promised to praise the merits of the work to the king.

Sitting on the throne was Charles XI, still at this time a young, inexperienced, and remarkably insecure monarch. The worldly Italian diplomat Lorenzo Magalotti described his first encounter with the new king on his visit in 1674. He was told to avoid engaging the king in conversation, so as not to embarrass or perplex him, or otherwise cause him any discomfort in trying to think of a response. Unexpectedly, however, the king offered his hand to the Florentine nobleman. Obeying convention, the diplomat kissed it. The flustered king then acted

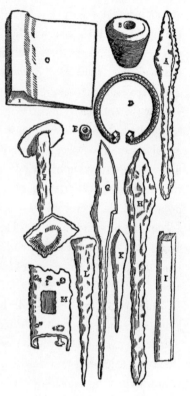

Knives, ax heads, and other artifacts supposedly of Atlantis were on display in Rudbeck's museum.

in a distinctly unroyal manner: he fled the room. Two years on the throne had not changed Sweden's ruler, who still appeared "shy and afraid of everything." "It looks as if he does not dare to look someone in the face, and he moves as if he walked on glass," Magalotti concluded.

Charles XI has not been remembered as Sweden's most cultured monarch, either. Despite high ambitions for his studies, one of the most grandiose plans ever devised for a Swedish prince, his education was "shamelessly neglected." Observers regularly noted that his progress was slow. He confused letters, reversed numbers, and spelled atrociously. The governor charged with overseeing his education, Christopher Horn, had hardly taken up his position with zest. He was given a room in the royal palace, where, instead of teaching, he indulged, his critics said, in eating, drinking, and displaying "all the qualities which incompetence can bring."

But the emphasis on the king's total lack of learning is very much overplayed. It also seems at least partly based on a misunderstanding of Charles XI's dyslexia, a condition he almost certainly had. Like many in his situation, the king would compensate with some exceptional talents in other areas. He excelled in hunting, riding, and outdoor activities, even collecting enough wild animals to open his own zoo in the Stockholm palace. He looked completely different when he sat on a horse. No longer timid, shy, reserved, or full of insecurity, Charles XI, on such occasions, as Magalotti put it, "really looks like a king."

Magnus Gabriel de la Gardie had known the monarch well, having led the regency government since 1660, when the crown prince was only four years old. Relying on years of trust, the count put in a good word for Rudbeck, and this was certainly a favorable moment for winning the king over to the extraordinary quest. In fact, Charles XI had just told De la Gardie how much he hated to turn away any good citizen who came in search of assistance. Given his potential, Rudbeck would surely be classified as one of these good citizens, and his search deemed worthy of royal support.

By a happy coincidence, Rudbeck was soon to come to the king's attention in his own memorable way. Although Charles XI had assumed power in 1672, he was not officially crowned until September 1675. For this occasion, Rudbeck, the discoverer of Atlantis, was asked to arrange the decorations and festivities in Uppsala Cathedral. Hurriedly the university was whipped into shape for the royal coronation. The Gustavianum was turned into a "house of nobility," the piles of trash beside the river were moved out of sight, and Rudbeck himself transported the dung piles near the horse stalls in the exercise hall to more secluded gardens.

No one knew it at the time, but this was to be one of the last great baroque ceremonies of Sweden's imperial age. And Rudbeck put on quite a show. He wrote the music for the king's coronation—and then sang the piece himself in Uppsala Cathedral in such a way that his thundering voice was said to overpower some twelve trumpets and four kettledrums playing with all their might.

Sure enough, the performance made a lasting impression on the young king. Reportedly, Rudbeck's emphasis on the loud and the bombastic was well advised, as Charles XI was then learning to play the drums, and seemed totally engrossed in what Rudbeck called his "little noise." Every time the king came to Uppsala for the rest of his life, it was said, he insisted on hearing Olof Rudbeck sing. More immediately, the king pledged additional funding, some five hundred *daler silvermynt,* for Rudbeck's adventure.

The same degree of success during the coronation, however, cannot be said for Magnus Gabriel de la Gardie. In the initial moments before the procession into the cathedral, the count's horse reared and threw him to the ground. The brand-new crimson velvet and ermine-trimmed robes unveiled on that occasion were stained, and De la Gardie's wig was tossed into the mud. The imperial orb fell out of his grip, banged on the cobblestones, and dented on impact. De la Gardie regained his composure for the rest of the ceremony, but the man who liked so much to party went home uncharacteristically early that night.

RUDBECK'S MUSIC at the coronation must have been a pleasant diversion for the young king on the silver throne. Nineteen years old and about to turn twenty in a couple of months, this awkward boy was nevertheless anxiously excited about the future. He had just been engaged to be married.

His bride-to-be was a Danish princess, Ulrika Eleonora, and, historically speaking, a radical choice. She was the sister of Christian V, king of Denmark, which had been Sweden's enemy for as long as anyone alive could remember. There was even a word in Swedish coined to describe this hostility, *Danskhat,* which roughly translates as "hatred of the Danes."

King Charles XI's own father, Charles X, had come to exemplify the high passions animating the northern rivalry. Back in the abnormally cold winter of 1658, when the waters separating the two kingdoms had frozen hard, Charles X had made the decision to march his army over the ice to Denmark. The plan was to kidnap the Danish royal family, disperse the ruling aristocracy, and raze Copenhagen to the ground. The Swedes intended literally to destroy the independence of Denmark.

Despite the sounds of cracking ice and the water seeping through their natural bridge, the seven thousand soldiers managed to cross the channel with surprisingly few losses. The Danes were taken by complete surprise. The Swedish king was prevented from obliterating his rival only by the timely intervention of foreign powers. He did, however, leave the negotiation table with new territories for his kingdom, rich provinces in the west and south that are still part of Sweden today (Skåne, Blekinge, Bohuslän, Halland, and others).

Now, less than fifteen years after Charles X's audacious march, his son was marrying the daughter of the man who had just barely escaped the attack. A sign of the changing times, this proposed marriage between the new Swedish king and the Danish princess aimed to bring the two constantly quarreling kingdoms closer together and seal a lasting peace treaty. This marriage would later be remembered as marking an important beginning to a long process of reconciliation between the two bitter Nordic belligerents.

So the engagement was made, the two kings looked happy, and the plan seemed to be working. But all the fireworks and merry toasts to eternal friendship could not stop the Danish king, only a few months later, from declaring war.

A few weeks after this royal engagement had been announced in June 1675, Swedish troops experienced an engagement of a different kind. Allied with the French, the Swedes were dragged into hostilities with one of Louis XIV's enemies in northern Germany, the Brandenburg prince Frederick William. They had not particularly wanted war, but, bound by treaty, they attacked anyway on the fields of Fehrbellin. To great surprise on all sides, the Swedes were repulsed. The German prince effectively exploited the orderly retreat to shout out to the world that the Swedes were no longer invincible.

Marriage proposal and celebrated engagement aside, the ever-vigilant king of Denmark, Christian V, sensed that this was too good an opportunity to miss. The current situation—a Swedish loss on the battlefield—surely constituted an exception to the general words of goodwill and reconciliation just pledged. Denmark had long wanted to regain the lost provinces, that valuable territory full of fortresses and fertile lands which Charles XI's dad had forced Christian V's dad to hand over. With Sweden distracted by the German enemy, now was their chance.

The Danes declared war immediately. Their allies, the Dutch, also found this logic persuasive, and followed suit, looking toward more control over the lucrative Baltic trade. As if this coalition with its combined naval strength were not difficult enough to fight, the Hapsburg emperor also saw the possibility of finally kicking out the Swedes from nearby German territories—lands that he thought he could better dominate by himself.

As formidable enemies were mobilizing their troops on a frankly nightmarish number of fronts, the previous nonchalance at the loss at Fehrbellin started to undergo a real change. When De la Gardie finally showed up in Stockholm again, three weeks after that defeat, he found a rather irate group of *Riksråd* (Council) and parliamentary officials. Serious questions were posed about the actions of the old regency government and the man who stood at its center, namely, De la Gardie himself.

With *Riksråd* and parliamentary leaders distancing themselves from the past, there came a call for an official investigation. Many wanted to know how Sweden had entered into this alliance with France and had then agreed to fight in a war for which they were so obviously ill prepared. After only fourteen years of peace, statesmen also demanded to know why the Swedish military had fallen into such a poor condition. Again eyes turned to De la Gardie's leadership. What on earth had happened to the army that only a few years ago was the feared hammer of the north?

In the midst of the uproar and hysteria, more accusations were leveled against the chancellor. High-ranking men of society came forward claiming to have heard De la Gardie utter some treacherous words about the king, calling him a "rascal" and urging his removal. Led by Claes Rålamb, Stockholm's highest official, and Knut Kurck, president of the Commerce College, the politicians took their information straight to the king.

The count fell on his knees and begged his innocence. Their words were all lies and hearsay, he pleaded, and in turn, he accused the rivals of spreading false rumors. With such prominent people on both sides of the issue, the inexperienced king was uncertain how to proceed. Prudently, though, he steered a middle course. He refused to consider this a matter of state, and suggested that the two sides settle the dispute between themselves.

But as both sides were conscripting allies in the autumn of 1675 for what would certainly have been a vicious struggle, something happened that would sway many of the remaining undecided opinions.

EARLIER THAT SUMMER the king had ordered the Royal Navy to launch a preemptive strike on the Danish and Dutch warships gathering in the south. Three months and countless delays later, the

Swedes were still preparing for the attack. By late October, as sailing conditions were rapidly deteriorating, sixty-six large and well-armed vessels sailed out in one of the largest fleets ever assembled on the Baltic. This Swedish armada was to put a stop to the malicious designs of the Danes and their ill-advised declaration of war.

Ten days later the first ships were seen creaking back to shore, sails torn, ropes rotten, and anchors lost. And they had not even met an enemy. A nasty storm had emerged on the choppy Baltic Sea, causing dismal visibility and disrupting established means of communication. Some ships literally crashed into each other. Many supplies, including the stores of food, went overboard. It was an embarrassing performance, and the admiral, Gustaf Otto Stenbock, was fired for his incompetence. Prior to his appointment as admiral, it turned out, he had never even been to sea.

As much as this disaster hurt De la Gardie's prestige, things did not unfortunately improve. At the next opportunity, the summer of 1676, the Swedes pulled out their greatest weapon, the flagship *Kronan* (*Crown*). Drawing on the most advanced naval architecture developed by the great maritime powers England and Holland, *Kronan* was one of the largest and best-armed ships of its day. About 180 feet in length and forty-three in width, the man-of-war boasted a terrifying 126 cannon, including some highly regarded thirty- and thirty-six-pounders.

As *Kronan* started to attack near the Baltic island of Öland on the first day of June 1676, one of the Swedish naval officers sent a message to his superior, the admiral Lorentz Creutz. Now, the admiral was new, and he had never fought a battle, with his previous experience consisting mainly of prosecuting witches. In the general confusion of the melee, Creutz misunderstood his officer's message. Instead of continuing the fight as signaled, he ordered the monstrous ship to set a new course. At the same time, the inexperienced commander seems to have forgotten to give the accompanying order to adjust the sails and close the gunports. The enemy Dutch and Danish commanders looked on in bewilderment at what happened next to Sweden's most feared warship: "*Kronan* careened, water poured in through the hatches, the cannons broke loose, a slow match ended up in the gunpowder stocks, and *Kronan* exploded and sank." Of a crew of 850, only forty-two were known to have survived.

A tragedy, a disaster, an embarrassment, and a stunning reversal — and it was not over yet. The second-largest ship in the navy, *Svärdet* (*Sword*), did not last much longer; and a third, *Äpplet* (*Apple*), went down as well. The commander of this ship, too, seems to have known frighteningly little of naval warfare. "He cannot even differentiate the forecastle and the poop," the minutes of the later trial revealed. Evidently the commander's previous position had been running a restaurant.

None of this reflected well on De la Gardie's stewardship. A total of eleven ships, including the three most impressive, went down with some three thousand sailors of the Swedish Royal Navy. In the wake of this overwhelming loss, Swedish defenses lay prostrate. It was only a matter of time before an all-out Danish invasion would begin.

Morale had sunk very low in Stockholm, and the new king seemed manifestly depressed. Although he had long trusted De la Gardie, he was now inclined to listen to the pleas of the furious and the disenchanted who blamed the overall sorry state of the navy on De la Gardie's government. For twelve years it had concentrated power too much, blocked access to the king, and, some suspected, kept the monarch in a state of ignorance about the true conditions of the kingdom.

Sweden was now paying the price for these faults in the naval fiascoes and criminally ill-prepared forces. Soon it would also have to face a Danish invasion, one certain to be as bold, determined, and set on revenge as had been the Swedes who marched over the ice. Count Magnus Gabriel de la Gardie watched helplessly as the king reluctantly ordered an investigation into the charges of widespread misrule. Rudbeck, too, was anxious about these developments. Neither the war nor the prosecution of his patron boded well for his hunt for Atlantis.

ALL OARS TO ATLANTIS

As time went by our need to fight for the ideal increased to an unquestioning possession, riding with spur and rein over our doubts.

—T. E. LAWRENCE, *SEVEN PILLARS OF WISDOM*

TIMES WERE UNCERTAIN indeed, but Rudbeck poured his soul into the search. Soon he had turned up no less than 102 pieces of evidence of why Atlantis had actually been in Sweden. Many prominent landmarks—the rivers, the mountains, the temple, and the racetrack—had already been identified in Old Uppsala. Even the thick forests surrounding the capital were said to be the heavily wooded areas outside of Uppsala. Rudbeck was growing absolutely convinced. His countrymen were walking in the shadows of Plato's lost world.

The Swedish physician, however, was hardly the first to seek Atlantis. As the fantasy of such an extraordinary discovery tightened its grip, Rudbeck's search would become a dialogue with rival visions of the vanished world. He would learn from, and at the same time compete with, the many theories that flourished in his day and before.

The modern rediscovery of Atlantis had begun unexpectedly in the fateful and traumatic encounter between the Old and New Worlds in the Age of Discovery. Sixteenth-century Europeans came armed with muskets and portable cannon that roared as if the "dyvels of hell" had been loosed on the world. Mounted on horses, animals never seen before, the Spanish conquistadores must have looked to the indigenous peoples of Central and South America like strange, menacing beasts, perhaps like the half-man, half-horse centaurs who roamed the mythic hills of Arcadia.

Driven by a complex set of motives, the first European explorers had set sail down the uncharted west coast of Africa. Many hoped to tap the ultimate source of gold that crossed the Saharan desert and enriched the coffers of trading cities like Venice or Genoa. Others saw the opportunity to win new converts to the faith, and possibly find the legendary Christian prince Prester John, who ruled somewhere in a sea of the heathen. Still others wanted to earn an honored name, gain eternal fame, or even fathom the "secrets of these parts" that had so long been "hidden from other men."

The initial gold rush broadened into a veritable spice race—and the frontiers of the search expanded from the coasts of Africa to the distant worlds of India, Ceylon, China, and beyond. Such "grains of paradise" not only preserved meat from spoilage, but also added variety to the diet and made bad meals on European tables less appalling. Spices were a valuable addition to the medicine chest, as well, combating coughs, countering colds, and preventing everything, it was said, from earache to the plague. The Portuguese were yet again the first to take tentative steps in securing this lucrative market. Important ports like Calcutta, strategic straits like Malacca, and waterways like the Bay of Bengal lay in their hands.

Laden with pepper, cinnamon, ginger, mace, cloves, and nutmeg— the last of these literally worth more than its weight in gold—caravel triumphs were unimaginably profitable. They began to attract the attentions of ambitious neighbors. In this context, the Genoese sailor Cristóbal Colón, more commonly known as Christopher Columbus, devised a somewhat unconventional plan to reach the riches of the East by sailing in the opposite direction. Medieval legends seemed to confirm the vague possibilities of success in this "foolish mad" venture, and, significantly, learned miscalculations vastly underestimated the actual distances involved. The ancient geographer Ptolemy's classic maps of the world, for example, which had recently been published, cut over six thousand miles from the journey, and played no small role in strengthening Columbus's already legendary indomitable will.

After countless rejections from several European heads of state, Columbus finally managed to persuade the rulers of Spain, King Ferdinand and Queen Isabella, to finance his voyage. So, in October 1492, after a thirty-three-day voyage from the Canaries, the captain and his crew struck land on the Bahamian island of San Salvador (today Guanahaní). Three more successful voyages followed, to Cuba, to Jamaica, and along the coast of Central America—all of which, Columbus thought, were the East Indies, the entrance to Japan, China, and the fabulous riches of the East. The navigator went to his death absolutely certain that he had glimpsed these oriental mysteries.

Columbus did not, as we now know, discover the East Indies. As explorers ventured farther inland and mapmakers struggled to incorporate the discoveries on the latest maps, it gradually became clear that he had actually stumbled upon a brand-new continent. Two of them, as a matter of fact (though despite common belief today, Columbus himself never set foot on the continent in the north, i.e., today's United States). Also, daring seafarers who most probably made the oceanic voyages before him include everyone from adventurous Vikings to Irish monks, though their exploits had faded from memory and were not rediscovered until later scholars started peering into the old manuscripts again. This time, however, with the printing press and rumors promising almost endless opportunities for power, profit, prestige, and preaching, it would be different.

This discovery of a new continent was to have a tremendous impact on the Old World, not least in that it sparked new and lively speculation about the lost civilization of Atlantis. Hadn't Plato written about a mysterious island somewhere in the far west, beyond the pillars of Hercules? Hadn't the philosopher also placed it at a "distant point in the Atlantic"? Maybe it had not been destroyed after all, but had only fallen out of common knowledge. Could this "brave new world," as Shakespeare called the enchanted isle that formed the setting of *The Tempest,* actually be the lost continent of Atlantis?

In the period immediately after 1492, this seemed a likely option. It was made more so in the 1550s, when Ferdinand Magellan's daring circumnavigation of the world proved for the first time that this America was an entirely unknown continent. As the old assurance of a three-continent Earth crumbled, Plato's story about a former powerful island civilization in the far west no longer seemed all that far-fetched.

In fact, Renaissance thinkers were quick to place new discoveries in the context of the old classical traditions, and the New World seemed to have many things in common with Plato's Atlantis. For one thing, travelers' reports told of the continent's overwhelming size. Like Atlantis, it seemed "larger than Libya and Asia together," enjoying all the natural advantages that the philosopher Plato attributed to Atlas's isle. Explorers indeed strained their descriptive abilities to paint an accurate portrait of the many new birds, animals, and plants inhabiting this lush *novus mundus.* For those who refused to believe the stories about the Americas—and those tales were often outlandish—the goods that flowed into European harbors provided a more tangible confirmation: potatoes for the tables, chocolate for the cups, tobacco for the pipes, and sugar for almost everything else.

The vibrant culture, too, seemed remarkably Atlantean. One civilization the Spanish encountered, the Aztecs, showed a close resemblance to Plato's descriptions of the islanders' great talent for engineering projects. The capital, Tenochtitlán, appeared to rise out of a lake of salt, and bridges looped over a system of canals that crisscrossed the land. Grand structures commanded attention, particu-

larly the stone-terraced pyramids and the temples gilded with offerings and stained with the blood of many human sacrifices. Fountains
in the gardens and baths in the palace further suggested the sophisti-
cation and luxury that readers had come to expect of old Atlantis.

Most dramatically, the Aztec civilization shared a degree of wealth
comparable to the legendary treasures of Atlantis. As Plato described
it, the riches of the kingdom were so immense that "the like had
never been seen before in any royal house nor will ever easily be seen
again." From the very beginning, European explorers could hardly fail
to note the shining ornaments encircling the necks, dangling from
the ears, and decorating the bodies of the natives. Main buildings in
the Aztec capital glowed with bright white stucco, and gold adorned
the lavish temples. Escorted into the palace, the Spanish gaped at the
ostentatious display of the Aztec officials' wealth. Pearls, emeralds,
and other precious stones lined the clothes, covered the staffs, and
accompanied the "marvelously delicate" featherwork. Even the soles
of Montezuma's sandals were tipped in gold.

A few very bloody years later, the conquistadores had stripped off,
melted down, and carried back so much from their native hosts that
Spain was virtually swimming in Aztec gold. After Francisco Pizarro's
brutal campaign in Peru, and the discovery of rich mines high in the
Andes, the home country would also feast on Incan silver. So much
bullion poured in from the New World that it flowed like "rain on a
rooftop." Conservative estimates put the total cargo until 1650 at 181
tons of gold and 16,000 tons of silver, and this does not account for
the treasure lost to smuggling, piracy, and shipwreck. As one Aztec
put it, the strangers "longed and lusted for gold" so much that "their
bodies swelled with greed, . . . [and] they hungered like pigs."

So moved by the sights, one Spaniard paused from the plundering
to put his observations on record. This was Francisco López de
Gomara, the priest and private secretary of the "restless, haughty,
mischievous and given to quarreling" young man, the infamous con-
quistador Hernán Cortés. From his vantage point, Gomara wrote our

oldest account of the conquest of Mexico and the influential history of the Indies (1553), which remains today an invaluable source for understanding this brutal period of the past. Inside the work was an early statement placing Atlantis firmly in the Americas, a view that would be shared by many others in the sixteenth and seventeenth centuries.

Not everyone, of course, would find this a sound idea, let alone be convinced that the Spanish had stumbled upon old Atlantis. The famous French thinker Michel de Montaigne, for one, doubted this identification. In one of his essays (1580)—he was one of the first and most influential thinkers to popularize the essay as a literary genre in its own right—Montaigne acknowledged that it was "very probable" that a great flood had in fact destroyed Atlantis as Plato described. But he expressed his skepticism that the newly discovered continent was really Plato's world. "It is not very probable that the new world we have lately discovered is, in fact, that island."

Another popular rival theory places Atlantis precisely in the ocean where the island was said to have sunk. Although it sometimes appeared on medieval and early modern maps, such as the one by the learned Jesuit priest Athanasius Kircher in the 1660s, it was not until the late nineteenth century that this legendary civilization would be sought in the mid-Atlantic. This search was largely due to the influential work of an American thinker named Ignatius Donnelly. In the early 1880s Donnelly had just lost an agonizing political election, and the fifty-year-old former lieutenant governor of Minnesota and U.S. congressman felt he was beginning a forced retirement. With his political stock, as he put it, at "zero," Donnelly worked feverishly on a book he called *Atlantis: The Antediluvian World* (1882).

He believed that Plato's tale was not a "fable, but veritable history," detailing the fortunes of the island where "man first rose from a state of barbarism to civilization." From this world center in the middle of the Atlantic, Donnelly saw the civilizing influence of Atlantis pouring out in all directions, particularly affecting the Americas in the west and the nearby coastal regions of Africa and Europe in the east.

Positing the continent of Atlantis in the mid-Atlantic in fact helped explain many "intriguing similarities" between such far-flung continents. Africa and South America, for example, both had pyramids, hieroglyphics, mummies, and similar words for such things as sun, ax, and hawk. (Later historians have determined many differences; not the least of these is that some two thousand years separated the building of the Egyptian and Aztec pyramids, though Donnelly could not have known this fact.) Seeing the many correspondences, Donnelly went on drawing his conclusions, proposing that Atlantis had served as the origin of all our civilization. Ancient gods were originally kings and queens of Atlantis, just as all our arts and sciences came from this brilliant, sun-drenched home. Then Atlantis "perished in a terrible convulsion of nature, in which the whole island sank into the ocean, with nearly all its inhabitants."

If Donnelly was correct, then the French novelist Jules Verne's romantic adventure *Twenty Thousand Leagues under the Sea* (1870) evoked an image of what lay waiting to be discovered. As Captain Nemo and the crew of the double-hulled, iron-plated, and "truly marvelous" submarine *Nautilus* cruise through the Atlantic off the shores of Morocco, they chance upon a sight that is certainly no less marvelous. One of the observers, the cantankerous professor Arronax, describes what he saw:

> [There] before my very eyes, lay the ruins . . . its temples demolished, its arches in pieces, its columns on the ground, but its proportions were clearly outlined, reminding me of the stately architecture of Tuscany.

Other relics of the sunken civilization emerge: underwater aqueducts, "floating forms of a Parthenon," and "crumbled walls and long lines of wide, deserted streets." Here was Atlantis, an "ancient Pompeii, buried beneath the sea."

This was a vivid portrait of a lost world that prepared the way for the largely enthusiastic reception of Donnelly's vision of Atlantis. In the grand perspective, too, Verne's fictional account helped many late-nineteenth- and twentieth-century readers visualize the implications of the adventurous search. "Who shall say," Donnelly wrote in 1882, "that one hundred years from now the great museums of the world may not be adorned with gems, statues, arms and implements from Atlantis, while the libraries of the world shall contain translations of its inscriptions, throwing new light upon all the past history of the human race and all the great problems which now perplex the thinkers of our day?"

Donnelly's Atlantis—like Verne's classic science-fiction novel— was an instant smash hit. The author was inducted into the American Association of Science, and the city of New Orleans chose Atlantis as the theme for its Mardi Gras celebration in 1883. Besides that, Great Britain's prime minister William Gladstone wrote an enthusiastic four-page letter to the acclaimed American author. In his humble home in the small town of Niniger, Minnesota, Donnelly was overjoyed, and wrote:

> I looked down at myself and could not but smile at the appearance of the man, who in this little, snow-bound hamlet, was corresponding with the man whose word was fate anywhere in the British Empire.

The prime minister also spoke of seeking parliamentary funds for a naval expedition to find the legendary island. "I could have uttered a war hoop of exultation," said Donnelly, the man who was soon to be widely heralded as the "father of Atlantis studies," that is, after Plato himself.

Atlantis would, however, have a long fascinating life beyond these classic formulations. Later intriguing theories would place this lost civilization on the islands of Crete and Santorini, as well as in the desert (Sahara), high atop mountains (the Andes), underneath the ice (the Antarctic or Spitzbergen), or even in outer space. Not to mention the occult and mystical interpretations that have also flourished.

One last theory that did appear in Rudbeck's day looked for Atlantis not in America or at the bottom of the Atlantic Ocean, or anywhere else other than Plato's head. There was a sense that the philosopher had made it up, either for the sake of creating an imaginative fictional account or, more likely, as a philosophical discourse that set up a vision of an idealized world to portray the problems of humanity in general, or his Athens in particular. Such a view of Atlantis as fiction or fable continues to flourish in our day, though sometimes the creator of the story is said to be someone else: Solon, Egyptian priests, Egyptian tradition, and so on.

But Rudbeck was not convinced. After reading Plato's dialogues, he could not accept a theory that placed the lost civilization anywhere outside Sweden.

LOOKING FOR ATLANTIS in the Americas was, Rudbeck boldly proclaimed, pure vanity. The entire theory was predicated on a fundamental misreading of Plato.

One of the main arguments for locating Atlantis on a continent in the New World stemmed from the philosopher's description of the kingdom as "larger than Libya and Asia together." Rudbeck, however, cautioned that Plato did not necessarily mean the same things by the terms *Libya* and *Asia* that later generations did. The meanings of words change over time, and the duty of a historian is to capture the meaning of the word that prevailed when the philosopher used it.

In Plato's day, the name *Asia* did not refer to the entire continent that runs through the territories of Russia to the far reaches of Siberia, China, and Korea. Rather, "Asia was taken by the old writers to mean only the little Asia, which stretches from the Mediterranean Sea in the south to the Black Sea in the north." Relying on his love of maps, Rudbeck supported his hypothesis with a slew of ancient geographers. Each authority confirmed that the ancient word *Asia* meant only the much smaller, far western part of the continent, or the area historians call "Asia Minor." Likewise, Plato's word *Libya* did not mean all of the continent of Africa, as many had assumed. The word in the philosopher's time referred only to the far northern coast, basically the fertile regions and immediate outlying deserts surrounding ancient Egypt.

With this refreshingly historical effort to put Plato's vocabulary in the context of fourth-century-B.C. conventions of the Greek language, Rudbeck had uncovered a serious problem at the heart of understanding Atlantis. It was no longer necessary to seek this lost civilization in a land larger than the combined continents of Asia and Libya. Instead it should be sought in a place that corresponded to the meaning of the words in Plato's day, that is, a land larger than Asia Minor and northern Africa. In this one bold stroke, Rudbeck shattered one of the powerful arguments for placing the vanished continent in the New World, previously one of the very few places that could have satisfied the stringent conditions.

Besides that, drawing on his own experiences on tempestuous waters, with his commercial yacht and postal service, Rudbeck raised the eminently practical question that many theorists overlooked in their haste to place Atlantis somewhere in the Americas. This was directed less to the "learned, the wise, and the elite in the world" than to the common sailor:

> If such a great navy should cross from America, and attack all of Europe, Asia, and Libya some thousands of years ago, when no one knew how to sail with a compass, no one dared far from the coast with a little ship, and no

big ships were built which could withstand the waves of
the great ocean, how well would they have held up?

"If I asked such a thing," Rudbeck said, "I fear that the boatmen
would laugh at me."

For skeptics who questioned the testimony of a "common boatman," Rudbeck issued a further challenge. Read the explorer's accounts of the New World, take a look at the types of boats the natives
used, and try to figure out how they would have fared in such a difficult transatlantic voyage. Plato was after all speaking not of a single
isolated venture over the Atlantic, but a war of conquest that would
mean moving massive fleets across the hazardous waters of the high
seas. In an age before the invention of the compass or at least systematic knowledge of the use of stars for navigation, America was hardly
a realistic prospect for the home of the Atlanteans.

Taking the offensive on yet another front, assuming for the moment that the Atlanteans had somehow managed to make the perilous crossing from America, Rudbeck raised another embarrassing
point: "And should they have conquered Europe, Asia, and Libya in
the old days just as Plato speaks about, then there should reasonably
be some evidence of this Atlantis in their language, customs, laws,
worship, and such things."

The current war between Sweden and Denmark, for example, was
leaving many signs, not the least the "thousands" of independent accounts of its progress. Few wars in history occur without leaving any
trace, and it was thus not unreasonable to expect some survivals of
such a catastrophic war as Plato described. Yet in the many centuries
that had passed, Rudbeck reminded, no one had come up with any
real evidence of ancient American influence in any of the places
where the Atlanteans supposedly attacked.

So if Rudbeck was correct in his interpretation of Plato's words,
the existing knowledge of American boats, and the overwhelming

lack of evidence of any surviving influence anywhere they allegedly conquered, scholars were clearly looking in the wrong place. "Either Plato's Atlantis is a poem," Rudbeck said, "or it is true, in which case it must be understood as some other land or island" than the Americas.

While he was on the subject, there was another matter that needed to be cleared up. Plato spoke of Atlantis as an "island," but Rudbeck believed it was not quite so simple. Going back to the original language of the philosopher, Rudbeck noted that Plato used the Greek word *Nῆσos* (pronounced NAY-sos) to describe Atlantis. Scholars almost invariably translated this word as "island," though, he noted, this did not have to be the case. *Nῆσos* could also mean "peninsula," and for support, he simply pointed to the Peloponnesus in southern Greece.

This landmass was named using the Greek words *Pelops,* the wild chariot driver of classical mythology, and *Nῆσos,* the word in question. The Peloponnesus was, literally, "Pelop's island," and as anyone with a map knew, this was a peninsula. Clearly the term *Nῆσos* applied to islands as well as peninsulas — and as long as only one possible translation of *Nῆσos* was accepted, it was easy to miss many opportunities for finding Atlantis.

SIZE, SHAPE, TOPOGRAPHY, and even the blood-drenched ceremonies had all apparently agreed with Rudbeck's unusual solution to the timeless mystery. No less exciting, Rudbeck had found the symbolic leader of the sacrifices, the king of Atlantis himself.

According to the *Critias* dialogue, the first king of this powerful civilization had been a man named Atlas, whose name in fact lived on in the word *Atlantis* and in the name of its nearby ocean, the Atlantic (both derived from the genitive form, meaning, appropriately, "of Atlas"). For Rudbeck, this was a no-brainer. Atlas was none other than the Swedish king Atle!

Now Rudbeck was proposing to compare figures from different historic periods and vastly different cultural traditions, and, many

An ancient king of Atlantis with the honorary title Atlas.

sober critics would say, figures with almost nothing in common besides a vague similarity in their names. But that had never stopped him before. Like Atlas, Atle was a powerful king, as clearly seen in the Norse poems *Atla-kvíða* and *Atla-mál,* and other slight references in the eddas. Atle controlled a large empire and a flourishing civilization, and as Plato had said, he had been easily corrupted, falling victim to his love of treasure. Atle's kingdom was also utterly destroyed. His majestic halls with the "high-builded towers" and the "far-famed temples" disappeared forever, swept away in the "roaring flames."

This curious, shadowy figure of the Norse eddas was, again like Plato's Atlas, only dimly known (for Plato's Atlas is not Homer's Atlas, the Titan who was forced to hold the world on his shoulders; the two are often confused). Yet Rudbeck believed Atle must have made quite an impression. Pulling out a map of Sweden, he rattled off a long list of places where the name of the Atlantean king was supposedly enshrined. There was Atle's island (Atlesöö) on the beautiful lake Mälaren, just outside Stockholm and also in one of the country's oldest settlements. There were also Atle's lake (Atlesjö), Atle's village (Atleby or Alby), and a string of other places running throughout the kingdom. Sweden even had its own Atlas Mountains (Atlefjäll). Indeed, just as Plato had said, King Atlas had left his name all over the country. Most dramatic, of course, was an old name for Sweden: Atland, which Rudbeck immediately translated as "Atlantis" (and incorporated into the Swedish title of the book, *Atland eller Manheim*).

Even if the differences between the ancient Greek and Norse figures were many, and the similarities vague at best, Rudbeck was overflowing with excitement. Consumed by his theory, he was determined to make it work. When a solution did not immediately present itself, Rudbeck was unwavering, laboring passionately and compulsively. Fears for his own "sickly constitution" evaporated in the whirlwind of enthusiasm.

As he saw it, the task was to hammer out the small details of the larger, grand vision of Atlantis that, in his frenzy, seemed more accurate with each passing day. Rudbeck had an explanation, for instance, as to why Plato had used the name *Atlas* and all he himself could find was the Swedish *Atle*. His answer was lifted straight from Plato's own words:

> Since Solon was planning to make use of the story for his own poetry, he had found, on investigating the meaning of the names, that those Egyptians who had first written them down had translated them into their own tongue. So he himself in turn recovered the original sense of each name and, rendering it into our tongue, wrote it down so.

In other words, by the time the story was recorded in the 380s B.C., the name of King Atle had been transformed from the language of Atlantis (Swedish) to Egyptian and then to Greek. After that, it was at the mercy of Solon's discretionary interpretation and the whims of Critias's childhood memory. No wonder, Rudbeck said, the name had been somewhat garbled over time.

Meanwhile, other distinguishing features of Atlantis were starting to cause more problems. For one, Plato was pretty clear that Atlantis was situated near the famous Pillars of Hercules, traditionally located at the Strait of Gibraltar, the narrow waterway separating southern Spain from northern Africa. According to ancient myth, the hero Hercules had set them up as the "far-famed witnesses of the farthest limit of voyaging." Given such a position, it is no surprise that many had looked for the lost world in the mid-Atlantic or the Americas.

But Rudbeck soon had a proposal of his own. Forced back to the drawing board, he started repositioning his map of Atlantis. Placing the capital at Old Uppsala, with the kingdom stretching northward to the Arctic Kimmernes, the home of the Cimmerians at the halls of Hades and down to the southern tip of Skåne, Rudbeck must have watched with amazement. Right in front of his eyes, he saw the Pillars of Hercules.

The answer seemed so clear, so obvious, that he wondered why no one had proposed it before: the real pillars must have been the Öresund, the strategic waterway that separated the kingdoms of Denmark and Sweden, and one of the most perilous straits in Europe. Dutch and English traders knew the spot well, and had long been forced to pay hefty tolls to the Crown that controlled this enviable gateway to the Baltic. The narrow strip of sea was where, incidentally, Hamlet's castle was supposedly located, and where the lumbering Kronborg stands guard today.

Although he had no small confidence in his own mapmaking abilities, Rudbeck's proposal that the Pillars of Hercules lay in Scandinavia was radical to say the least. Why should one make recourse to a Nordic location, in the face of such widespread, almost unanimous, opinion that the pillars were found at the conjunction of Spain and northern Africa?

Reading through texts widely and energetically, in his customary fashion, Rudbeck must have been thrilled to come across the words of one of the most esteemed geographers of antiquity, Strabo. In the first book of his encyclopedic geography of the world, this first-century authority counted no less than seven different interpretations of the meaning and location of the Pillars of Hercules. One of them, actually, was the mythic "Crashing Rocks," the dangerous straits the Argonauts encountered on the quest for the Golden Fleece—and a location that must have been particularly appealing in light of Rudbeck's own unconventional ideas about Jason's voyage.

Another stimulating clue had, incidentally, come from the Roman historian Tacitus. In *Germania,* his account of the northern barbarian tribes, Tacitus records an observation from a Roman commander, Drusus Germanicus, exploring the north: "We have even ventured upon the Northern Ocean itself, and rumor has it that there are Pillars of Hercules in the far north."

Suddenly Rudbeck's suspicion that the location of the "Pillars of Hercules" was actually more complicated than usually presented seemed possible, hinted at by the historian and confirmed by the geographer. And once his mind got started on the matter, Rudbeck believed that the Swedish solution actually fulfilled the criteria more satisfactorily than the conventional site of Gibraltar.

After all, if the pillars had been set up to honor the glory of Hercules and mark the so-called limits of human endeavor, then why place them in a location where ancient peoples "sailed past them every year"? The far edge of the Mediterranean was certainly not the end of the world; ask the Phoenicians, ask the Carthaginians, ask anyone who presumably traded for the valuable tin found in Great Britain. This traditional Gibraltar location hardly made sense in either geographical or psychological terms. Sweden, on the other hand, offered another possibility.

Here rough, frigid, sometimes icy waters made sailing difficult if not impossible at certain times of the year, a fact that made this Scandinavian option a more likely place for the "limits of the ancient world" than Gibraltar. Here, too, right in the very spot that Rudbeck was proposing, were many place-names preserving the memory of a much older name.

All around the Öresund were small villages whose names, coincidentally, bore the root of *Hercules:* Herhal, Herhamber, and a host of others, including one as far away as Stockholm called Hercul. Rudbeck was growing so confident that he was on the right track with his new theory about the Pillars of Hercules that he would soon pronounce, in full stride, that the club-toting strongman and antiquity's greatest warrior had originally been a Swede. His real name, found in many sagas and rune stones, was Härkolle, which meant literally "warrior chief" or perhaps "one dressed in a warrior's clothes." (Rudbeck contrasted his theory with one leading etymology that derived the name Hercules from the Greek words meaning "the glory of Hera"—an "unsatisfactory guess," he said, when Hera hated Hercules' guts.) Much more would indeed follow about the Swedish Hercules. For now the importance was clear. All these place-names near the Öresund were surviving memories of the original "Pillars of Hercules," the treacherous northern straits that once marked the entrance to the kingdom of Atlantis.

With Plato's distinct words and his own painstaking exploration fueled by a splendid imagination, Rudbeck could only marvel with joy at how well it all seemed to fall into place. For that was now becoming the method, relentlessly marching forward, and if each new discovery unleashed countless additional problems, then Rudbeck would figure it out, somehow, as he always did. He was also growing bolder in the process—more convinced of how little the past had really been understood, and more confident in his own ability to recover the lost truth.

Indeed, as Rudbeck looked at Atlantis, it seemed as if Plato had personally been to Sweden, and had patiently dictated the dimensions of its countryside in exact detail. The philosopher had mentioned many specific characteristics about its location and the landscape. "Not a single one," Rudbeck was glad to say, "conflicted with the land of Sweden as it can still be seen today."

Swept away by elation, Rudbeck described the adventure:

> This island of Atlantis, which no one for some thousands of years has dared to try and find, because of the heavy mud, numerous pirates, infinite islets and rocks, and moving drift-ice that have troubled its Atlantic sea, making for the voyager a dark way and difficult to find, I have now by God's help dared to pass with a boat equipped with 102 Platonic oars, and found her.

This map, drawn by one of Rudbeck's talented students, Philip Thelott, shows the locations of Atlantis, Hades, and some of the many other discoveries about ancient Sweden.

AS RUDBECK CHASED Atlantis, Sweden was waiting nervously for the imminent foreign invasion. Recent Swedish losses on the battlefield had revived some bitter memories of past insults and humiliations. Just when the performances of Gustavus Adolphus, Queen Christina, and Charles X Gustav seemed to have relegated these painful experiences to the "dustbin of the past," Danish advances were bringing them disgracefully back to mind.

In late June 1676, the Danes landed on Swedish soil. Three hundred ships dropped almost fifteen thousand well-armed enemy troops onto a highly exposed Swedish coast. Towns near the present-day Norwegian border, such as Vänersborg, were going up in flames, and stray forces were plundering unopposed in the countryside. Rushed out to the west coast, Count Magnus Gabriel de la Gardie was hastily assembling some means of defense.

Occasional victories came to the count, the very first for Sweden in this horrible war. For the most part, however, those successes were small and far too infrequent to have much effect. Most of the early engagements ended instead decidedly in the Danes' favor, sometimes indeed in simply a rout. Compared with the invaders, the rounded-up makeshift Swedish forces were quite inexperienced. "Naked and barefoot" was how one observer described them.

In places with better defenses, such as Skåne in the south, the truth was no less harsh. Not only were the people succumbing to the attacks, but a frightening number were even joining the Danish invaders. Many families in this region, which had long been a part of the Danish kingdom, resented the forced changes that came with the union with Sweden, the seemingly never-ending stream of orders from the distant capital. Within a few months it looked as if this rich province of fertile lands, deep forests, and enviable fishing grounds was well on its way to being restored to Denmark.

The people were, in the meantime, suffering as prices for basic necessities rose to exorbitant heights, and taxes remained at their crushing levels. As the Danes penetrated farther into the Swedish kingdom, confusion was everywhere, and so was the desperation of the people. At one point a band of peasants actually attacked the Swedish king's personal supplies. Nine of the king's guards were killed, and the peasants dragged away food, drink, trophies (including the royal tent), and money to the tune of fifty thousand *daler silvermynt*.

By the end of autumn 1676, the Danes had burned and pillaged widely in the west, and taken all but one of the strategic fortresses in the south, the fortress at Malmö. If things continued in this way, one historian noted, there was a fear that "the king would not only lose his mind, but also his crown." The many setbacks severely strained the Swedes, and certainly must have increased Rudbeck's own anxieties.

However bleak the prospects looked in the darkest days of the 1670s, Rudbeck could reassure himself and his fellow Swedes that a great, powerful civilization had once flourished in their beleaguered country. Ancient heroes and poets had made pilgrimages to this glorious civilization, and had sought its wisdom. Yet it was not just a matter of seeking solace in a distant, imagined past.

Rudbeck's investigations also made him feel that he had found a recipe for surviving this time of crisis. As the country faced its worst emergency in modern history, the Swedes could look back for guidance to their ancestors, who had loved justice, given their sacred oaths of loyalty to the kingdom, and elevated a life of virtue to an art form. The Atlanteans cherished truth, dignity, and goodness, holding honor in the strictest regard.

This was a clarion call for his fellow Swedes to heed the lessons from their Atlantean ancestors. All the happiness and wisdom that flourished in their society had begun with the individual Atlanteans, who, in their prime, "thought scorn of everything save virtue." Despite enjoying great riches, they were not so "drunk with pride . . . that they lost control of themselves and went to ruin." The problems had only begun when they lost this enlightened perspective. As Plato put it, the old "divinity within them" was gradually extinguished, causing the once mighty civilization to succumb to its worst excesses.

The same malady was once again threatening the Atlanteans' descendants. As Sweden was suffering a losing war, a struggling economy, popular unrest, treasonous support of the invaders, and a sense of hopelessness, Rudbeck believed that it was absolutely urgent to rekindle the wisdom of Atlantis. Nothing less would prevent Sweden from sinking for a second time into the decadence that came with too much lusting for power, wealth, and worldly ambition.

11

OLYMPUS STORMED

❧

Now the Olympian magic mountain opens itself before us,
showing us its very roots.

—FRIEDRICH NIETZSCHE, *THE BIRTH OF TRAGEDY*

*N*O PROPOSED SITE has ever fit Atlantis perfectly, and the challenges of finding a site in Sweden were, to say the least, daunting. Confidence, hope, and determination would be vital, because some of the difficulties were significant indeed.

No matter how hard Rudbeck and his land-surveying students tried, the exact size of the plain surrounding the legendary capital city could not be found. Very few Atlantis theories have satisfactorily resolved this dilemma—and with the vast dimensions, three thousand by two thousand stadia (approaching some 550 kilometers by 365 kilometers), it is not difficult to see why. The intricate web of canals that encircled the imposing city was also problematic, though Rudbeck's answer was inventive.

As he saw it, Atlantis's complex system of waterways was really the maze of channels formed within the thousands of islands and islets dotting the Stockholm archipelago. "The whole world together," Rudbeck said, "probably did not have more islands than this peninsula

[Sweden]." Later he would add a fascinating discussion of these narrow sea lanes and excellent rocky hideaways, showing how well they had served Swedish raiders and traders for centuries, from Atlantis to the Viking era to the present. Yet, however provocative a solution, these natural formations were still a far cry from Plato's artificial, geometrically designed network of canals.

Studying the landscape also helped Rudbeck's search for Atlantis's grand royal palace. Although there was clearly no such building in sight, Rudbeck could trace out the bare outlines of its old foundation following Plato's description of its location near the temple, the grove, and the springs, as well as the encouraging coincidence that the area was in fact known locally as *Kungsgård,* or royal garden. So Rudbeck marked the likely spot, and then looked on admiringly, imagining how the royal palace of Atlantis once rose out of the middle of Old Uppsala.

Looking in vain for any surviving physical traces of the magnificent edifice, Rudbeck ventured an explanation for the conspicuous absence. There were good reasons, he thought, why tangible remains were not readily at hand. When the palace was originally constructed, the Atlanteans would have used a combination of materials relying primarily on stone or wood. If they had preferred wood, then it was hardly surprising that the palace had not survived—the Norse sagas had made it perfectly clear that Atle's great hall had burned. Even without a fire, though, few timber structures could have withstood so many centuries of exposure to the elements.

If the Atlanteans had opted for stone, as Plato indicated, then the gradually decaying building would have been quarried long ago for construction projects. Certainly Rudbeck knew many elderly gentlemen who remembered hearing tales in their childhood about how desperate the town dwellers had been to obtain all the necessary materials for building the large Vasa castle in Uppsala. Ransacking old monuments was unfortunately a timeless practice (Hadorph's pioneering law had only recently granted the vulnerable monuments protection, at least legally). In any case the ruins of the Atlantis palace were probably lost for good, either consumed by the flames or recycled within the walls of nearby castles and churches.

One thing Rudbeck was sure about, though, was that the palace had not been destroyed exactly as Plato had claimed, swept away along with the rest of Atlantis in a massive earthquake and flood. Rudbeck was in fact amazed that anyone could believe that this part of Plato's story was literally true. For instance, Plato had claimed that the destruction buried the civilization, leaving only "a barrier of impassable mud which prevents those who are sailing out from here to the ocean beyond from proceeding further."

How could such a cataclysm produce so much mud that would, centuries later, still be unsettled, and make the nearby ocean an unnavigable graveyard? This, Rudbeck said, was "an explanation for children." For readers who did not share Rudbeck's interest or expertise in natural history, he provided another argument.

Plato's words, quite simply, conflicted with sacred history. The book of Genesis recorded God's promise never to flood the world again with another overwhelming deluge: "Never again will all life be cut off by the waters of a flood; never again will there be a flood to destroy the earth."

According to Rudbeck, both sacred and natural history ruled out an actual annihilation of Atlantis. It made much more sense, he argued, to see Plato's words as describing the figurative destruction of a society sinking into decline and oblivion—a degeneration brought on by their love of war and their tragic slide into corruption.

Discussing the last days of the old kingdom brought Rudbeck back to another challenge that has long bedeviled Atlantis hunters: the chronology of the events. In *Critias,* Plato dated the war with Atlantis about nine thousand years in the past, millennia before any advanced civilization is known to have flourished. But unlike many theorists who have attempted to solve this problem by simply dropping a zero to obtain a more workable nine hundred years, Rudbeck actually offered an explanation for his chronological acrobatics. He also, refreshingly, avoided attributing this significant change to a simple error in memory, transcription, or translation, or some other form of carelessness.

There was no reason to assume that the Atlanteans had used the Gregorian calendar or the older, less accurate Julian calendar, Rudbeck rightly noted. In fact it was highly unlikely. A calendar based on the sun was far from the easiest to discover, or even, for that matter, the most natural to use. Ancient astronomers were much more likely, Rudbeck the stargazer argued correctly, to devise a system of time reckoning based upon the moon. Unlike the sun, the moon passes through easily visible and predictable phases. At such an early time in history, there was no recorded evidence that the solar year had even been discovered.

As a result, the chronology of the Atlanteans could be much better explained as consisting of periods of time based on the regular movements of the moon. If this was correct, then a quick calculation reduced Plato's 9400 B.C., at one stroke, to about 1350 B.C. (Plato's "nine thousand years in the past" divided by twelve converts to 750 solar years, which is then added to the starting point, which Rudbeck traced back to Solon's discussion with the Egyptian priests, about 600 B.C.). This calculation also inserts neatly into Rudbeck's reconstructed chronology of ancient Sweden, based on measuring the distinctions in the soil around the oldest ruins. The Atlanteans' war and destruction would have occurred around 1350 B.C., about one thousand years after Sweden was first settled.

Despite some manifest difficulties that still needed to be ironed out, Rudbeck believed that Plato's words described Sweden "as clear as day." No other place on earth had even a fraction of the evidence for Atlantis that he had found in Sweden. So close was the fit that, Rudbeck said, a Swedish blind man hearing the tale could sense with his cane the very landscape of Atlantis under his feet. Ten years later Rudbeck would still be proclaiming his theory with even more evidence and greater enthusiasm, gladly taking visitors to Uppsala on a guided tour of the lost world of Atlantis. Another ten years into the search, Rudbeck would issue a challenge to any scholar in Europe to come to Sweden and prove him wrong. Rudbeck would, he said, cover the expenses.

Yet no matter how many tours he would give, or challenges he would offer, some difficulties still remained, as if to taunt him. Rudbeck was virtually incapable of resting as long as any doubt or ambiguity lingered about his Atlantis. Even the slightest hint of uncertainty would be assaulted with an astonishing vigor, as if the search itself were under threat. Such striving for perfection drove Rudbeck deeper into the labyrinths of myth, and further into the realm of obsession.

ENJOYING THE THRILL of the search, Rudbeck was spending less time at the medical school. His lectures were languishing, and university authorities were once again warning him about neglecting his duties. Fortunately for Rudbeck, his old friend Professor Petrus Hoffvenius was picking up the slack, though it was clear that he could not continue to do so indefinitely.

Rudbeck's waterworks system, meanwhile, had broken down; its pipes had burst in a severe winter a few years earlier. His anatomy theater needed a new roof, and one of his suspension bridges over the town river had collapsed in a recent spring flood. There were many matters that needed attention, but Rudbeck had first to be satisfied with his work on Atlantis.

Hunting down every possible claim about the legendary civilization, Rudbeck came across one of the great unsung heroes in the tradition of Atlantis: the first-century-B.C. historian Diodorus Siculus.

Writing during the bloody upheavals that tore Rome apart during the last days of the republic, this Sicilian-born scholar spent three decades gathering materials for his monumental work, the *Library of*

History. Originally spanning forty books, Diodorus's collection aimed to present an overall sweep of the past, a universal history that began with the earliest recorded events and made its way up to Julius Caesar's Gallic Wars (58–50 B.C.). The ten surviving books show a certain idiosyncrasy in the selection and treatment of its subject matter. Indeed, for this historian, the citizens of Atlantis were just as real as the Romans, Greeks, Gauls, or any other ancient people he discussed.

Although Diodorus does not earn much praise today as a reliable authority, he nevertheless preserved many invaluable traditions that would otherwise have been lost. By the time his eccentric chronicle reached the history of Atlantis, he essentially took Plato's vision of an advanced civilization and magnified it considerably. Even more, Diodorus added a twist to the tale; he claimed to have access to the traditions of the Atlanteans themselves.

After this rather surprising revelation, Diodorus really dropped a bomb. Zeus, Poseidon, and the gods of ancient Greece had, according to these same records, come originally from the island of Atlantis! Such a claim was "in agreement with the most renowned of the Greek poets, Homer." In the *Iliad*, for instance, the Olympian goddess Hera thus announces her plans for an upcoming journey: "I am going to the ends of the fruitful earth to visit Ocean, the forebear of the gods, and Mother Tethys, who treated me kindly and brought me up in their home." And this "Mother Tethys" was, Diodorus added, an ancient queen of Atlantis.

From the vantage point of 1670s Sweden, these were extraordinary words. In the version of the classical myth most widely known, Tethys was an important though hazy figure who had married Oceanus and played at least some role in raising Hera, if not also the other gods as Homer sometimes seems to suggest. Now the assiduous collector of old traditions, Diodorus Siculus, had preserved some vague legend that connected Tethys to the island of Atlantis. Rudbeck could only wonder about how well this information fitted with his own emerging vision of the past. For Tethys sounded strangely close to a place on his Atlantis, called Tethis Fiord, which was located firmly in the far north, at the sixty-eighth meridian, indeed, as Homer put it, "at the ends of the fruitful earth."

But Tethys was also known to be a Titan, and some descriptions of this powerful race of giants have actually survived. In the oldest extant account that offers some detail, the eighth-century-B.C. Greek poet Hesiod described their home as "hidden under misty gloom, in a dank place where are the ends of the huge earth." The shepherd poet further described their "awful home of murky Night wrapped in dark clouds." Where Tethys and the Titans dwelt, "the glowing Sun never looks upon them with his beams," just as actually happens, every winter, at Tethis Fiord in northern Scandinavia.

DIODORUS SICULUS WAS not only greatly encouraging the Swedish doctor, but now also helping direct his enormous energies. Rudbeck had started to follow some fascinating leads, particularly about the classical gods and those vague, supposed traditions connecting them with the kingdom of Atlantis.

Zeus, Apollo, and the other gods of Mount Olympus were known to every educated person in Rudbeck's day. Needless to say, nowhere the Olympians were said to have lived, visited, or otherwise had anything to do with Sweden or with the Scandinavian far north. All the oldest surviving accounts clearly place the Olympians somewhere within the ancient Greek world. Tradition associated Zeus with Crete, Hera with Argos and Mycenae, and Aphrodite with Cyprus; Hephaestus "fell" on the island of Lemnos; and so on. The locations of their birth, the sites of many of their known deeds, and their main shrines all were placed mainly within the limits of the ancient Mediterranean.

Yet the idea of the Swedish origin of the classical gods had caught Rudbeck's attention, and the flamboyant Renaissance man could not let go of this possibility. Faint signs of uncertainty and dissension about the gods, however subtle and hinted, would be chased down and pounced upon with an overwhelming fixation, as Rudbeck obsessively tried to root up Mount Olympus and situate it in his homeland, not far from where he had reconstructed ancient Atlantis. His imagination could, as one scholar put it, take on a frightening quality.

Years later, for instance, when Sweden was considering a comprehensive reform of its calendar, a committee of experts requested Rudbeck's opinion. He agreed that the old Julian calendar needed to be abandoned, but unexpectedly he did not favor switching over to the Gregorian, as many European countries had already done. Instead Rudbeck proposed that Sweden adopt a calendar based on the runes of Atlantis! This rather unusual choice would mean losing a few minutes every year, but that did not really matter, Rudbeck said, because the end of the world was near anyway. The committee had difficulty determining whether he was serious, and his imaginative proposal was politely turned down.

Back in the search for the classical gods, two important traditions were probably guiding Rudbeck in his ever-growing ambition. The first was a nearly universal belief that traced the ancestry of the classical gods back to the Titans. Usually the parents were identified as Cronos and Rhea, though some preferred another minor and perhaps older tradition that suggested Oceanus and Tethys. At any rate, the oldest Olympians were in all accounts the children of the Titans.

The second tradition was a popular way of viewing mythology that had flourished for centuries, now called Euhemerism after the early-third-century-B.C. philosopher Euhemerus of Messene, who sought real historical figures behind the stories of the gods. They were, in other words, kings, queens, heroes, sages, or people who had performed such memorable deeds that they were, with the passage of time, remembered as gods. And for Rudbeck, looking at the ancient gods and working within this tradition, the temptations must have been irresistible.

For, according to standard accounts of classical mythology, especially Hesiod's *Theogony*, the Titans once ruled the universe. Fearing the loss of power, the leader of the Titans, Cronos, decided to launch a preemptive strike. He would eat his children. Hestia, Poseidon, Hades, Demeter, Hera—the entire family of Olympians—were swallowed. By the time the sixth and youngest child, Zeus, had been born, the Titan mother Rhea had had enough. When Cronos prepared to devour her new son in the usual fashion, Rhea tricked him by presenting a stone wrapped up as an infant. In the meantime she smuggled the baby Zeus to safety on the island of Crete.

After reaching maturity, Zeus rescued his siblings, who were magically disgorged unharmed, and rallied them to victory over Cronos and the whole Titan lot. That is, except his mother, Rhea, who would move into the new home of the gods on Mount Olympus. Oceanus and Tethys also escaped the harsh punishment. The ultimate reason is not specifically stated, though this was probably because of Olympian loyalty to their kind rearers, as hinted in the *Iliad,* or perhaps it was gratitude for their valuable services in the war against the Titans.

Now Rudbeck put the fragmented pieces together into a stunning proposition. Could it be that, after winning this war of liberation, Zeus and the gods left their Titan overseers imprisoned in the dark abode at the ends of the earth, that is, around the arctic Tethis Fiord, and then made their way, for the first time, into Crete, Mycenae, Argos, and all the places that held their early sanctuaries and that were also undoubtedly some of the oldest known settlements of the ancient Greek world? Could memories of these events still be encoded in the oldest, most obscure stories of classical mythology?

To Rudbeck, who was willing to entertain any potential solution, even the most daring and revolutionary, this was certainly a possibility. Soon his enthusiasm would make it a probability, indeed almost a certainty, in the unfolding vision of the past that he was desperately trying to capture on paper. Yet before he could pursue this specific

point further, there was another idea that must have struck his imagination and convinced him even more of the Atlantis-Titans-Sweden
connection.

All the whimsical and wrathful Olympians who usually displayed
the full gamut of human passions looked like another rowdy, boister-
ous gang Rudbeck had come across. Unlike the classical gods, however, this was a family that was known only to a select few who had
access to their adventures, recorded in some of the world's rarest
books and still unpublished manuscripts housed in Scandinavia: the
gods of Asgard.

How similar were the classical gods who feasted on nectar and
ambrosia atop snowy Mount Olympus to the Norse gods who dined
on mead and boar in Valhalla! How similar, too, were Zeus, Poseidon,
and the classical gods who fought the Titans to Odin, Thor, and the
Norse gods who waged war against their archenemies, the monstrous
giants! Once again, Rudbeck's head swirled as he contemplated the
possible implications.

What were those "Atlantean traditions" that Diodorus Siculus
had mentioned, anyway? Could they have been preserved in Sweden,
where, after all, Rudbeck had found Atlantis and, it seemed, a possible home for the Titan Tethys? Could they have anything to do with
those mysterious runes carved on stone, wood, and metal? Better yet,
could they have something to do with the much more elaborate
Norse sagas and eddas that Rudbeck was starting to appreciate with a
new passion? Although most were obviously written down in the
Middle Ages, could these brittle manuscripts contain memories of
older, lost Atlantean stories, perhaps fragments of fragments? Even if
Diodorus was not the most authoritative of sources, must he necessarily be wrong about every single point?

It was time to investigate the worlds of Olympus and Valhalla.
Looking to learn everything he could, Rudbeck pored over the oldest
and most authoritative accounts of ancient history and mythology.
After rowing with 102 Platonic oars to Atlantis, Rudbeck would ef-

fectively "hoist sail with Homer" and embark on his own maverick odyssey into the dreamy world of his own creation.

EVEN BEFORE RUDBECK had stumbled upon the quest for Atlantis and attempted to storm Mount Olympus, there was an unmistakable sense of urgency about the venture. He was already six hundred pages deep in the writing of the work, and, as he started to worry, he had not even made it a quarter of the way through to the desired end. Rushing to cram all his new discoveries, which were expanding exponentially almost each way he turned, Rudbeck could not work fast enough to keep up the hectic pace. Seven hundred pages into the text, there was still no end in sight.

Raising the stakes in this race against time, Rudbeck had earlier taken the advice of his friend Olaus Verelius. He had decided to begin printing as early as February 1675, though the many new discoveries had delayed it further, not to mention the firing of Curio the printer and the uproar over the subsequent lawsuits. The legal manipulations and the suit, however, were not looking all that good. "Only the Lord knows what will happen to him," Rudbeck said to his friend Count de la Gardie as the prospects in the case looked worse and worse.

Given the looming uncertainty, the prudent thing, Verelius and Rudbeck agreed, was to start printing at once. As soon as new pages were written, they were immediately rushed to Curio's press. *Atlantica,* as the work would be called after Rudbeck's discovery of Atland or Atlantis, would be printed a few pages at a time, sheet by sheet, right after he finished writing them.

Regardless of Curio's fate, which Rudbeck's clever maneuvering had at least for the moment managed to forestall, the costs of the search for the lost world were quickly adding up. He had taken Verelius's advice about another matter as well. Originally Rudbeck had planned to publish the *Atlantica* only in Swedish, and if the scholarly community deemed his work worthwhile, then he was confident that someone would come along to translate it into the more accessible Latin or French "just as often happens to other men's books."

Verelius, however, had insisted that Rudbeck adorn the work with a Latin translation, and other scholars at Uppsala who read the drafts agreed. "A good friend," Rudbeck said, was recruited for the task. Rudbeck hardly had the time for this translation himself, not to mention the fact that he had "long since stopped worrying his head with such grammatical curiosities."

The unnamed friend who would assume the task of translating this unwieldy volume was most likely the classical scholar and professor of eloquence Anders Norcopensis. A child prodigy with a wonderful grasp of Latin, he certainly added much with his translation of the work. By all accounts, it was a stellar performance. Few have failed to notice how Norcopensis sometimes "cleaned up" Rudbeck's rather hurried and idiosyncratic text, written as it was in an almost stream-of-consciousness style under great pressure of time.

Within a few years this choice of translator would in another respect be of no small consequence. In the 1680s, Norcopensis would be appointed personal tutor to the Swedish crown prince, the future king Charles XII, the romantic and quite controversial ruler who would be the last of Sweden's warrior kings.

In the meantime, however, if Verelius's advice about fitting the text with a Latin translation helped ensure a much wider readership, it also significantly increased the strains in an already monumental undertaking.

LOOKING INTO THE intricate genealogies of ancient mythology, one of the most promising leads in the search for the Olympians was the god Apollo. Armed with golden lyre and silver bow, shining Apollo was the healing, music-loving god of reason and archery. To many scholars today, he seems the "most Greek" of the classical pantheon.

To Rudbeck, on the other hand, Apollo looked as Swedish as Gustavus Adolphus.

Rudbeck already knew that this god was held in special reverence among the Hyperboreans. Virtually every ancient source touching on the legendary northerners agreed on this fact, and many told the story that Apollo's mother, Leto, had actually been a Hyperborean. In his book *The Nature of the Gods,* the first-century Roman prince of orators, Cicero, was still aware of this tale, writing, "This is Apollo who tradition says came to Delphi from the land of the Hyperboreans."

Whether he was born on the Greek isle of Delos or came into the Mediterranean from a distant land "beyond the north wind," the conclusion was essentially the same. Would this not make Apollo seem, in Rudbeckian logic, at least partially Hyperborean, or Swedish, indeed Atlantean, since Diodorus's tradition had said that the gods came from there anyway?

Yet, aside from this string of hypotheticals, were there any possible reasons to believe that Apollo had actually been Swedish? For Rudbeck, the answer was obvious, almost instantaneously showing itself in the old manuscripts through the Norse god Balder. The similarities, at least at first glance, were many.

Just as the ancients praised Apollo for his justice and beauty, a child "lovely above all the sons of heaven," Balder was noticeably hailed in Norse accounts as the most just and the most beautiful of the gods. Both were known for their gift of prophecy. When Homer sang in the *Iliad* that "the past, the present, and the future held no secrets" for Apollo, Balder the Good "dreamed great dreams" about future dangers, terrible premonitions that prompted his mother Frigg to fear for his life and seek the oath of every living thing not to harm her child (again perhaps the basis for the fears that forced Apollo's mom, Leto, to travel around seeking a safe haven to give birth to her children).

Additionally, both figures were related in other fundamental ways. While Apollo was the god of light, and some later traditions even associated him with the sun, Balder was "so fair in appearance and so bright that light shines from him." Apollo's justice, reasoning, and clear logical thought were echoed in Balder's fame as "the wisest of the Aesir," and Apollo's eloquence likewise made its appearance when the *Edda* knew Balder as "the most beautifully spoken." As for Apollo's celebrated magnificence, attested to by the number of his shrines and sanctuaries, Balder was also "the most merciful," and as the *Edda* put it, the "best and all praise him." And so on.

Despite the obvious lack of correspondence in every possible tradition, Rudbeck saw enough key similarities between the classical and Norse figures to think that he was on the trail of the original Olympian that, as Diodorus's lost sources allegedly claimed, came from Atlantis to the Mediterranean. Besides, the oldest and most complete genealogies available about the classical gods made the question even more provocative.

Apollo's reputed Hyperborean heritage could be found to have deeper roots. His mother, Leto, it turned out, not only was regarded as a Hyperborean, but also was the daughter of a Titan—a Titan who lived in dark, "misty gloom . . . at the ends of the huge earth," and actually a brother of Tethys, whose name Rudbeck thought had survived in the name of Tethis Fiord, which is located at the actual dark "ends of the huge earth." With the testimony of the oldest known works in classical mythology, all these coincidences could only reinforce Rudbeck's suspicion, indeed his conviction, that he was on the right track. The classical Apollo was merely a pale reflection of an original Balder cult that came from the far north.

"I could still put forth endless reasons," Rudbeck said, "but I will save them for another place." Given Rudbeck's tremendous ability to make connections, no matter how far removed, this was no idle boast. Elaborations about the northern elements surviving in the classical myth of Apollo would indeed be plentiful, but they would have to wait. So much else was on the agenda in this bizarre hunt for the Swedish Olympians.

❧

IF APOLLO WAS Swedish, and his mother Swedish, what about the father—could Zeus also be Swedish? Logically, building upon the Apollo-Balder identity, you might think that Rudbeck would look for Apollo's dad in Balder's dad, the Norse god Odin.

After all, both Zeus and Odin were regarded as the chiefs of their respective worlds, Olympus and Valhalla. With long white beards and unrivaled authority, Zeus and Odin alike sat on their thrones, beholding the vast panorama of divine and human events as they unfolded. They had also reached this lofty summit in a similar way, that is, with the violent overthrow of their rivals. Even the means of destruction were similar. Zeus had disposed of the Titan Cronos in a gruesome way, usually depicted as castration, and Odin had likewise, as the *Edda* tells us, "dismembered" the frost giant Ymir.

But Rudbeck did not make the Zeus-Odin connection, probably because the difficulties of trying to reconcile such formidable figures would soon have been overwhelming. For the more one looks into the stories about Zeus and Odin, the more different they seem. Zeus was insatiable in his lust, chasing goddesses, mortals, and indeed just about anything that moved. This sex-crazed god was almost literally the father of all things. Although Odin was also known to engage in a few affairs and was specifically called "All-Father," this Norse god was admittedly something of a contrast.

Odin often seemed far away from the moment, brooding over the terrible things that awaited. He took less pleasure in his food, eating no meat and, unlike his fellow gods, drinking only wine. The stern figure just gave his portions to the two wolves at his side, and listened attentively to the two ravens perched on his shoulder who returned to the great hall each night at dinner with tidings from around the world. Odin's great loves seemed to be knowledge and poetry, with no better illustration than the time he gave one of his eyes in exchange for a drink at the well of wit and wisdom. On inspection, the two chiefs of Olympus and Valhalla indeed marched in different directions: Zeus the protector of the laws, and Odin the patron god of thieves, outlaws, and the hanged. In so many important ways, one-eyed Odin, who spoke only in rhyme, seemed quite a bit different from the hardheaded Zeus.

So with Rudbeck's dexterity very much at work, another possibility would not have been far away, and this one had unlimited potential. For in many ways, an intriguing counterpart to Zeus could be seen in the Norse god Thor.

Thor had the strength that was often attributed to the Olympian. "What lunatics, to quarrel with Zeus!" Hera said at one point in the *Iliad.* "For brute strength he is beyond question first among the gods." Zeus was not above confirming his own prowess, bragging about how he could easily take on all the other gods put together. Thor worked better than Odin here, as a strong god, stronger than Odin, and, in the words of the *Edda,* quite simply the "strongest of all the gods."

Also, Zeus and Thor were quite close in temper and disposition. Both had violent outbursts and warlike spirits, and when the situation became dire, they would be called upon by the other gods for rescue. Again and again, in the battles with enemies, in both cases giants, the gods were staying alive, sometimes barely so, only because Thor or Zeus tipped the balance with his robust deeds.

So when Zeus "the cloud gatherer" storms, Thor thunders—reveling in letting his own brand of "white-hot thunderbolts" fly, scorching his enemies to a crisp. He seems to enjoy nothing more than a good fight, bashing skulls and splitting heads. Thor was a wild force of nature, unpredictable in his explosions, and at times, like Zeus, with more than his share of the comical. Thor was more simple-minded than the subtle and crafty Odin; Thor's immediate reaction was usually to swing his mighty hammer Miollnir, so "well-known to the frost-giants and the mountain-giants." And for Zeus as well as Thor, this was the ultimate protector of order in the universe, and held in highest regard for preserving divine justice.

Given all this and more, Rudbeck believed that Zeus and Thor had originally been the same figure. Indeed, in Rudbeck's opinion, *Zeus* was a Swedish word, deriving from an old-fashioned term that meant, appropriately enough, "god." Scholars had speculated for centuries on the meaning of Zeus's name, proposing everything from "living," "fertile," and, referring perhaps to the lightning bolts, "heat." None of these really impressed Rudbeck, who saw them as contradictory, incomplete, or just plain unsatisfactory, and wrote, "It is no wonder that they have made so many uncertain guesses on this matter, as Thor was foreign to them."

Had classical scholars been able to read Swedish and the Norse stories about Thor, they could have recognized Zeus long ago, realizing his name came from *Thius,* two compounds of "god" and "earth" (*dy-*), and son (someone born). In the meantime, if Thor was Zeus, as he believed he had proved, where did that leave Odin?

Placing the stories side by side, and plotting out the various relationships, there was one glaring possibility for Odin in the king of the Underworld, Hades. The two, Hades and Odin, shared more than might at first appear. Like Hades ruling over the dead in classical mythology, Odin was the patron of dead soldiers, with his winged companions, the Valkyries, riding out to battlefields and choosing the slain to come to Odin's hall, Valhalla, literally "hall of the slain." After all, Rudbeck had already found the kingdom of Hades in the far north, indeed where the Norse sagas had arguably placed Odin's halls. Rudbeck would mine classical and Norse mythologies for every similarity he could find to bring the dark, brooding Hades into Odin's Valhalla.

By linking the Swedish Thor to the Greek Zeus, and the Swedish Odin to the classical Hades, not to mention the sea god Niord to the classical Neptune or Poseidon, Rudbeck had come full circle in his investigation, all the way back to Plato and the dialogues on lost Atlantis, when the armies of the power-crazed kingdom undertook ambitious wars of expansion. Could these ancient Greek figures,

The Norse gods Odin, Thor, and Frigge, once rulers of Atlantis.

Zeus, Apollo, and the other Olympians, be surviving memories of that Atlantean aggression which Rudbeck believed had brought the Swedes to the banks of the Nile and the rocky hills of Athens?

To the bitter end, Rudbeck would be convinced of this startling revision of world history, and see it as yet further evidence that Atlantis, despite some temporary missing links, had been found in Sweden.

SUCH SENSATIONAL DISCOVERIES were undoubtedly affecting Rudbeck's behavior. He began to dress more simply than ever, much as he envisioned the ideals of the ancient Swedes before their fall. Quite radically, he decided to print university programs in Swedish, not Latin, as he believed that this Atlantic, or Swedish, language lay at the root of both Latin and Greek. Rudbeck was one of the first scholars ever to use Swedish so prominently at a university. He explained his reasoning thus: since he had not yet discovered "that Aristotle or Cicero ever honored the Gothic or Scythian tongue (which is the oldest)," Rudbeck planned to do the same. He would address the university "in good, pure Swedish, our mother tongue."

Such maverick disregard for tradition outraged many of his enemies, who feared that foreign scholars would mock Uppsala for discarding the international language of the learned. As one member of the College of Antiquities grumbled, "They will think this is only a school for children."

As was often the case with Rudbeck, his ambitions would grow with time, and one can only wonder at his plans for the future. For if he could not find the palace of Atlantis in Old Uppsala, then perhaps he felt he could at least build it in the heart of the university. His design for the new main university building, which he had been asked to draw up, shows more than a passing resemblance to the great royal palace of Atlantis. It was enormous like the palace Plato had described; and the decorations for the new university building were Atlantean right down to the Nereids, the sea nymphs riding dolphins that were to adorn the columns of the magnificent façade.

The project was, however, never fulfilled, given the great expenses involved and the sluggish economy of the 1670s. Unfortunately the same forces were straining Rudbeck's search for Atlantis, and threatening to make it end up like his unrealized plans for the university building.

Almost immediately after his book went to press, in March 1677, enormous sums of money were being consumed by this antiquarian project. By April the investment was costing a staggering fifty-four *daler* a week just to keep the production running, and soon even this did not suffice. By November, eight months later, Rudbeck had already pledged two thousand *daler sílvermynt* to cover the labor of the printer and another thousand for purchasing the huge stacks of paper required to print the bulging text—in both Swedish and Latin parallel texts—with an ambitious initial print run of five hundred copies.

Another couple of hundred *daler silvermynt* went for larger-sized paper to be used in the lavish volume of images and maps. After all, with the Argonauts' reconstructed voyage, the finds at the capital city of Atlantis, and the images from the expedition to the Underworld, these once luxurious accessories were quickly becoming a necessity, perhaps even a priority. New maps of ancient Sweden were also drafted, and none of this was exactly cheap. Together they added another two thousand *daler silvermynt* for the wood and copper engravings, as well as six hundred in wages for the assistants in the printer's shop.

Rudbeck's salary as a professor simply could not cover all these expenses. Just six months after *Atlantica* went to press, the costs of printing ran to almost six thousand *daler silvermynt*—and this at a time when a professor's annual earnings were about seven hundred! At the same time, nothing in this figure even remotely made allowances for all the time and energy that Rudbeck had devoted to the project, or his own personal financing of the expeditions to the Underworld, or to observe the Hyperborean mountains.

Given the epic proportions of the search and the equally colossal costs, what had initially looked like a dream now seemed a nightmare. The professor could not ask the count for the shortfall. Although always generous with his gold, De la Gardie no longer had so much to give; the combination of lavish lifestyle and a severe downturn in the Swedish economy had considerably reduced his treasury. Worse by far were the nasty politics of the time. The losses in the war were blamed on the regency, and increasingly De la Gardie took most of the responsibility for the sorry state of affairs.

And one year after the king's coronation in 1675, the financial support promised by Charles XI had not arrived. "Times were difficult," Rudbeck tried to explain, and a lot of people in town were on edge, waiting for him to pay off the debts he had accumulated. Another year passed and Rudbeck was still politely asking the count to remind the king of the money. Unfortunately, though, De la Gardie was finding himself far outside the royal inner circle. As the war with Denmark intensified and Sweden strove to marshal available resources, the prospects of receiving the king's gold seemed more distant than ever.

But the project must not die. As though it were a gigantic puzzle, Rudbeck was finding novel solutions to some of the oldest, most perplexing problems in ancient history — and gradually putting together the missing pieces to form a spectacular picture of the past. Classical mythology continued to bend under the weight of Rudbeck's erudition, his enthusiasm, and indeed his obsession. In his mind, everything pointed to this ancient golden age of ice and frost under the North Star.

With the count mired in his difficulties and the king's money nowhere to be found, Rudbeck scrambled to keep the search afloat. He borrowed money from friends, sold paper he had set aside for his books, begged for extra time in paying the printing costs, and even took loans from students — anything to prevent the work from suffering an early death. In the end Rudbeck even pawned the family silver.

His frantic actions kept the project alive for the moment, but trouble came from an unexpected source.

HANGING BY A THREAD

Dorian is far too wise not to do foolish things now and then, my dear Basil.

—OSCAR WILDE, *THE PICTURE OF DORIAN GRAY*

ESPITE ANGERED COUNCIL members, theologians retrenched for battle, and antiquarians still grumbling over Rudbeck's audacious moves to protect his printer, the new challenge was not to come from the most likely camps. Nor was it even that someone was offended when the Swedish physician dared to place the halls of Hades in their homeland, or pulled the pagan temple of Atlantis out from the walls of a prominent church. The problem, actually, was worse.

This was a simple, nonpartisan objection that was inspired at first by largely intellectual motivations. Back in the 1650s, while Rudbeck was still busy avoiding his anatomy lectures and dabbling in his new botanical garden, a celebrated classical scholar named Johannes Schefferus had begun his own investigations into the early history of Uppsala.

A short man with a long nose, who reportedly always wore a silk cape, Schefferus was probably Sweden's most prominent classical humanist. He had married the daughter of Professor Loccenius, the president of the College of Antiquities, and on the occasion of his wedding ceremony, he danced for the only time in his life. Like his father-in-law, Schefferus was another serious, talented German thinker who had come over to Uppsala University and found himself smitten by the glowing patriotism of his adopted country. Locking himself in his study overlooking the river, Schefferus devoted almost every waking hour to unhampered scholarship.

With this love of learning, Schefferus had tackled the early history of Uppsala, publishing his discoveries in a lavish work of scholarship, *Upsalia* (1666). The product of over a decade of study, *Upsalia* traced the history of the university town from its pagan origins through the conversion to Christianity and the flourishing of the modern diocese centered in the majestic cathedral. In this work, Schefferus advanced an argument that the famous temple of Old Uppsala had not actually been in Old Uppsala. It had stood instead, he claimed, right in the heart of the modern town of Uppsala, down from the cathedral and near the present Trinity Church.

In fact, by the time Schefferus was through with his study, Old Uppsala itself was not even *in* Old Uppsala—that, too, was located in the modern university town. Although this theory is now known to be incorrect, Schefferus's revision was certainly still plausible in the seventeenth century. And with a forceful advocate in Professor Schefferus, this rival theory could potentially have much appeal in the learned world. It could also, undoubtedly, cause considerable trouble for Olof Rudbeck, making his work in progress, as he would later say, "not worth reading, much less printing."

The first salvos in this controversy had been fired by Olaus Verelius when he published his edition of the *Hervararsaga* in 1672. While he was working on his scholarly notes for this Norse tale, Verelius found many shortcomings with Schefferus's theory, which he thought relied too heavily on late evidence of questionable value. Indeed it was fairly easy for him to undermine the basis of Schefferus's position.

Verelius also received help from Rudbeck, whose investigations of the Old Uppsala burial mounds satisfactorily showed the great antiquity of the Swedish civilization. Rudbeck's new staff confirmed that there were no older burial mounds than those found at the traditional location. No fewer than 665 burial mounds dated back almost four thousand years, to 2100 B.C., years before the outbreak of the Trojan War and the brilliant flowering of classical civilization.

This very point made Schefferus's work all the more indigestible. When placing the old temple and the town in modern Uppsala, Schefferus had also claimed that the famous pagan temple was not really all that old. He pointed to the historical sources, such as the Norse chronicler Snorri Sturluson, who claimed that the temple had not been founded until the reign of King Frei, that is, just before the birth of Christ. And if this temple dated back only to the first century, how could it have been, as Rudbeck was in the process of claiming, the lost golden temple of Atlantis? Besides, what would Schefferus's claim, if proved, have to say about the reliability of Rudbeck's archaeological dating methods, which had repeatedly confirmed a much greater antiquity?

Schefferus's *Upsalia,* in other words, challenged the very basis of Rudbeck's work in progress. Initially the dispute was conducted in the usual scholarly fashion of debate and discussion. Schefferus pointed to his sources, which were mainly medieval textual references to the Old Uppsala temple. Verelius was quick to answer with powerful counterarguments, complete with support from even older Norse manuscripts in De la Gardie's collection, which Schefferus had not seen, and supplemented further by Rudbeck's discoveries in the field. At this point, in the late spring of 1677, Schefferus opted for a different strategy. He asked the chancellor of Uppsala University, Count de la Gardie, to impose an act of censorship, strictly forbidding any further discussion of this issue.

This was an excellent time for Schefferus's unexpected request. De la Gardie could not have been more distracted, given the war, his fears of his enemies' plots in Stockholm, and his obvious unease as these same rivals were making themselves indispensable to the young king. In May 1677 the count's reply reached Uppsala. Magnus Gabriel de la Gardie expressed his displeasure at the behavior of the dueling scholars Verelius and Schefferus. Then he stressed the importance, indeed the necessity, of putting a stop to this incessant quarreling. He felt so "tired and sorry" about the state of affairs at the academy, with the scholarly disputes so "inconveniently and unreasonably" feeding on each other. No longer would any printer be allowed to churn the presses to contribute to this rotten state. The count ordered an immediate ban on the printing of materials related to this dispute.

What must have particularly upset Rudbeck and Verelius was that immediately before making this appeal, Professor Schefferus had finished writing his own commentary on the controversy and then rushed it out of town to be printed secretly in Stockholm. Without following the customary procedures, Schefferus raced the work from the printer to the market at a "dizzying speed."

The *Epistola defensoria,* a seventy-page pamphlet, did not actually add much new material. But that made little difference. Bringing together the older arguments into one place with a cogent, articulate punch, the *Epistola* was intended to be the last word before the prohibition was scheduled to go into effect—a ploy worthy of the intrigues found in the works of the Roman historians Schefferus so much loved reading. The man who was responsible for lecturing on the art of politics knew how to play the game when he wanted.

When the chancellor's ban was announced in May 1677, Schefferus's work had already been in circulation for about two weeks. Uppsala's scholars responded to the news in a mixed fashion. Verelius burst out, "I have not written anything that I cannot defend, nor anything prohibited by the censor," reaffirming the strength of his case, which he had built up with the help of the best historical evidence. The old Norse manuscripts that supported the traditional view were in fact much more genuine than the documents Schefferus relied upon, copies that were written down centuries after the sagas.

Referring also to the efforts he made to avoid offense, Verelius detailed how he had sent his arguments on the controversy to many friends for advance inspection. He asked each reader to mark an X next to anything that should be stricken from publication. From the royal censor to Professor Rudbeck, many had read the words and approved of his (uncustomarily) genteel approach, including Count de la Gardie, who now banned its printing. Even Professor Loccenius, Schefferus's own father-in-law, had proofread the comments in advance. Verelius felt such bitter disappointment at Schefferus's actions and the count's prohibition that privately he swore he would never publish a scholarly work again.

As Verelius raved about the merits of his arguments, Professor of Medicine Hoffvenius responded like the Cartesian many suspected he was: Since this was a dispute about such tangible matters, why not make an official expedition to Old Uppsala and settle this once and for all?

The stakes in the matter were clear: the implications extended far beyond the debate about Old Uppsala. They struck at the heart of Rudbeck's personal quest.

In a private letter to the count, written a few days after the prohibition was announced at Uppsala, Rudbeck put the importance of an expedition bluntly:

> If this cannot be true, which still today stands in front of everyone's eyes, then everything that I want to show in my work from our oldest poets and eddas, and the very oldest Greek, Latin, Egyptian, and Chaldean and Arabic writings about the size of the temple, its construction, its style of columns, its proximity to Lake Mälaren, the three springs, the mounds, the racetrack, etc., the exo-

dus of the gods and kings from Sweden and the entire
chronology will fall and not be worth reading, much less
printing.

A trip to Old Uppsala would surely settle the matter to everyone's
satisfaction, indeed just as Professor Hoffvenius proposed.

But the other professors refused to participate in such an excursion. They did not wish to provoke Schefferus, a very respected figure
in town, let alone blatantly contradict the letter and spirit of the
chancellor's decree. Undiscouraged, Rudbeck and his supporters decided to go ahead anyway. If the Uppsala professors on the council
would not come, they would find other judges. And indeed they did.
One May afternoon in 1677 they brought along a band of thirteen
Germans—twelve army officers and a priest—who all had served in
the Danish army and had been captured as prisoners of war.

Deemed neutral and impartial, these prisoners were released on
the grounds around the Old Uppsala church and burial mounds. At
the end of their explorations, they confirmed Rudbeck's position: the
foundation of the pagan temple was clearly seen in the existing
church and hence, by deduction, this must have been part of the original Old Uppsala.

Even if few outside the most fanatical believers would accept the
testimony of these handpicked German prisoners as independent or
of decisive importance in the controversy, Rudbeck knew the value of
such an expedition. Scholars were debating about words in texts,
when the actual place stood there for examination. "No documents
are more certain about the truth of a thing than the thing itself,"
Rudbeck wrote to the count. The fact that he was deeply convinced
that Schefferus was wrong and highly confident that he could prove it
made the situation more frustrating.

While this quixotic outing to Old Uppsala was apparently having no
significant effect in overturning the prohibition, Rudbeck emphasized

the seriousness of the issue. "The life of our antiquities," he said, "seems to hang by a thread." But then something happened that has raised eyebrows ever since.

DURING THIS TIME OF confusion, probably late 1677 and definitely by early 1678, a curious document turned up in Uppsala. This was a loose manuscript, supposedly a summary of an older lost chronicle written by a thirteenth-century bishop of Västerås. Bishop Karl's Chronicle, as the document came to be known, had much to say about the controversy.

According to this newly discovered chronicle, the construction of Sweden's first cathedral had begun in the year 1138, and its bishop, Sverker the Elder, had chosen the site of Old Uppsala. Additionally, this document confirmed that the builders had used the ruins of the old pagan temple, which another ruler, Yggemund, had destroyed.

What a dramatic find—and it simply could not have come to light at a better time. Here, all of a sudden, was an old authority, a bishop no less, who seemed almost miraculously to confirm Rudbeck's basic assumption about the location of Old Uppsala. Curiously, too, this document was found in a suspicious place: it had been inserted in the pages of an old medieval herbal treatise shelved in Olof Rudbeck's own library.

No wonder questions have been raised about the authenticity of the so-called Bishop Karl's Chronicle. Could Rudbeck and Verelius really have enjoyed the good fortune of stumbling on such valuable evidence in this time of need? For many, it was simply too convenient. Schefferus, for one, smelled a rat, and cried forgery.

Why, after all, did the bishop of Västerås spend so much time writing about Uppsala, a town outside his administration? Who could help but notice that this so-called thirteenth-century account managed to address just about every concern of the current debate in 1677—and displayed little interest in matters beyond this controversy? Other oddities, too, arose upon inspection of this document. Bishop Karl showed an unusual preference for some seventeenth-century terms, as opposed to the words often favored by medieval chroniclers. Most glaringly, the ink on the old manuscript seemed suspiciously modern.

All these questions were buzzing in the late spring of 1678 when Olaus Verelius decided to disregard the ban and publish the discovery. Verelius's annotated excerpts of Bishop Karl's Chronicle, *Annotationes ex scriptis Karoli episcopi Arosiensis excerptae* (*Bishop Karl's Annotations*), reignited the old debate, unequivocally heralding this document as confirmation of the location of the pagan temple and town in Old Uppsala.

Schefferus was enraged. He was convinced that the entire manuscript was a forgery, "a most foul-ugly fraud" about to be imposed on the learned world (*turpissimam fraudem et imposturam*), and the biggest question on his mind was who had done it. The immediate suspect was of course Olaus Verelius. He had been utterly disappointed in the way Schefferus had managed to stifle discussion, and he was not exactly the person to sit idly by, allowing his grievance to fester. Indeed he had taken Schefferus's manipulation personally, a fact that had not helped his already strained relationship with his former friend.

As Schefferus knew all too well, recent problems between the two scholars were still fresh in Verelius's mind. Just as Rudbeck no longer felt welcome in the council chamber, Verelius had been experiencing his own ostracism from the College of Antiquities. Bitterly he had complained that several members of this body acted like "sworn enemies," contriving to remove him from the scene. They held meetings, he charged, without bothering to invite him or even to notify him of the date, time, and location. He also felt that Schefferus and his fellow antiquarians made sure that he did not receive his promised salary. For his work as Professor of the Fatherland's Antiquities, Verelius had been paid only two times in the last fifteen years.

From the college's perspective, it was all a misunderstanding. The withholding of his salary was unfortunately true, but that was not an isolated case, and reflected only the overall financial problems that the college faced. Verelius, they said, was the one who showed no interest in the meetings. He would not take time to come into the university to check on the society's events, and when he happened to be in town, he always seemed too preoccupied to attend the gatherings. Accusations flew from both sides of this heated dispute. Whatever the merits of his complaints, most certainly exaggerated, one thing was clear: Verelius felt hostility and a sense of persecution, which at times seemed to run on parallel lines with Rudbeck's own impressions, drawing the two even closer together.

So, given how much these resentments were breaking apart the former friends in the College of Antiquities, Schefferus could only wonder if Verelius had orchestrated this strange episode of Bishop Karl's Chronicle. He certainly had a motive. The printing of the old manuscript would promote his own work, settle the score over past animosities, and help his friend Rudbeck, whose own theory about Old Uppsala was threatening to come apart.

As the controversy simmered during the spring and summer of 1678, with the publication of *Bishop Karl's Annotations* being eagerly read and Schefferus's suspicions heard, Verelius felt compelled to defend himself. In a private letter to Count de la Gardie, he explained his actions. Schefferus was, in his opinion, trying unceremoniously to implicate him in a scandal of which he claimed complete innocence. Bishop Karl's notes were not based on a spurious manuscript, he stated firmly. The document was genuine, and he wanted an official inquiry into the matter, with a jury staffed by members of the Royal Chancellery. All of the wild claims about an unadulterated fabrication were simply the product of "Schefferus's delirium."

A more likely culprit might be Olof Rudbeck himself. Would he not have more to gain than Verelius, who could, if he were exposed, forever be remembered for having edited and commented on a forged script? Rudbeck also had quite an authoritarian streak, and often found it difficult to control himself when he felt challenged or provoked. Given the articulate doubts of Sweden's most esteemed humanist, it is not difficult to imagine Rudbeck becoming defensive with an almost explosive zeal. So much money, so much time, so much energy had already been committed, and Rudbeck felt that he was on the brink of finding that essential, irrefutable piece of evidence which would establish without doubt the truth of his lost world.

Besides, Rudbeck was famous for finding, or creating, loopholes and ways out of the worst predicaments. Here was a document that was not specifically forbidden by the chancellor's prohibition. It could help him respond to Schefferus's errors, indeed dangerous errors that threatened to keep knowledge of Old Uppsala, or Atlantis, out of public knowledge.

Stacks and stacks of halfway printed books littering the printer's shop were not to be in vain. Nor was Rudbeck's rash abandonment of university affairs, or his hasty, somewhat impulsive plunge into the complex study of the past. Rudbeck was driven to bolder, more audacious acts of desperation. Otherwise his *Atlantica* might come crashing down, indeed even before a single copy had been finished.

But, for some reason, no one has ever seriously accused Rudbeck of forging this document. Such a claim would imply many things that are hard to establish, especially the difficulty of imagining Rudbeck using his friend Verelius in this manner. Given the lack of supporting evidence, not to mention the fact that the original *Bishop Karl's Annotations* is not known to have survived, it would be harsh to lay the blame squarely at Rudbeck's feet.

Indeed, before his death in 1679, Schefferus would absolve Rudbeck of any possible guilt in the matter, and Verelius would go to his grave passionately affirming his own innocence. It is actually possible that both Rudbeck and Verelius were innocent. There was another man who was increasingly seen at Rudbeck's side, his good friend Carl Lundius, an ambitious thirty-nine-year-old scholar who had married Vendela's sister Gertrude. Lundius is overwhelmingly associated with a number of questionable documents. At this time, however, his reputation was impeccable.

Pursuing his lifelong goal of becoming a lawyer like his father, Carl Lundius was a professor of law quickly rising in esteem. He excelled in jurisprudence, Swedish law, Roman law, and influential natural-law doctrines of the day. Previously he had shown his legal finesse as an energetic member of the Witchcraft Commission for the northern province of Hälsingland. Historians are fond of telling the story of the time when Lundius came home after a long day at the witch trials and found, he claimed, an uninvited guest in his chamber: the Prince of Darkness himself.

Lundius was every bit as reckless as Rudbeck, often accompanying him on explorations of the supposed Atlantis. He was known in fact to have been present during one of those crucial visits to Old Uppsala during the tense period of May 1677 immediately after the chancellor's prohibition. Looking at the works Lundius would publish over the next thirty years, one might conclude that he was even "more Rudbeckian" than the author of the *Atlantica* himself. Given his close relationship with the Rudbecks, he could also conceivably have smuggled this document into a place in the library where Rudbeck was bound to look.

Yet tracing this document back to Lundius is no simple matter. In fact, after a long time of assuming that this was an unabashed forgery, or some combination of fraud, faith, and a willingness to be deluded, some scholars have concluded that Bishop Karl's Chronicle was probably, after all, a genuine document. According to the Swedish historian of science Sten Lindroth, the bulk of the evidence actually weighs in favor of its authenticity. Other solid, meticulous studies, though, have favored Schefferus's conviction that it was a forgery.

At any rate, in this messy, complex scenario, with the question of forgery still very much in the air, the irony is that Rudbeck, Verelius,

Lundius, and their supporters were actually correct about the main point in the debate. Old Uppsala was certainly situated where they thought, and where they also believed they had seen Atlantis. Given archaeological work done in the twentieth century, Rudbeck was probably also right about the site of the old pagan temple underneath the historic Christian church. The archaeologist Sune Lindqvist found traces of the foundation on the precise spot where Rudbeck envisioned it.

As for Schefferus, who was undoubtedly much more knowledgeable, experienced, and talented as a classical humanist scholar, he had relied too heavily on the authority of late sources, mostly fifteenth-century accounts that were written centuries after the flourishing of the pagan temple. It is quite odd to see this critical scholar misled by the sources. One historian put it more sharply: "That a man with Schefferus's good head and historical education did not realize the weakness in such evidence, is undeniably peculiar." Schefferus could hardly have avoided "realizing that this information about the pagan temple was completely worthless." Such a strongly defensive posture was perhaps explained by a "not uncommon unwillingness to abandon an opinion."

The same thing should also be said about Olof Rudbeck. Abrasive, relentless, and fanatical as he was in pursuing his quest, the strains of the crushing debts and the desperate attempts to pay them had made him even less willing to compromise.

Within a year after the publication of *Bishop Karl Annotations,* which were now, ironically, protected by the prohibition, some high-placed antiquarians were writing long letters attempting to persuade the count to overturn his decision. Schefferus's close friend, the antiquarian scholar Johan Hadorph, wrote an impassioned appeal for loosing the ban. Arguing and pleading, they were desperate to slay the monster that they had gladly helped create.

13

ET VOS HOMINES

❧

But there's nothing remarkable about it. All you have to do is to look around you.

—PIERRE AUGUSTE RENOIR, IN RESPONSE TO
AN ADMIRER OF HIS PAINTING

*B*ACK IN THE halcyon days of the late 1650s and the early 1660s, Count de la Gardie had amassed a splendid collection of medieval Icelandic manuscripts. With sixty-four sagas and eddas, many in their oldest known form, including Snorri's *Edda*, this was undoubtedly one of the most valuable sets of documents illuminating the Viking heritage anywhere in the world. And in early 1669, on Rudbeck's prompting, they were packed up and sent to Uppsala University as a gift.

Along with them came a bound set of purple-tinted pages of parchment inscribed with gold and silver letters. This was the legendary *Codex argenteus*, or "Silver Bible," captured in 1648 when Swedish troops looted Prague in a last-minute dash before the ink could dry on the peace treaty ending the Thirty Years' War.

An early-sixth-century translation of the Gospels of the New Testament into the Gothic language, the Silver Bible was the rarest of treasures. Probably kept in the royal chamber of the barbarian Gothic king Theodoric, this beautiful manuscript is still today considered the oldest surviving work in any Germanic language. De la Gardie had purchased it in 1662 from one of Queen Christina's former librarians, who, in a financial crisis, had received the book instead of his perennially late salary.

Actually, when it went up for sale, it was no longer a book. Minds more enterprising than scholarly had long ago decided to break up the priceless manuscript and sell it page by page. De la Gardie bought all the sheets that were left, some 187 leaves of an estimated total of 336, for a sum of five hundred *riksdaler,* enjoying the pleasure of outbidding, ironically, Queen Christina, who had earlier humiliated him. On the voyage home after the auction, however, the new Swedish treasure narrowly missed being lost in a shipwreck amid the treacherous waters outside Amsterdam. It was saved only by its sturdy oak chest.

As with the Norse sagas, it was on Rudbeck's inspired suggestion that the Gothic Bible made its way to a cozy home at Uppsala University. There it has remained to this day—for the most part, that is. One afternoon in the spring of 1995, two men entered the library with a large hammer. Taking advantage of the noise and chaos accompanying a student election that was being held in the lobby, they confidently walked over to a glass case protecting a few leaves from the priceless Bible. Eight or nine wallops later, they had managed to smash open the display and snatch its contents. A canister of tear gas added to the disorientation, as the thieves ran off with their prize, including the silver case that De la Gardie had added to his donation (the same beautiful case that gives the book the alternative name "Silver Bible"). One month later, after much anguish over the loss, an anonymous phone call led authorities to a coin-locker at the central Stockholm train station, where the stolen goods were found and then promptly returned to Uppsala.

With such original old manuscripts moving out from showcases in De la Gardie's castle, there was now more material available for studying the Swedish past than ever before. Given their antiquity and rarity, these were fantastically valuable aids as Rudbeck started to immerse himself in the world of ancient languages. Soon he was keeping the sagas, eddas, and the other original manuscripts on extended, virtually permanent loan at his house. And in one of the manuscripts—the Gothic Bible, no less—there are unmistakable signs of tampering.

This time there can be no dispute about the attempted fabrications. Scrapings over letters and signs of a newer, lighter silver ink applied to the purplish red parchment make that all too clear. Most notoriously, in the Gospel of Saint John, someone had scribbled in changes to the passage "and Jesus was in the temple area walking in Solomon's Colonnade" (10:23). The Gothic word for the colonnade in the temple, *Ubizvai*, was rubbed over, and repainted in silver ink to read *Ubizali*, that is, a word pronounced, as it sounds, "Uppsala."

Such a reading of *Ubizali* as a pillared hall or portico was of tremendous importance. It would confirm yet again Rudbeck's theory about Atlantis lying in Old Uppsala. In the original dialogues, Plato spoke of the famous temple to Poseidon on Atlantis as an "open temple," which Rudbeck eagerly derived from the name Uppsala, *upp* (or *opp*) meaning "open" and *sal* "space" or "hall."

We know that Rudbeck used the Silver Bible in his research, and that he specifically cited this passage in his discussion about his discovery of Atlantis. But would his passion make him resort to forging sources—and would his growing obsession make him do so in the oldest survival of any Germanic language, and in Sweden's most treasured manuscript?

OF COURSE, it is possible that the letters had already been doctored by the time Rudbeck stumbled across the passage, and he was so blinded by his obsession that he failed to detect the tampering. Out of all the people who would have had access to the Gothic Bible on its long wandering before it reached his study—in Queen Christina's library, the Dutch scholar's home, De la Gardie's castle, and through the various loans to professors before the count's donation in 1669 — it would be unfair to single Rudbeck out as the culprit in the crime, that is, without clear evidence linking him to the alteration. Surely Rudbeck the master technician would have made the changes in a more dexterous and artful manner than the way they appear. The possibility of another actor should at least be entertained.

For scholars who have investigated this controversy, the name most often mentioned is again Rudbeck's energetic brother-in-law, Carl Lundius. Sometimes it seems that Professor Lundius is still, three centuries later, deflecting blame for the unscrupulous forgeries away from Rudbeck or some other close friend.

Lundius had an undeniably strong desire to push forward the frontiers of the search for Atlantis. He would certainly have had the knowledge of variant readings of *Ubizvai*, as well as the necessary access to the Silver Bible. More suspiciously, his own work on the laws of ancient Sweden unquestionably relies on sources that no known scholar had used before or has since.

In his *Zamolxis*, for instance, a work discussing the legendary first Gothic lawgiver mentioned briefly by Herodotus, Lundius cited some curious documents that would supposedly place Zamolxis's home in Sweden. His name in "our scrolls" was Samolses, and Lundius applauded Herodotus for his accuracy, "the perfect agreement and harmony [with] the incunabula of the ancient Goths." But grander and more dramatic claims would follow from his controversial waxed tablets. For example: "We have in evidence a number of literary monuments having a completely overwhelming convincing force, attesting to the Greeks having taken from the Goth (Geta), in every particular, the essential element of the Athenian legislation." Unfortunately, no one has ever seen any of these manuscripts.

Maybe all these documents preserving the ancient Swedish-Greek cultural links were destroyed in one of the fires that ravaged

Uppsala over the years, or were somehow lost over time. Even if we assume the best of intentions, however, and make the most cautious conclusions, Lundius's scrolls remain very much in doubt.

Nevertheless there is still good reason not to rush into accusing this zealous law professor. It is certainly possible that Lundius was not so much the deceiver as the deceived. The scrapings and repaintings in the Gothic Bible are in fact only the most prominent of a series of questionable and nefarious activities on the fringes of Rudbeck's search for Atlantis. Some have pointed to an entire "forgery factory" in operation somewhere in the gabled university town.

Could the culprit be a certain one of Professor Lundius's friends and colleagues, now known to have been a forger, manipulating old manuscripts with a deliberate attempt to deceive? After all, this friend was arguably the most talented and prolific of all *known* forgers in Scandinavian history: a priest named Nils Rabenius.

What little is certain about Rabenius's life gives the impression of a checkered career. Suspended from his duties, criticized for flagrant disobedience, and reprimanded for routine drunkenness, this renegade priest even spent a night or two in jail. Unscrupulous and highly unstable, Rabenius seems to have reveled in mischief, with his antics earning him a degree of notoriety and, oddly enough, also a position as court preacher in Stockholm for the very devout king Charles XI.

Rabenius was an avid collector of medieval manuscripts, and a notorious editor of the documents he accumulated. He was particularly prone to inserting exploits of his own family. Any mention of someone in the "Rabbe" family in a medieval document is today considered a good reason to question its authenticity. So one can only wonder about Rabenius the champion forger, his well-known connections with Lundius, and the parchments circulating around Uppsala supposedly chronicling Zeus's adventures in Sweden.

As far as the forgeries in the Gothic Bible are concerned, another intriguing option put forth by the Swedish scholar Gunnar Eriksson changes the terms of the debate somewhat. As the discovery of the tampering is not known to have been made until the 1730s, years after the death of Rudbeck and the other principal characters in this story, it is possible that the changes in the Silver Bible were made *after* the *Atlantica* was printed. This may sound paradoxical, but as Eriksson correctly points out, when Rudbeck linked *Ubizvai* to Uppsala, he was not relying on the Silver Bible. He was using instead a manuscript in De la Gardie's collection, now lost. In other words, it could have been Lundius, Rabenius, or a later reader who had access to the work at the university library—and then decided to "correct" the Silver Bible to make it agree with Rudbeck's *Atlantica.*

At any rate, regardless of who actually made the changes, the forged manuscripts and the fabricated passages in the Gothic Bible illustrate the great difficulty Rudbeck and his supporters were starting to face in the search for Atlantis. They also show just how far some would go to find the necessary yet elusive evidence, even if it meant unscrupulously tampering with the material. Expectations for Rudbeck's quest were high, and already rising. Each new finding only increased the plausibility of the sweeping vision, while at the same time intensifying the demand for greater, more exciting breakthroughs.

BY THE END of 1678, Sweden had emerged as the original home of the classical gods, and the land often visited by ancient heroes in search of wisdom and enlightenment. One of the last discoveries that Rudbeck managed to fit into his bulging volume of *Atlantica* was no less impressive.

His theory involved the runes, best known today perhaps as a language of elves, dwarves, and hobbits in the fantasy realm of Middle Earth. But as J. R. R. Tolkien, Bosworth Chair of Anglo-Saxon at Oxford University, knew, the runes were once a functioning alphabetic script found in Scandinavia and northern Europe. The sharp, angular symbols could be scratched into wooden staffs, cut into helmets, inscribed on whalebone, or, more often, carved on large standing stones, usually adorned with intertwining snakes or dragons. Just over three thousand inscriptions are known today in Sweden, by far the most in any country. A full thousand are found in the area around Uppsala alone, most of which had already been discovered by the late seventeenth century.

Interpreting these runes is a thrilling and at times very difficult challenge. Scholars have not been able to agree about many things, including for instance where the letters originated. Strong arguments have been put forward in favor of Sweden, Denmark, the Black Sea region, and somewhere high atop the Alps. Not even the basic chronology can be convincingly determined. The most commonly proposed time of invention points to the first century A.D., though alternative estimates range from a remote period of the past to as late as the fourth century A.D. It is appropriate, then, that the word *rune* means literally "mystery" or "secret."

No less mystery enveloped these rare carvings in Rudbeck's day, and his own growing infatuation would bring him into contact with the pioneering scholars in the history of the runes. As with the revival of the Old Norse sagas and eddas, the "runic renaissance" had begun to flourish in the sixteenth and seventeenth centuries. Scholars at the forefront of this movement were again Scandinavians, among others the Swedish scholar Johan Bureus and the Danish royal physician Olaus Wormius.

These highly original thinkers traveled the countryside looking for runic inscriptions, meticulously copying them down, and trying to decipher their possible meanings. Significantly, they were also helped by the fact that knowledge of the runes had, in some places, never completely died out. The last surviving "rune masters," the name for the craftsmen skilled in the art of carving the letters, would live on in certain parts of the Scandinavian peninsula to as late as the early twentieth century. Elsewhere this knowledge had been gradually forgotten or, in some cases, as in Iceland, ruthlessly suppressed for its presumed magical, superstitious qualities.

In Rudbeck's own study of the runes, the single greatest inspiration was one of these early thinkers, his fellow Swede Johan Bureus, already a valuable source for his theories about the Hyperboreans. With his long white beard and strong mystical leanings, Bureus looked like one of the legendary rune masters whose art he had studied so energetically. Like many mystics of the late sixteenth and early seventeenth centuries, Bureus believed that a harmonious order governed the universe, literally breathed into existence at the beginning of time and encoded in all creation. This divine wisdom had survived the Flood, the confusion at Babel, and the many great upheavals of the past, though at times it had only done so by going underground, flourishing among a select group of thinkers. True prophets and sages had been privy to the secret "hermetic" tradition that, by Rudbeck's time, was communicated only to the initiated. Bureus spent his entire life trying to penetrate this wisdom, and that was certainly one of the main reasons for his fascination with the runes.

For Bureus saw the enigmatic runic symbols as possibly capturing this original wisdom (one of their many levels and functions in ancient society). They were the oldest language in the world, that is, after Hebrew, though later in his life he would reverse the order, giving precedence to the Scandinavian letters. Bureus's enthusiasm was certainly infectious. King Charles IX had selected him to teach history to the young prince and future king Gustavus Adolphus, who, when he came to power, welcomed the scholar into his inner circle.

In one of his typically bold plans, Bureus had once proposed that Sweden replace its current alphabet with a revived form of the older, nobler, and more mystical runes. He thought the Latin-derived Swedish script was too closely bound up with the Roman Catholic Church, whose triumphant march had gone hand in hand with the progress of the Latin language. Returning to the runes, Bureus argued, would spark a new renaissance in Sweden and unlock enormous creative energies. One law was actually passed in 1611 forbidding the publication of the regular Swedish grammar books in favor of the runes, and Bureus worked on inventing a more flexible, cursive form. But otherwise this dreamy plan does not seem to have gotten very far.

Neither, for that matter, did most of Bureus's literary works. He had a very difficult time completing his projects, and so, at the time of his death in 1652, virtually the entire bulk of his life's work remained buried in unfinished manuscripts. Rudbeck, however, was more than glad to continue investigating the runes where Bureus and his successors had stopped.

APPLYING HIS MEASURING staff to the soil around the stones, Rudbeck read the layers of humus, the accumulations of the rich fertile soil that, given their position, could have gathered only after the erection of the pillars. The age of the stones varied tremendously. Some were set up rather late, during the period A.D. 600–1100, a very conventional date for the many late Viking inscriptions found around Uppsala. But other inscriptions, Rudbeck was convinced, must have been significantly older. Some, he thought, dated all the way back to 2300–2200 B.C. And if this calculation was accurate, then the findings would be extraordinary.

This would mean that the Swedes had started carving the runic letters only a few hundred years after they had arrived in the land around Uppsala. Given conventional chronologies, this was an exceptionally early date, about one thousand years before the Trojan War or the first Olympic games. In other words, if Rudbeck's measurements were correct—and a reported twelve thousand tests had convinced him they were an "infallible" method of dating—then Bureus had been right: Sweden had one of the oldest alphabets in the world.

Further explorations in the countryside followed, and other surprising implications ensued. After closely reading the inscriptions found on the runic monoliths, Rudbeck had come to believe that these mysterious letters were actually the *origin* of the ancient Greek alphabet. A little historical detective work started the chain of reasoning that led to this stunning conclusion about the Swedish runes, the Hyperborean hieroglyphics.

One crucial piece of evidence came from the first-century Roman natural historian Pliny, who discussed the history of the Greek language in his multivolume *Natural History.* This ardent searcher of secrets had noted some intriguing facts about the development of the ancient language. Most interestingly, the Greek alphabet did not always have twenty-four letters. Pliny had concluded that in its earliest period of formation, before the Trojan War, the Greek language had had only sixteen letters. As Rudbeck looked further into the claim, which was based on many older sources, he agreed. From Plutarch to Aristotle, the ancients "spoke with one mouth" that there were at first only sixteen letters. The earliest Greek alphabet had consisted of the following:

Α Β Γ Δ Ε Ι Κ Λ Μ Ν Ο Π Ρ Σ Τ Υ

The other eight letters—Θ Ξ Φ Χ Ζ Η Ψ Ω—were added later.

This piece of information from the cautious collector came as a revelation to Olof Rudbeck. He began to wonder even more about traditional accounts of the origins of the ancient Greek alphabet. According to these, the Greeks developed their letters from the Phoenicians, the ancient Semitic people living on the far eastern shores of the Mediterranean and still today credited with creating the oldest alphabet. But Pliny's passing comment raised an intriguing question. If the Phoenician script had twenty-two letters, as modern authorities from Joseph Scaliger to Samuel Bochart knew, then Rudbeck asked: How did the Greeks end up with only sixteen of the twenty-two letters they had supposedly borrowed? Why would they prefer to take only part of a script, and what happened to the other Phoenician letters?

It was highly unlikely, Rudbeck ventured, that the ancients would take a more complete and self-sufficient script and turn it into a truncated and incomplete one. No one would do that, he said, in his pragmatic approach to the question. Additionally, there was the strange case of the letters that the Greeks certainly had but were nowhere to be found in Phoenician. How, for instance, did the Greeks end up with alpha (A), epsilon (E), iota (I), upsilon (Y), or any other vowel, when no such letters existed among the Phoenicians? Besides, Rudbeck's crash initiation into eastern antiquities, together with his typically unapologetic directness, made him think that the Greek letters were simply too different from their alleged counterparts to conclude that they were at one time the same letters. The runes adorning the standing stones in the Swedish landscape, on the other hand, were an altogether different matter.

To Rudbeck, the sixteen original Greek letters seemed very similar to the sixteen symbols that he believed to be the oldest runic script. Placing the two alphabets side by side, Rudbeck saw, through his Atlantis-tinted glasses, a string of correspondences between the Greek and the runic. How similar they sounded! How similar the letters looked! How similarly they were drawn! The short, simple angular thrusts, in linear fashion, without any adornment, made Rudbeck absolutely sure that Swedish runic and ancient Greek were once the same script.

Alpha (A), beta (B), gamma (Γ), delta (Δ), right down the list, no less than thirteen of the original sixteen Greek letters fit like a glove (see table on facing page). The last three letters, E, K, and Π, however, were not as easily found.

Unable to solve this riddle, Rudbeck began to look at specific Greek words that used these letters and then compare them with words in Old Swedish that meant the same thing. In this way, for instance, Rudbeck came to believe that the Greek K (kappa) was de-

Rudbeck's table highlights the similarities between the runic and the ancient Greek alphabets.

rived from the Swedish H. The Swedish word for "heart," *hiarta,* as the anatomist suggested, had become the Greek *kardia.*

The Greek pi (Π) likewise revealed itself in the Swedish F. Rudbeck saw common words such as *father,* or *fader,* become the Greek *pater* (πατήρ), sensing what is now a well-established link shared among Indo-European languages. The famous figure of Greek mythology, Pan, or πάν, the horned, goat-legged, and mischievous god of antiquity, known for startling travelers (hence a "panic"), was originally the Swedish Fan, another horned, goat-legged figure who haunted the forests, and whose name is the word that today still is used in Swedish for "devil." However ludicrous this may sound, Rudbeck had not lost his mind. What he had lost was perspective and, all too often, a sense of reality. And so Rudbeck went on happily deriving many Greek words from a Swedish origin, each one adding to the accumulating pile of evidence about the Swedish impact on the ancient past, and each one, at the same time, showing how ingenious his delusions could be.

PROBABLY ONE OF the most creative pieces of evidence about the runic origins of ancient Greek developed naturally from Rudbeck's previous work on the Olympian god Hermes.

As the half-brother of Apollo, and the herald of Zeus, both already found in Sweden, Hermes must have seemed a natural candidate for a Swedish Atlantean. Equipped with his golden winged sandals and winged hat, he was also the chosen guide for escorting many souls through the "dank ways," over the "snowy rock," and past the "narrows of the sunset," to the "wastes at the world's end," that is, to the kingdom of the Underworld, which Rudbeck had also already located in the Arctic north.

Sure enough, Rudbeck believed that he had come across the original inspiration for the Olympian Hermes in the north: the Aesir god Heimdall. Like Hermes, who was praised for keeping watch over the house, the business, the family (perhaps explaining why Hermes was the most often sculptured of all the classical gods), "splendid Heimdall" was the watchman for the Norse Aesir. As Hermes relayed messages to mortals and immortals alike, Heimdall was the communicator for the Aesir gods. The similarities between the classical and Norse deities continued, though Rudbeck had to force them somewhat.

With his position as herald, guide, messenger, interpreter, and even diplomat of the gods, Hermes held a position of great responsibility. This "sophisticated rogue" had effectively developed into the favorite servant of Zeus. Such great importance for Hermes was, in Rudbeck's vision, based on the esteem of Heimdall, whose official functions had been enshrined in his name, which drew on the Swedish words *hemlig* and *taler,* meaning "secret" and "speaker." Heimdall was a *Heimtaler,* "a secret speaker" entrusted with sensitive information and then sent to carry out various special missions.

Rudbeck believed that Hermes' Swedish origins were seen clearly in another unexpected place: the god's famous staff, the caduceus. In classical mythology, Hermes, or Mercury as the Romans called him, carried a staff encircled by two intertwined snakes. According to Rudbeck, the image of the intertwined snakes was common in the north in the distant past, and a perfect microcosm of the runes. In fact, on examination, each letter of the runic alphabet could actually be seen encoded in the god's emblem. If one relied on various angles formed by the snakes around the staff, every single rune could indeed be crafted.

Affixing numbers to various points on the staff and the snakes, Rudbeck provided directions for marking the runes by using Mercury's caduceus. The basic rune, I, was drawn by moving the pen from position 1 to 2. Another rune, ↑, was made by moving from 2 to 5, 9 to 10, and a more complicated one, *, was made using the formula 1 to 7, 11 to 6, 4 to 8. And so on.

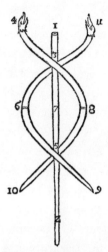

Mercury's staff, reproduced in the first volume of Rudbeck's Atlantica.

What a device for encoding the letters, and for transmitting this knowledge! Rudbeck's discovery looks even more exciting when it is remembered that Hermes was, according to traditional accounts of classical mythology, the god who brought the alphabet into many places in antiquity, from Egypt to Arcadia. So Rudbeck concluded that the god's staff was the handy means of teaching the art of the runes. And along with these Hyperborean hieroglyphics, the magical, mystical, and secret learning of the north would also be transmitted to the wise men of the Mediterranean.

Developing this insight—how, when, where, why, and what it all meant—was to be one of the central functions of Rudbeck's *Atlantica*. The first volume was nearly finished, but Rudbeck would try for the rest of his life to elaborate on the many achievements of ancient Sweden. As matters looked worse for his country, and as his own personal affairs continued to deteriorate, Rudbeck's sense of mission only became stronger, and his fantasy ran amok. Concealed in old manuscripts and carved on standing stones, Rudbeck was everywhere seeing a dazzling image of the ancient north.

As the monumental work came to a close, some nine hundred pages detailing his dramatic revision of the past, Rudbeck ended *Atlantica* with two rather surreal stories. The first was about a peasant with a big nose who went to see a doctor.

Afflicted by an imaginary disease, the peasant somehow came to fear that the unusually large size of his nose caused death to anyone who happened to touch it. After many unsuccessful attempts to find treatment, he was finally cured. Both impressed with and curious about the doctor's success, the peasant asked for permission to attend one of the anatomical dissections that were then so much in vogue in the learned world. But when he went to the anatomy theater, the peasant watched with surprise and horror.

As one physician demonstrated beyond doubt the circulation of the blood, some of the older, more learned doctors refused to accept this controversial new claim. The blood does not circulate, they said, repeating the certainties they had known since the beginning of their medical studies. By the end of the demonstration, the peasant thanked God that he was not so learned as the distinguished physicians in the theater, and so sure of his learning that he could not understand what he saw with his own eyes.

Rudbeck told this story as part of his final appeal to the reader not to be misled by conventional thought, traditional authorities, and the many prejudices that cloud our judgment. All of these things can lead to maladies from which we do not even know we suffer. Instead, Rudbeck wanted his readers, like the simple peasant, to look at the facts with their own eyes and judge with an open mind. Doing so, he was sure, would enable the unbiased observer to see how everything did in fact fit together. Like the discovery that the blood circulated throughout the body, the unthinkable had once again occurred and shattered our old certainties. Atlantis had been found in Sweden.

Then, in his second story, Rudbeck told the reader about a gar-

dener who had witnessed all kinds of sweet-smelling spices and exotic animals coming into Europe from the new worlds in the East and
West Indies. Curious, the gardener wanted to see the lands that produced such remarkable things. As Rudbeck described it, "He went
out. Came back. Wrote a book in his simplicity, according to what he
had experienced himself." Some learned men, however, were enraged
that a common gardener would dare to publish his own account.
They had already described these spices and animals, adorning them
"wonderfully with their eloquent tongues" and scorning the rather
plain attempts of this simple observer. So they took their discontent
to the patron of the creative arts, identified in this story as Apollo,
and asked him to forbid the gardener's work.

After listening to their complaint, Apollo ordered the book
brought to him and called an assembly of the gods to discuss the matter. As the deities were about to agree with the learned professionals,
and planned to outlaw its dissemination, Apollo asked to look at the
gardener's work himself.

He opened the book, and saw the bold words on the first page: ET
NOS HOMINES. Struck by the wisdom in these words — "we, too, are
human" — the gods decided to journey to the land of the spices and investigate for themselves. As Rudbeck concluded the tale, "[They] found
that the gardener with his own experience and simple writing better
found the truth than those who just adorn the writings of another."

It is appropriate that Rudbeck closed *Atlantica* with these stories,
which fairly well capture his insistence on observation, experience,
and firsthand engagement with the ancient world. Indeed, with one
foot in the garden himself, Rudbeck was like the simple cultivator
who always wanted to remember the words *et vos homines*. "You, too,
are human": the theories you craft, however learned and ingenious,
can still be wrong. But Rudbeck was also like the peasant in the
anatomy theater with the rich imagination. He knew what he saw,
what he heard, and what he thought. And by now, no amount of
learning would ever convince him otherwise.

14

ON NOTHING

How much more rabidly, too, will he believe in his cause when he sees you and people like you not only coming in crowds but with smiles of congratulation on your faces?

—CICERO, WRITING IN A LETTER TO HIS FRIEND ATTICUS ABOUT JULIUS CAESAR, 49 B.C.

O N A SNOWY DAY in late March 1679, the first bound copy of Rudbeck's work rolled off Curio's press. Emblazoned triumphantly on the title page was the word *Atlantica,* the Latin name for the central discovery of the text. The Swedish title elaborated somewhat, adding another twenty-seven of the most prominent findings Rudbeck had made in the course of his investigations. The full title filled almost the entire first page:

> Olof Rudbeck's Atland or Manheim, from which come
> the descendants of Japhet, the most prominent impe-
> rial and royal families governing the whole world, and
> from which also poured out the following peoples,
> namely the Scythians, Barbarians, Aesir, Giants, Goths,
> Phrygians, Trojans, Amazons, Thracians, Libyans Mauer,
> Tussar, Gauls, Cimbrians, Cimmerians, Saxons, Ger-

mans, Swedes, Longobards, Vandals, Heruli, Gepar, Angles, Picts, Danes, and Sea Peoples, and many others which shall be proven in the work.

As soon as the inclement weather lifted, Rudbeck sent over the almost nine-hundred-page volume to his patron, Count Magnus Gabriel de la Gardie, in the count's castle outside Stockholm. The young man chosen to transport this bulky package was Anders Goeding, a "diligent and learned student" who had spent the last seven years at university reading philosophy and theology. He was a close friend, a promising logician, and also the future husband of Rudbeck's daughter Johanna Kristina.

In the eyes of Rudbeck, approaching his fiftieth birthday, the publication of *Atlantica* marked the highlight of his career. Not even his discovery of the lymphatic glands, the observation of comets, or the design of many buildings could compare with the fantastic succession of breakthroughs he had made about the ancient world.

To Rudbeck's delight, many contemporaries agreed. Two German visitors, for example, came across Rudbeck's *Atlantica* in Stockholm that spring, and each bought a copy. Deciding to make a journey out to Old Uppsala to see the sights of Atlantis themselves, they were so impressed that, Rudbeck joked, he believed one of them was probably "still there and kissing the old walls and big mounds."

This was a sign of things to come. After a slow beginning, with only a few letters of appreciation trickling in over the summer, the pace picked up in the autumn. Rudbeck would be celebrated as the "Atlas of the northern skies," a pioneer who blazed a heroic trail into the past. According to one enthusiastic reader, Rudbeck was a "Swedish Heracles" who had accomplished his own personal Herculean labor, and restored light where dark Cimmerian mists had formerly prevailed. To another admirer, Rudbeck had solved one of the great riddles of the past, proving how so many peoples had come out of Sweden "as if from a Trojan horse."

His adversaries, on the other hand, were appalled at such praise. They had hoped to see Rudbeck's work flop. Some were even haunted by envy, as if, one contemporary said, pursued by the Furies, those dark mythic creatures with "heads wreathed in swarming serpents" that hounded their victims to madness. And to the horror of these scholars, words of praise, gratitude, and encouragement would continue to reach Uppsala from many different places.

Merchants discussed the work in the busy port of Gothenburg, and vicars in magnificent Stockholm churches testified to Rudbeck's "immeasurable labor, wonderful genius and manner of expression." One reader, the director of the Witchcraft Commission for three northern provinces, Anders Stiernhöök, claimed that he simply could not put the book down. He was undertaking daily studies throughout the fall of 1679, and the joy of the readings, he said, scarcely left him in control of his senses.

Appreciation for the "oracle of the north" also raged outside Sweden. The famous polymath, Kiel's own walking encyclopedia, D. G. Morhof, described his own experience with Rudbeck's mammoth work: "I completely devoured the book in one unbroken reading." He enclosed a poem on the merits of the "divine *Atlantica*," admiring how Rudbeck made the dirt speak and the stones of the north proclaim their unrivaled antiquity. Rudbeck, he added, painted "his genius in most beautiful hues."

Similarly, glowing testimony arrived from no less than London's Royal Society, the famous gathering of natural philosophers and gentleman dilettantes that included Robert Hooke, Isaac Newton, and Samuel Pepys. With Christopher Wren in the presidential chair, the Royal Society sent Rudbeck the following words: "We are not able to admire enough the power of genius and the abundance of learning . . . by which you uncover the secrets of the past."

At least three times during the fall and winter of 1681–82, Rudbeck's theories were discussed in the chambers of the Royal Society. *Atlantica* was also chosen to be reviewed in the Royal Society's journal, *Philosophical Transactions.* In the issue dated January 10, 1681/82 (the double year because Britain was still refusing to adopt the Gregorian calendar and, as a result, was ten days behind most of Europe), the reviewer proclaimed, "This deservedly famous Author has here undertaken a great Work, and much to the honor of his Country, to set forth the Rise and Progress of the kingdom of Sweeden, from Japhet the first king and Possessor thereof in the times nearest the Flood, to Charles now at present Reigning. . . ."

The reviewer went on, praising Rudbeck's work on the earliest civilization as flourishing first in Sweden, referring afterwards to the "expedition of the gods" from Sweden, and the establishment of colonies all over the Mediterranean. All of this was mentioned without criticism, even the Swedish conquests over "most of Europe, Asia, the Indies to Aegypt and the parts thereabout." Such a favorable review no doubt helped disseminate the news and excitement of Rudbeck's bold theory throughout the international Republic of Letters.

Accolades for the Swedish physician went further still. At the Royal Society's meeting held December 14, 1681, Rudbeck was proposed as a member. It was in fact an expert on the ancient world, former Cambridge University Regius Professor of Greek Thomas Gale, who officially proposed Rudbeck to the Royal Society. In his enthusiasm, seconded by the physicist Robert Hooke, he nominated *Atlantica's* deliveryman for membership as well.

DESPITE THE HONOR, Rudbeck never showed any signs of interest in joining the distinguished society, or in engaging in regular correspondence with its members. He was far too preoccupied, busying himself with his own search, as the mysteries of the past had not ceased to unfold. Many new pieces of evidence were still turning up to support his claims, and in some cases, entirely new discoveries were being made along the way.

By now, too, Rudbeck had, incredibly, launched another massive project, a botanical work called *Campus Elysii*, which attempted to describe all the plants of the world, complete with life-size reproductions. This work received its name from the Elysian Fields, the ancient paradise lands that Rudbeck had earlier found in Sweden. Since his sons and daughters were now old enough to help, Rudbeck's adventure was becoming a family enterprise. Olof junior, Johanna Kristina, and young Vendela in particular helped with the project, working on many of the woodcuts of the plants. This collaboration with his children, along with the recognition he had received for his *Atlantica*, must have provided a powerful boost.

But the last few years had not only seen glowing tributes to *Atlantica*, and poetic fanfares to its wonderful, bewildering genius. There were those who had been less than impressed. Schefferus, Rudbeck's rival in the Old Uppsala dispute, had received a copy straight from the press while he lay on his deathbed in March 1679, and had said, "God knows where he got all this he has written! I did not think Rudbeck was capable of such a work."

When Rudbeck heard this, he took it as a compliment, a sign that the former contender had finally been brought around by the sheer force of the argument. One of Schefferus's friends at his bedside, however, knew otherwise, because the dying scholar had added, "For there is much craziness in it, too."

Indeed, from the very beginning, even before the long-awaited publication of the book, all sorts of rumors about Rudbeck and his integrity were circulated by his enemies at Uppsala University. One of the worst was a savage satire of *Atlantica*'s author as a buffoon who "knew nothing." Written as a pamphlet, this "censura gravissima" pretended to be a proclamation issued by the classical god Apollo high atop Mount Parnassus. Transcribed from "the protocols" by his secretary Mercury, another god of Swedish descent in *Atlantica*, this anonymous pamphleteer launched into a tirade against "the very celebrated Herr Olof Rudbeck." The jack of all trades was now pro-

Wisdom pours out of the ancient north, and Europeans catch the overflow. Some, however, try to devour more than they can stomach.

nounced, in the words of Apollo, incompetent in each of his areas: "In theology as well as jurisprudence, as well as medicine, chemistry, philosophy, Herr Rudbeck knows nothing."

Undismayed on the surface, but not known for taking criticism well, Rudbeck responded by announcing his upcoming lecture series at the university; he would teach the greatest, most profound subject, and his self-proclaimed specialty: nothing.

So imagine the surprise of students, not to mention the officials, when they read the formal lecture catalog for Uppsala University for the fall term 1679. Next to botany, anatomy, theology, and the familiar academic subjects, there was the following offering:

> Olof Rudbeck is going to treat his listeners to a very useful, very intricate, and very subtle subject that is never praised enough: Nothing.

Surprise, laughter, and probably some cheers for one of Uppsala's perennially favorite teachers. Rudbeck was once again having fun at his enemies' expense. As the university catalog went on to describe the course, Rudbeck kept playing with his rivals' own Aristotelian terms in a mocking fashion. "He is going to show how Nothing arose and fell, and trace its unending affections, virtues, and deficiencies as well as its multifaceted uses in theology, law, medicine, philosophy, all mechanical arts, and daily life."

Needless to say, few of his Uppsala colleagues were amused by this prank. University officials were upset at this "tasteless gesture," with one professor saying, "Each and every person who tastelessly cracks jokes about a serious matter knows nothing about good manners and culture; but Olof Rudbeck does this in the Uppsala professors' lecture catalog; therefore he knows nothing about education."

Some professors evidently worried about the effects on young people. Would this not bring the educational mission into disrepute, or perhaps give the impression that there was no such thing as knowledge? Even the archbishop, Johannes Baazius the Younger, agreed that this prank was insulting and went a little too far.

Again Rudbeck was forced to explain himself, both at the council meeting and to the university chancellor. No, he said, this lecture series "On Nothing" was not meant to insult his colleagues or deny the existence of knowledge. He had only intended to offer some reflections on the many uses of "nothing" in the sciences. From medicine to pharmacy to physics, he saw nothing, and nothing everywhere. This was, as he put it, an attempt at a "true science of nothing."

Was Rudbeck speaking of experiments with vacuum, then in vogue among some natural philosophers? Was he hinting at a sharper mystical turn? Or was this just another attempt to get out of trouble? That is hard to say, though it was probably a little bit of each. De la Gardie, at any rate, accepted Rudbeck's explanation. The count also acknowledged that Rudbeck had behaved somewhat inconsiderately with his announced program.

For Rudbeck, the critiques—just like the words of encouragement—acted like powerful stimulants, urging him forward, a man driven and not exactly known for his sense of moderation. When the objections moved beyond the realm of personal attacks, they could be even more beneficial. Sometimes they helped him identify unforeseen problems with his theory about Atlantis, or pinpoint areas that needed more fiddling. And Rudbeck would almost invariably proceed to solve them, at least to his own satisfaction.

Spurred on by encouragement and criticism in equal measure, not to mention his own inner drive to perfect the theory, Rudbeck made so many advances that he dreamed of publishing "a small addition" to *Atlantica*. The problem, however, was that he was deep in debt, and despite the many positive reviews, the sales of the book had been unexpectedly slow.

"Wish what Your Excellence said had been true," Rudbeck wrote to De la Gardie, referring to the count's prediction that there would soon not be enough copies to satisfy the demand. Most of the initial print run of some five hundred copies, with one hundred special, lav-ishly produced copies, was still available for purchase.

Frustratingly, after two weeks on the market, only sixty copies of the special presentation copies had been sold. He had set aside forty of them for the high-ranking figures at court, or leaders in the king's government, but not a single volume was sold until the fourth of April, when the governor of the province of Geflve bought his copy.

Sales were so slow, in fact, that it is almost possible to count them as they occurred. In the first weeks, only about one dozen of the reg-ular copies of *Atlantica* were sold anywhere in the kingdom. Rudbeck's brother-in-law Professor Carl Lundius bought one of the first copies to come off the press. So did the professor of medicine Petrus Hoffvenius, his longtime friend, as well as the classical scholar Anders Norcopensis, who had translated the volume. Several noble-men and officials had also bought their own copies of *Atlantica*, but somewhat disappointingly they tended to opt for the cheaper vol-umes. Also, as Rudbeck complained, "when one person buys it, he loans it to everyone."

None of these trends boded well for narrowing the gulf between the glowing praise and the glaring lack of sales. Over the summer of 1679, the number of copies sold was, according to his own testimony, a grand total of one. Weary from worry, Rudbeck reported a few months later that, despite all his efforts, he had not managed to sell more than 120 copies. Given the huge debts he had assumed to print the work, Rudbeck hoped and prayed that the dismal slump would come to a speedy end. At this rate he was inching closer to financial disaster.

Sadly, one of the great sources of inspiration in his life, his dear friend Olaus Verelius, had fallen gravely ill. He had shown signs of deterioration for a while now. Rudbeck noted how his colleague would come over to his house and stand there in the doorway, nearly out of breath from the walk up the flight of stairs. The day Rudbeck had long dreaded came in early January 1682, and Rudbeck took a break from his own sorrows to write his friend's epitaph, *Corona virtutis* ("crown of virtue"):

> *. . . the one who knows what has happened in the oldest times*
> *He is as aged as the times*
> *And has a big trace of God's image;*
> *Whose foremost property is*
> *An unfathomable wisdom*

Such words reveal a great amount about Rudbeck and his relationship with Verelius, not to mention his appreciation of the wisdom that was to be mined from the past. And every bit of this wisdom would be needed for what awaited him.

BETWEEN THE TIME *Atlantica* was published and when it reached the Royal Society two years later, Rudbeck's country had undergone some dramatic changes in the dramatic century that many historians call the "Swedish Age of Greatness."

The young king Charles XI, so uncertain when he first sat on the throne, had matured considerably during the last four years, which he had spent almost completely on mud-soaked battlefields. In 1680, now that the war was over and Sweden had finally repulsed the Danish invaders, he was back in his royal palace in Stockholm. Coaxed by his new associates, the twenty-five-year-old king declared himself absolute ruler of Sweden.

No longer would he promise to seek the advice of the council before making decisions of consequence. The old council had in fact been disgraced by the poor showing in the war, deemed irrelevant, and, eventually, denounced as dangerously incompetent. Other traditional limitations on royal power were likewise to be swept away, at least in theory. Although the king had assumed many more powers during the humiliations and crises of the recent war, keeping real decision-making within his small circle of favorites in the camp, Charles XI was now, by law, answerable only to God in heaven.

For the vast majority of Swedes laboring under the severe strains of the state military machine, the king's assumption of absolute power would not make all that much difference. They would continue to toil away on the farms and fields, struggling desperately with harsh winters, crushing taxes, and the ever-present threat of famine. For the small middle class, growing steadily though still much smaller than that in Britain, the Netherlands, or France, there would be more opportunities for joining the growing administration and serving the state. But the impact of the new system would be felt most by the high aristocracy, and for some the experience would be catastrophic.

With the Swedish navy annihilated and the countryside devastated, the setbacks of the last war had shown the sorry state to which the country had fallen. Sweden was, in the words of the king, like a poorly equipped ship that had just managed to survive the stormy waters to creep back into harbor. It was vastly in need of repairs, though there was no money available to make them, let alone repay all its enormous debts. There wasn't even money to pay the crew, the loyal state employees who were keeping the creaking ship afloat.

"We know that the country is in desperate straits, and that everyone serves without wages," one government official expressed his concern in one of the lively debates in Parliament held during the turbulent fall of 1680. Meanwhile, "a handful of persons," he added, "own all the land in the kingdom." At this cue, another member chimed in, "And what happens is that the poor among us have to pay up, but the rich and the powerful, who own the nation's land, have done nothing; this is something that ought to be looked into."

The new absolute power planned to do exactly that, and the result was radical, to say the least. The king's men would examine every undertaking of the regency government—every single decision, expense, or gift bestowed in the last few decades would be scrutinized with the aim of discovering the "source of all the disorder." And that source, it was added ominously, would be held accountable.

What had long been murmured was now written as the law of the realm. The members of the regency, the old elite who steered the country, were officially blamed for the "miserable condition of the finances" and the great disasters of the 1670s that nearly destroyed the kingdom. Now they would have to pay—and the price, it was decided, would be their own property.

Along with this punishment, the king decided to establish a "Chamber of Liquidation." Far too many gifts and donations had been awarded to court favorites, seriously eroding the government's sources of income. The king's chamber was to make sure that all such grants were returned to the Crown. This was known as the reduction. With remarkably few exceptions, any major royal gift provided for any reason since 1632 was now judged to have been illegal and ordered to be returned immediately, with interest.

Such a sweeping plan was necessary, its proponents argued, to rescue Sweden from a state of emergency. To the high aristocracy targeted, however, *reduction* was just a fancy word for vengeful robbery perpetrated by the king and his advisers.

Unfortunately for Rudbeck and his hopes of continuing his search for Atlantis, one of the hardest hit was Magnus Gabriel de la Gardie. After steadily losing his influence with the king and his position of power, the count was nevertheless still unprepared for the nightmare that followed.

The king's men finalized the scrutiny of De la Gardie's actions as Chancellor of the Realm, and judged that he owed the state a total of some 352,159 *daler silvermynt*, a sum that could pay the annual salary of no fewer than eight hundred officials in the state bureaucracy.

Considering the extent of the count's property and assets, this fine might not have been so devastating. The problem was that the vast majority of his wealth consisted of land, not cash, and many of his transferable valuables, such as jewels, had already been mortgaged in an effort to maintain his lavish lifestyle and patronage. In one case, the count had even pawned an entire castle, Makalös, which stood just across the water from the royal palace and one of the most impressive in all of Stockholm. Far worse than all this, however, was the verdict of the Liquidation Chamber.

De la Gardie would watch helplessly as castle after castle, estate after estate, and jewel after jewel disappeared from his grasp. By the time the chamber finished its work, roughly three dozen castles, two hundred estates, and one thousand farms were lost, leaving the count literally with only one single castle, Venngarn.

In this bitter turn of events, De la Gardie turned to his last source of consolation: religious faith. One of the spiritual poems he composed at this time, when he was subjected to such wild extremes of fortune, is still a part of Sweden's Lutheran hymnal.

> *I from life's stormy ocean come*
> *Home to a friendly strand.*
> *What though my flesh lie in the tomb?*
> *My soul is in God's hand.*
> *From darkness into light I move,*
> *From poverty to wealth of love,*
> *From strife to rest eternal.*

By the end of the reduction, many other aristocratic families had also been plundered and devastated. The Brahes, the Oxenstiernas, and the De la Gardies, who together once owned about one-twentieth of all land in Sweden, saw much of their wealth depleted. Others left the country in 1680 for good, moving to the Netherlands, Britain, the Hapsburg lands, or anywhere away from the Liquidation Chamber of Charles XI's Sweden.

Although some families would bounce back to prominence, many would never recover from such an unprecedented transfer of castles

and properties. The winners in the royal lottery would be the growing state, its new civil servants, and the emerging businessmen with
money to buy the new, relatively cheap castles that temporarily
flooded the market. And ultimately, it was said, the country at large
would benefit. Land ownership in Sweden would never be the same;
a transformation had begun that would gradually allow this Scandinavian country to have one of the most equal distributions of land
ownership anywhere in the world.

At the time, though, chaos prevailed, and De la Gardie was not
one of those who would live to see their families reemerge after the
upheaval. From the depths of an unofficial political exile, he had
fallen straight into the abyss. Very disillusioned by the cruel swings of
fortune, the count was further embittered when he saw many of his
former friends forget the services he had previously rendered them.
Time after time, he was abandoned by those he had promoted into
power.

But Rudbeck would never forget the count's past favors. There is
no change in the tone of his letters, or in the volume of pages that he
sent to his friend. In fact, if anything, it seems that Rudbeck was trying to overcompensate. For De la Gardie, *Atlantica*'s greatest supporter and Sweden's greatest patron of the arts in that century, was
on his way to a poor, almost penniless, and, with a few exceptions,
pretty much unmourned death.

And Then the Snake Thawed

ᨳ

Just as I never cease to be vain in seeking something new to ponder, I am now trying to figure out how, with a good mind, I can learn patience. . . . I hope to find this invention, then I would have found the greatest treasure on earth.

—Olof Rudbeck

CONFRONTED WITH SLOW sales, crushing debts, the passing of Verelius, and the attacks on Count de la Gardie, Rudbeck saw no signs of improvement. In fact, the prospects looked worse when he learned of the contender vying for Verelius's influential position as librarian of Uppsala University.

This was Henrik Schütz, a professor who was quickly emerging as a powerful force in the coalition against Rudbeck. As a trained theologian, Schütz had heard many horror stories about the Rudbeck ogre: his stance as a wicked Cartesian, the scandalous behavior in the Curio lawsuit, and the shameless critiques of the Aristotelian principles enshrined at the heart of the university training.

Schütz was not exactly bred to take this blatant opposition silently. As one leading cultural historian described him, he was a "quarrelsome person and a game cock, who was unparalleled even in this time [for being] vindictive, possessing good memory, and quick to his guns." His personality was indeed volcanic. Professor Schütz was known, as Count de la Gardie put it, for "scouring the neighborhood farms with a pistol to silence the horses and pigs just because they bothered him."

Domineering and uncompromising, Schütz was also one of the most unpopular professors in town. He cursed, swore, and scolded in almost equal measure. When he was supposed to preach sermons, they were often given behind closed doors. The reason, De la Gardie suggested, was to hide his incompetence. Although this assessment was rather harsh, many did in fact seem to agree with the count's portrait of a difficult man who wanted things done in only one particular way. Some absolutely abhorred him and his severity. Once when he lay sick, unsympathetic students assembled in the night to play funeral music outside his window.

And when Verelius was lying on his deathbed in early January 1682, Schütz had hurried off to Stockholm to seek the influential and presumably soon to be vacant position as librarian of Uppsala University. The rival candidate for this powerful post, the university soon learned, was Olof Rudbeck.

For some time, Rudbeck had been tiring of all the medical duties. Not that he had been actively engaged the last few years—indeed, since his search for Atlantis had become a full-blown obsession, Rudbeck's disregard of his lecturing duties had reached almost legendary proportions. Such anatomy lessons, which had once been his love, were now just frustratingly inconvenient and distracting. Besides, referring to the sometimes macabre spectacle of dissecting bodies, Rudbeck said that his stomach no longer tolerated "the fresh steaks."

Taking charge of the library would be much more amenable to his antiquarian pursuits, which he regarded as his truly important work. The position of librarian, moreover, traditionally went to an older professor as an unofficial reward for long and beneficial service to the university. Loccenius, Schefferus, and Verelius had all in turn been appointed, and Rudbeck wanted to be next.

None of the authorities dragged his feet in making the decision, and the announcement was ready the day after Verelius died on January 3, 1682. Much to the surprise of university insiders, the king announced that the new director of the library would be Professor Henrik Schütz.

Only thirty-three years old, Schütz did not have much experience with manuscripts. He did not seem to have the literary achievements, either, that would command respect when he was showing visitors around the halls. Far from having given long service to the university, Schütz had graduated just one or two years before. Why the king took such a liking to this professor is puzzling. Perhaps it was Schütz's strong personality, or, as some have suggested, his influential friends and relatives at court.

When the appointment was announced, Rudbeck in fact made a sudden counteroffer. He proposed to do all the work as librarian, and yet allow the salary and the honors of the title to be given to Professor Schütz.

But this was all to no avail, and yet another attempt to secure the position for Rudbeck was made. In this last-minute move, De la Gardie called Schütz to Venngarn and told him bluntly, "There is no way that you can have the job, it is going to Rudbeck." At this point, Schütz left the castle and reported the situation to the king. In late January 1682, Charles XI issued a strongly worded order that left no doubt that Schütz should be named director of the library immediately.

This news came as a shock and a disappointment to Rudbeck. There were also serious practical implications of his unsuccessful bid for the post. Once again Rudbeck's own cavalier disregard of university rules had placed him in an uncomfortable position. Ever since he had started his work on *Atlantica,* he had treated the holdings of the library as if they were his own, borrowing with little concern for the official procedures and sometimes jotting his own commentaries to the texts in the margins. Many books were in fact held at his house on virtually indefinite loan. Evidently Rudbeck did not think this state of affairs was all that strange. The greatest treasures at the library, the Gothic Silver Bible and the early manuscripts of the Norse sagas, had, after all, come there on his suggestion.

Also, Rudbeck had been performing a range of services for the library, from drawing the designs for its new building free of charge to showing constant vigilance in expanding its collections. One of the most dramatic examples of this service was his proposal, back in 1665, to send Verelius's student Jonas Rugman on a trip to Iceland to seek out additional manuscripts for the university. Such a voyage seemed an attractive alternative to buying the manuscripts already ferreted out and put up for sale in the book markets. The count had even agreed to fund the venture, back when he still had his wealth. Unfortunately, however, the somewhat unpredictable "Icelandic Jonas" ended up spending most of the funding on alcohol and women. He never made it any farther than Copenhagen's rollicking taverns.

Despite that particular mishap, indicative of his ambitions as well as his willingness to take risks to achieve them, Rudbeck felt a strong sense of pride for and perhaps even entitlement to the ancient manuscripts housed in Uppsala's library. They had played a pivotal role in his discovery of Atlantis, and they seemed to have an almost unlimited potential for leading this curious hunter to new findings in his remarkable search. But now, with Professor Schütz's new authority over the ancient manuscripts and other library holdings, the atmosphere was about to change.

The first thing that Schütz would do was to order an immediate recall of library materials. All books and manuscripts were to be returned at once in his sweeping reform of the library procedures. There was to be a complete overhaul of the old, relaxed system, with its indulgence of professors like Rudbeck who ordered books by proxy, sent assistants to fetch them, and then carelessly lost the "tickets" or receipts documenting the transaction. But before Schütz could make his reforms, and indeed before he could do anything in his new job at all, he had to reckon with some unusual resistance. According to official complaints, Olof Rudbeck had hidden the keys to the library.

This childish prank hardly seemed becoming for a professor of Rudbeck's stature, as his critics were quick to point out. On another occasion just a few years before, too, when his enemy Professor Arrhenius was selected as rector of Uppsala, Rudbeck had infuriated the authorities by hiding university keys. On the other side of that locked door were all the musical instruments, many of which Rudbeck had donated to the university and now refused to allow in the inauguration, normally the most stately event on the university calendar. Professor Arrhenius was installed with pomp, though little fanfare, in that conspicuously silent ceremony.

Why was Rudbeck going around hiding keys, this time to the university library? As his critics saw it, Rudbeck was showing his usual lack of good judgment and again behaving in an outrageously inappropriate manner. Rudbeck, of course, explained it otherwise: Verelius had turned the keys over to him on his deathbed, one of his last wishes, literally, being that Rudbeck should hang on to them until an official inventory could be taken of the library stock. So this act of desperation, an obvious attempt to release some bottled-up frustration, was, Rudbeck said, intended to preserve the integrity of the library and honor the wish of his dying friend.

At any rate, with Schütz finally secure in his post by the end of February, the recall of the library books began in the middle of March 1682. Rudbeck protested. There was no possible way to write the book he intended, the second volume of *Atlantica*, without significant access to these sources. He could not simply return them because that would destroy the delicate order arranged in his study, he said, in another attempt to stall for time. Now Rudbeck had come across a man just as stubborn as he was, and Schütz would not back down. Besides, he would never forget his frivolous hazing.

JOINING SCHÜTZ'S TAUNTING circus was an influential member of the College of Antiquities, Johan Hadorph, who years before had caused so much trouble for Curio, when the printer was fired, fined, and sent for a brief stay in the local prison. Hadorph was a formidable opponent who made no secret of his disdain for *Atlantica,* with its wild conclusions and eccentric methods.

For Rudbeck's *Atlantica* was causing concern at the college, and it was not simply because of some annoyingly outlandish claims. Rudbeck's vision was drawing increasing praise among readers. In some circles the adoration was really over the top. Uppsala students returned with reports of unrestrained enthusiasm they had encountered on their travels on the Continent. One student told of meeting a gentleman in Germany with a magnificent library. After the student complimented him on his taste, the host asked if he would like to see something more impressive. He escorted the young man into a secret chamber that held only two books: the Holy Bible and Rudbeck's *Atlantica.*

Rumors of such overwhelming praise were floating around in the courts and salons of the kingdom, and they began to rankle the members of the college. Hadorph and his colleagues had also worked very hard on their antiquarian works, though they seemed to draw only a fraction of this attention. *Atlantica,* however, threatened more than just a fragile self-esteem.

Whereas the antiquarian scholars tended to take a more sober approach, based on a more cautious methodology and a more restrained use of source material, Rudbeck was relying on his overwhelming confidence in his intuition to find astonishing solutions to some of the oldest and most intricate "riddles" of the ancient world. His powerful

As Rudbeck declared that the gods and goddesses of classical mythology were Swedish, his enemies grew impatient with the increasingly outrageous claims.

creative mind helped him make some dazzling combinations of history and myth, just as his stubborn determination made sure he pursued each lead to virtual exhaustion. Pieces of the great Swedish puzzle were being fitted together with frightening ease. Rudbeck's towering "cloud castle" soared higher and higher. Worse still, as the antiquarians feared, his "fables and errors" were attracting increasing devotion in some circles.

All of this had a direct impact on the College of Antiquities, which, in the early 1680s, stood in a precarious situation. The budget was insecure, the small salaries of its members were still for the most part unpaid, and rumor had it that some influential figures were heard speculating that the annual funds for the struggling research institution might be better served financing Olof Rudbeck's detestable tragicomic search for Atlantis.

ℰ

ALMOST IMMEDIATELY AFTER taking office, Schütz began looking through the accounts of the library, and stumbled across some serious problems. There were many contradictions, unexplained omissions, numbers refusing to add up. It was a total mess. Most of the problems had existed for a long time, dating back to sloppy accounting and embezzlement by librarians during the booming 1650s. Verelius had been shocked when he took over in 1679, and in his desperation he had recruited Olof Rudbeck to help sort out the chaos.

Reconciling confusing numbers was for Rudbeck much like reading the "riddles" of ancient mythology, and that was why Verelius had gladly handed him one set of the books. By the time of Verelius's death, however, Rudbeck was still not done with the most complicated problems in his comprehensive audit. Fresh in his new office, Schütz was understandably eager to get to work. Predictably, given the tenor of their previous encounters, Schütz ordered all the account books returned at once. Rudbeck refused.

He was not done, he reminded Schütz, and he had no desire to stop in the middle of things, especially in view of how much time he had already invested. Worse than that, Schütz seemed, in Rudbeck's mind, a little too keen to show off the failures of the previous librarians. The reputation of his friends Loccenius, Schefferus, and Verelius would suffer, though they had, Rudbeck was sure, been guilty of little more than inheriting a chaotic situation that they could not bring under control.

When Rudbeck finally finished his account of the library books in 1683, the council approved his reconciliation. All the university officials seemed satisfied, and even the Arrhenius brothers signed their names to the bottom of the audit. But Professor Schütz, who had abstained from the special sessions in the council, was far from pleased. He accused Rudbeck of falsification.

At the sound of this serious allegation, both Jacob and Claes

Arrhenius promptly removed their names from the approval. Outraged, Rudbeck demanded to be allowed to defend himself. Schütz, however, did everything he could to prevent Rudbeck from having this opportunity. He obtained, in fact, an official summons from the King's Judicial Board for Public Lands and Funds, ordering Rudbeck to return every library receipt, bill, and document in his possession. Count Magnus Gabriel de la Gardie tried to protest, emphasizing that Rudbeck should at least be allowed access to the records to defend himself against the irresponsible charges of falsification. Nobody listened to the count.

Stormy sessions followed in the university council during the entire spring of 1684. Strong words were heard from both sides, shouting being perhaps a more accurate description. Each party presented its own version of the story, outlining the problems that had plagued the library over the last thirty years. This tense dispute culminated one year later, when Schütz sent two men over with orders to confiscate all of Rudbeck's account books, and with permission to use force, if necessary. Undisturbed by their threats, Rudbeck tried to stall further, while one of his friends furiously made copies of everything for the defense. After a three-day standoff, Rudbeck finally handed over the books.

The whole complicated affair is perhaps best summed up by the Swedish historian who wrote its authoritative account: "It is completely impossible now to arrive at any certainty in the matter, but Schütz's information did contain many mistakes, which Rudbeck had already pointed out."

One thing is sure: had any information been found in the disputed accounts incriminating Rudbeck, official censure and punishment would have been the result.

But Rudbeck had been put on the defensive again, forced to answer many questions about his actions. He was, moreover, appalled by Schütz's behavior. So was the chancellor, who was moved to write a letter to one of the king's trusted advisers to complain about the problematic professor. As Count de la Gardie put it, Schütz had formed an alliance and basically usurped power on the council, pushing through policies at will. God, he said, had punished Uppsala with this theologian. Schütz regularly acted without the knowledge or approval of the council, not to mention bypassing the chancellor of the university.

De la Gardie's comments probably reflect just as much his own frustration and anger, and bitter memories of Schütz's disregard of the count's nominal authority, as they do Schütz's personality. Yet they were stuck with the difficult professor, and unfortunately it was this Professor Schütz who was actually next in line to take the rotating position of rector, one of the most powerful posts in the university. Give Schütz six months, De la Gardie feared, and he would bring the entire university of Uppsala into chaos.

Sure enough, as rector of the university, Schütz would have even more power when he joined Rudbeck's old enemies Claes and Jacob Arrhenius. Zealous and articulate, Claes, now an aristocrat under the name Örnhielm, was enjoying greater clout and influence. His younger brother, Jacob, had been named treasurer of Uppsala University. He was an austere, ambitious official with an almost fanatical desire to trace problems back to Olof Rudbeck. What they decided to do about the library accounts came as a shock, a "thunderbolt to the unprepared council" and to a university clueless about their secretive planning.

The new rector and his treasurer had managed to secure royal authority to create an "Inquisition Commission" and launch a full-scale investigation of the university. Rudbeck and De la Gardie were bewildered at the king's announcement, wondering along with the rest of Uppsala about the eerie sense of déjà vu. Would this commission, led by its fiery "grand inquisitor" and meticulous number-cruncher out to reform the university, lead to a reenactment of the Liquidation Commission, with its hunger for scapegoats and its appetite for retribution?

✍

SET TO BEGIN operation in the first month of 1685, the Inquisition was a three-man commission consisting of Rector Schütz, Treasurer Jacob Arrhenius, and a third figure in the background, Professor Wolf. Their expressed aims were to determine the causes of the distresses plaguing the university and to find some immediate solutions. Unofficially, insiders knew that their secret intention was to remove Olof Rudbeck from the scene. In establishing this powerful institution (and certainly without any idea of their intended target), the king had made it perfectly clear that full cooperation would be expected. Anyone who resisted the Inquisition's authority would meet with a severe punishment that, according to the king's letter, would serve as a warning to others.

With this enormous authority, largely without clear limits, and backed by the power of the absolute king, the Inquisition forced Olof Rudbeck to account for his early activities at Uppsala. No one else would be hounded like him. The commission demanded detailed accounts of events that, at the time, were almost thirty years in the past. Rudbeck answered with a long and considered testimony describing his earliest connections to the university, including his days as a student, his invitation to Queen Christina's court, the royal scholarship to the Netherlands, and the circumstances surrounding the establishment of the botanical garden and anatomy theater. This defense was not the end but only the beginning of the ordeal.

Two weeks later the Inquisition Commission ordered an official explanation of Rudbeck's work with the botanical garden: a full account of its budgets, its legal status, its benefits, and the use of its materials since its founding and association with the university. Drafted on February 14, the letter ordered Rudbeck to gather all the materials and deliver his defense to the commission no later than March 1.

This investigation of the botanical garden shows the emerging pattern. The Inquisition would issue a statement requiring Rudbeck to respond at great length to some very broad subject that took place many years in the past and sometimes stretched over a significant span of time. When Rudbeck's defense arrived, almost invariably showing how much he had given of his time and services (and sometimes also materials), the Inquisition would pour over every sentence, and then, once again, issue another sweeping request, granting very little time to gather all the materials. Rudbeck's many other activities at the university were also slated to be scrutinized:

Anatomy theater	March 3
Waterworks project	March 3
Exercise house	March 7
Community house	March 7
Factory and mill	March 9
New library	March 12
College of Antiquities building	March 19

As if the many demands and the early deadlines did not make the task hard enough, access to university records was denied. Access to the minutes of the council meetings was also forbidden. When Rudbeck asked for permission to use them between 7:00 p.m. and 6:00 a.m., when no official would need them, the commission refused this as well. Rudbeck declared, ironically, that if he could not vouch for the honor of the professors on the Inquisition, he would believe that they were trying to make him convict himself.

No matter how nonchalant he tried to be, the terrible stresses of the Inquisition took their toll on the aging professor. The work was grueling, and the threat, backed by royal decree, serious. Each of the thirteen investigations called for a long, detailed, and carefully written defense. To comply, Rudbeck had to spend almost every waking hour laboring at his desk. Moreover, an accident several months before, when a castle gate crashed down on his carriage, had triggered vertigo, causing him to suffer from periodic onslaughts of dizziness.

For a man who had long seen enemies everywhere, real and imagined, his worst fears had come to life. He started to see his health fail, and sense that he was, again, in his last days, "every hour nearer to sickness and the grave."

AS THE INQUISITION looked into every conceivable aspect of Rudbeck's long relationship with the university, the front lines of the conflict were unexpectedly reopened elsewhere. Along with his elevation to the leadership of the university library, Professor Schütz was given another influential post: *inspector typographiae,* a title that gave the professor royal authority to scrutinize all printed materials produced in the Swedish kingdom. During the spring of 1685, Schütz decided to exercise this right.

Professor Schütz had heard that Rudbeck was about to print some unflattering comments about the College of Antiquities. What Rudbeck was in fact printing was a short but controversial collection of overwhelmingly positive reviews of his *Atlantica,* which his friends had assiduously accumulated over the last six years. He was hoping to drum up publicity and increase sales, and at the same time probably vent some frustration at the way he had been treated. He wanted to defend his reputation, once and for all. Schütz, by contrast, did not see it that way at all. He deplored the outrageous "bad taste" of printing such self-praise, and he particularly resented one letter that he heard would be included.

This entry, written by a monk named Sven Sithellius, not only praised *Atlantica* in radiant terms, but also emphasized, very bluntly, how much it surpassed the entire body of work that had so far been written about the Swedish past, including, by implication, everything from the state-funded College of Antiquities. In fact, the monk went on to propose that some special funding enjoyed by the college would be more profitably invested in Rudbeck's more noble and valuable quest. Such comments no doubt irked the college; the belligerent words played further on their anxieties about their already meager budgets and uncertain future.

So, in the first week of April 1685, Schütz stormed the press, imposed his authority as *inspector typographiae,* and demanded an immediate halt to Curio's machines. He literally ripped the sheets out of the hands of the printer, sealed them up, and took them to the university authorities, acting, as Rudbeck said, like "prosecutor, judge, and executioner all at once."

Arrhenius, Hadorph, and other enemies of Rudbeck at the college were elated at how decisively the censor had acted. To them, the shameless self-promotion, the underhanded insult to their honor, and the calculated appeal for royal subsidies all deserved, even demanded, such an action. Rudbeck, of course, protested the censorship, complaining that such an intrusion into his affairs was unwarranted. It was just another abuse of power, and a thinly veiled attempt by the opposition to maintain their control over the past. Besides, if the efforts to stop publication of his *testimonia* succeeded, Rudbeck knew what the "incompetent and passionate censors" had in mind for his *Atlantica.*

But even assuming for the moment that he could escape the censorship, there were some formidable economic obstacles standing in the way of his dream of completing the search for Atlantis. The self-reflection forced by the Inquisition had made the costs of his crusade all too clear. He had patently jeopardized his family's financial security. The costs of producing *Atlantica* were calculated at some 9,700 *daler kopparmynt,* not counting his own investment of time and energy in the search. Although sales of the folio volume had picked up quite a bit in the early 1680s, Rudbeck was still dangerously in debt. Six years after its publication, Rudbeck owed some 1,560 *daler kopparmynt* borrowed from a "good friend" and another thousand borrowed from a student society at the university. His family silver was still pawned.

Times were difficult, he said, and one had to advance cautiously. Again he saw his death approaching quickly, and feared that his family would have to "sigh for his grave." Mentally and physically fatigued, he felt too shy to beg and no longer had the strength to quarrel. It was simply not possible to continue in this manner, sacrificing everything for the sake of his search. As the Inquisition tightened its grip and he felt the economic pressures, Rudbeck did not dare to "string the bow any tighter." *Atlantica* looked doomed, destined to be engulfed by larger, uncontrollable forces, much like Plato's fabled isle.

Almost as disheartening, perhaps, Rudbeck saw many of his colleagues lured over to the Schütz and Arrhenius faction. After helping thirty-two people gain positions in the university faculties during the last two decades, Rudbeck was sad to see how little support he received from the professors as he faced the attacks from the Inquisition and the censor. Almost everyone, it seemed, was thinking only of his own career. Rudbeck compared his feelings of betrayal to the "peasant who stumbled upon a frozen snake." Never having seen such an object, the peasant reached down, picked it up, held it to his bosom to warm it, and saved its life. But when the snake thawed, its poisonous fangs lunged for his heart.

16

THE ELYSIAN FIELDS

What cared we for outward visions, when Agamemnon, Achilles, and
a thousand other heroes of the great Past were marching in ghostly procession
through our fancies?

—MARK TWAIN, *THE INNOCENTS ABROAD*

ON MAY 13, 1685, the dispute over the controversial collection of reviews was finally resolved. An order from King Charles XI freed Rudbeck personally from the clutches of the censor. One of Count de la Gardie's well-placed contacts had promised to help and did in fact manage to secure this royal exemption. Rudbeck's merits, according to the official statement, had earned him this special privilege, as someone whose "integrity and experience assured that his work does not contain anything harmful, irritating, and offensive." Rudbeck had won, at least the first battle. But the College of Antiquities immediately prepared another way to discredit the jolly nemesis who had invaded their turf.

Johan Hadorph and Claes Arrhenius, the true leaders of the college, shifted from censorship to public attack. In a letter to the university council, unsigned yet bearing the official seal of the college, the scholars accused Rudbeck of belittling their antiquarian work. They followed with a second letter to the university chancellor, criticizing Rudbeck's bad taste in publishing self-praise, a presumptuous and misleading enterprise that could, if necessary, be countered with a publication of the work's many flaws.

As additional ammunition, Hadorph also planned to print a peculiar historical manuscript that had long lain unfinished. Titled *Dissertation on the Hyperboreans,* this was a treatise penned by the esteemed poet and lethargic first president of the College of Antiquities, Georg Stiernhielm. In this work, Stiernhielm had outlined many of his arguments about the Hyperboreans, a people he believed had once lived in Sweden and had spoken the world's oldest language. Ironically, Hadorph had never liked the work. He printed the dissertation, it seems, only to show how much Rudbeck owed to his predecessors. During the tense spring and summer of 1685, Stiernhielm's posthumous, uncompleted, and unrevised manuscript went to press.

Rudbeck knew this work well and had certainly been influenced by its claims about the Hyperboreans. There is even reason to suspect that Verelius had loaned him the manuscript in the early days of the search, something that would have helped him as he entered the field of classical studies. But Rudbeck had gone much further in his conclusions than Stiernhielm or other patriotic historians. His search had culminated in a spectacular vision of the lost civilization of Atlantis and in his indefatigable efforts to bring the wide variety of theories together, more or less, into one unified picture of ancient Sweden. Still, by printing this work, Hadorph hoped to deflate Rudbeck's overblown esteem, and to show that *Atlantica* was not as breathlessly original as its admirers believed.

So, if the efforts of the censor had failed, then perhaps an attack on Rudbeck's credibility would succeed. Publication of Stiernhielm's manuscript and the latest accusations against Rudbeck were two features of the college's campaign to tarnish his reputation. Rudbeck was likened to the crow in the Aesop's classic fable who pretended to be a peacock, a plain bird achieving his impressive appearance only by relying on borrowed plumage. Unfortunately, too, with his many loans, he had gotten it all wrong, producing an erroneous monstrosity. Rudbeck should have stuck to medicine, his first profession. Surely "a deeper and truer history," Arrhenius wrote, could be written, and supported by state funds.

The College of Antiquities, its leaders believed, was doing just that, illustrating the history of Sweden with erudite treatises that far surpassed the "fables and errors" that decorated the pages of Rudbeck's *Atlantica.* Indeed, with confidence in the merits of their own work, it is not difficult to understand why the antiquarians deeply resented Rudbeck's printing of the *testimonia,* particularly the letter by the priest Sithellius. How wrong this monk must have seemed, praising Rudbeck's achievements while unfairly dismissing their own. How inappropriate it had been for him to suggest that the college's budget be used to finance Rudbeck's search. And printing such a letter only seemed to confirm their suspicions: Rudbeck secretly harbored designs on their funding.

When the college filed an official complaint against this alleged scheming, Rudbeck read the charges with amazement, and wrote of his reaction, "I began, from the very first to the end, to smile, as if I had drunk the best liquor. I could never have imagined that such a letter would come from a College."

The antiquarians, Rudbeck charged, had distorted the words of the priest's letter beyond all recognition, and derived meanings that were in no way intended. He did not want the college's money, nor did he wish to hinder their work in any way. In fact, Rudbeck recalled his many services on behalf of the college, promoting its members, supporting their research travels, drawing the designs for their planned building, and even being the one who suggested the very foundation of the institution. This assertion, though, Hadorph would vehemently dispute, claiming the honor for himself, which in turn ignited yet another source of tension between the two antiquarians.

Interestingly, when Rudbeck started to investigate matters for himself, he learned that some members of the college had no idea about the actions done in their name. Even its president, Professor Axelhielm, was surprised to hear of the attack. He claimed that he had been bypassed for years (and records show that his salary had actually been written out of the college's budget). Given this scenario, hinting of underlying dissension and intrigue, Rudbeck asked the chancellor to request that the plaintiffs sign the accusation personally. In this way he hoped to lure the disgruntled out from hiding under the authority of the college, an institution that he felt had been hijacked by some of its most domineering personalities.

But Rudbeck had never wanted *their* money, he emphasized. He wanted to claim only funds made available by the *tryckeritunna,* a special tax that had a complicated history. Designed as a tax on priests and parishes to raise money to publish the Swedish Bible, the famous Gustav Vasa Bible that cemented the kingdom's Reformation, the *tryckeritunna* (literally the "printing bushels") had been renewed in 1612 in efforts to fund another edition of the Scripture. But this time, when the Bible appeared (1618), the tax was not abolished. The king, Gustavus Adolphus, decided to use the fund for other purposes, including the publication of historical and literary works. Naturally the people paying the tax resented financing expensive books about ancient history. By the 1640s, the tax was allowed to fade away.

As for the college, its claims on this fund were quite recent, gained just a few years before, in 1674, when the defunct tax had again been revived, thanks to the successful lobbying of Johan Hadorph. He wanted the tax to support the college, its research activities, and its library, as well as to fund a team of copyists, artists, engravers, and woodcutters. Unfortunately for the college, what looked like a new, steady source of income had quickly dried up, an early casualty of the war with Denmark. The first year of its awarding would indeed be the last, that is, until Hadorph once again succeeded in having the tenuous rights reasserted in January 1682.

So the college's claim was effectively only three years old, and, even then, fiercely disputed. The archbishop had in fact protested the decision to award the *tryckeritunna* to the college, speaking on behalf of the parishes forced to pay the very unpopular tax. Those parishes resented taxation without representation. They had much preferred to use their own money for their own purposes, such as the schools, the poor, and the Church. A comparison of the salaries enjoyed by members of the College of Antiquities and the local vicars who were forced to pay the tax made the issue even more charged with emotion. Hadorph earned about 1,600 *daler silvermynt* a year (officially 2,200 *daler*) as an antiquarian, while many vicars made only about three hundred.

As for printing the praises of his *Atlantica,* Rudbeck stood by his action. He had never asked for any monetary gain, aristocratic titles, or membership in the prestigious College of Antiquities. The scholarly world's appreciation for the discovered Atlantis was his real salary. In this light, Rudbeck also defended the monk's outspoken comments about the relative merits of Sweden's historical works, writing, "I can't see that he [Sithellius] has sinned in that he desired something more to be completed of my work . . . and if he has sinned in this regard, then so have many others."

Sithellius was far from the only one to think in these terms, preferring *Atlantica* to the more obscure and dense antiquarian tomes. Privately Rudbeck confided to Count de la Gardie that he had been rather cautious, choosing not to print the more uninhibited praise he had received. He had not, for instance, published the words of the French ambassador, who, next to the Bible, preferred reading no other book than *Atlantica.* Moreover, less flattering portraits of the College of Antiquities could easily have been included, if Rudbeck had wanted.

All the college's critiques, Rudbeck concluded, essentially boiled down to an attempt to reassert its privileged position, and its desired control over the antiquarian arena. The college, on the other hand, saw Rudbeck as an author of fables unjustly maneuvering to gain its income. The judge in this dispute, it turns out, would be Count de la

Gardie. Although stripped of his castles, his wealth, and most of his status, he had one position of authority left: chancellor of Uppsala University. De la Gardie would now have to decide between the competing parties: *Atlantica,* which he had patronized, and the college he had founded.

Given his response, appearing in the middle of June 1685, the choice was not that difficult to make. The tone was set from the very beginning of the letter. Addressing himself to the "College in Upsala," De la Gardie was making explicit his hurt feelings about the college's past behavior. Immediately after the count had fallen from power, losing the chancellorship of the realm and his vast wealth in the liquidation, the College of Antiquities had sought out new, more influential patrons. It had even—without De la Gardie's approval or knowledge—moved its headquarters away from Uppsala.

De la Gardie proceeded to denounce how disgracefully the college had acted, "prostituting" its honor and selling itself so cheaply for the satisfaction of some private vendettas. Indeed it was not the entire college he now addressed, but rather only one or two offending scholars who had acted in its name, Hadorph and Arrhenius.

He was now really tired of all the scandalous insults he had heard about Olof Rudbeck, "impertinent and untrue judgments" enviously spread by members of the college. At the same time, De la Gardie did not approve of how the priest Sithellius had brushed aside the antiquarian's efforts, or of Rudbeck's indiscretion in printing the rebuff. Rudbeck had acted without caution or better judgment, something to which the count had never quite grown accustomed over the years in dealing with the flamboyant medical doctor.

Yet De la Gardie could not see how the printing of the letter had injured or reasonably upset the college. As a matter of fact, he hoped what the professors of the college said about themselves was true: namely that they wrote Swedish history with integrity, diligence, and industry. But despite their claims and their annual subsidies, the count added, "you cannot deny that for many years nothing has come to fruition." The only praiseworthy antiquarian works, he added, had been written by Olof Rudbeck.

Count de la Gardie announced his plan to go straight to the king's advisers and seek royal protection for Rudbeck, a man the college had long blamed and pursued without good reason. He would make sure that His Majesty was well informed of their "impertinent and indefensible behavior."

THE COLLEGE, HOWEVER, could not take the count's threats very seriously anymore. He was a fallen giant, humiliated and discredited. Far from distressed, Hadorph only increased his efforts to publish the catalog of errors, and wrote to his fellow antiquarian Claes Arrhenius advising him to stand firm, thereby robbing Rudbeck of the joy of feeling triumphant.

One month after the count uttered his threat to take the matters to a higher authority, Uppsala learned the fate of its printer Henrik Curio. After the case had spent ten years festering in law courts, Sweden's highest court, the Svea Hofrätt, rendered its judgment in the now notorious legal battle. Curio had lost his suit, and his post.

Effective immediately, Uppsala's printer would be turned out of office, ordered to repay the three hundred *riksdaler* (six hundred *daler silvermynt*) in loans for purchasing equipment, and forced to return all the machines in the condition in which he had received them. Even though De la Gardie's own son was serving as chief justice, the court had upheld the council's position completely. Curio would never see the nine hundred *daler silvermynt* that Rudbeck had promised, insisting that he had the university's permission to make the offer, though the council had always denied it.

In Rudbeck's eyes, the university had acted shamelessly. All of Curio's "troubles and pains" suffered on behalf of the academy were now harshly repaid. Tossed out of his position, with few prospects in a country that had only a few viable presses, Curio's future was, to say the least, uncertain. There was little hope he could pay back the additional three hundred *riksdaler* that he owed the university.

Rudbeck looked around for ways to help, hoping to arrange some agreement whereby Curio could start rebuilding his future. Perhaps he could repay the large fines with printed books, because, as Rudbeck said, "he does not have any other property." This request, though, was refused, with one of the strongest and most outspoken opponents being Rudbeck's nemesis, Professor Henrik Schütz.

Denied the opportunity to pay with his only available currency, Curio was in serious trouble, and Rudbeck tried once more "to carry his friend on his back." The plan was somehow to establish Curio as a printer and help him start working again, with the hope of earning enough income to support his family and pay the large fines to the university. The only question was how. If there was any chance of accomplishing this feat, Curio would need to hire some help. A minimum of two assistants would be needed to work the presses, a fraction of the staff at the university offices, when Curio, his wife, Disa, five apprentices, and a servant girl had run the operation. But even here the council balked. The university treasurer, Jacob Arrhenius, flatly refused Curio's request to hire any assistants until Curio first repaid his debts.

Taking the setbacks personally as usual, Rudbeck now had the added discomfort of feeling partly to blame for the ugly affair. It was mainly *his* enemies who were taking out their frustrations on his printer, just as they would soon be doing with his translator, Anders Norcopensis, who was also subjected to censorship. Rudbeck wanted desperately to find a way to help Curio and his family.

So one hundred copies of his *Atlantica* were pawned at twenty *daler kopparmynt* apiece, raising a total of two thousand *daler kopparmynt* (almost seven hundred *daler silvermynt*) for the cause. Curio followed suit, selling some of his stock of books to professors in town, netting an additional fifteen hundred *daler kopparmynt* (a fraction of their worth). Rudbeck also started selling his musical instruments. Even more generously, Rudbeck invited the printer and his family to move into the little stone house in his yard. There, Curio could hopefully open shop and work as Rudbeck's personal printer.

To the shock of his enemies, Rudbeck's grand scheme looked as if it might actually work. On October 6, 1685, King Charles XI did in fact grant Curio the right to publish, no mean feat in an age when royal sanction was a heavily guarded instrument in the Crown's efforts to control the press. Curio was also granted the right to import any new equipment from the Continent, free of the hefty customs tolls. Count Magnus Gabriel de la Gardie had after all been able to help, playing a large role in securing Curio the same privileges enjoyed by other printers and booksellers in the kingdom.

And over the next few years, Henrik Curio would again work as a printer in Uppsala. For a time he even rivaled the university press, because finding a successor to him was proving more difficult than the council had originally thought. It took time and intricate negotiations, and in the end the university had to grant a higher salary and better conditions to lure a new printer to town. After ten years of bitter litigation, reaching the highest court of the land and resulting in a heartbreaking loss, Curio's press had, in the end, only moved a few blocks away.

From this newly sanctioned press in the stone house in Rudbeck's yard, the two friends would publish many Norse sagas, including *Saint Olof's Saga, Arrow-Odd, Kaetil Haeng,* and *Egil's Saga.* A very early lexicon of Old Norse, which Verelius was working on until his death, was also published in 1691. In his spare time Rudbeck would often stop by the press, checking on its progress and tinkering with its equipment. He would even devise special blocks for printing the runic script. Rudbeck was indeed enjoying his work, being, as he put it, a "midwife" for the Norse sagas.

Now, with a press in place, Rudbeck was again trying to find a way to raise money for the continuation of his adored Atlantica project. As obsessed as ever with perfecting his theory, Rudbeck had many more clues to chase down, and more evidence to accumulate, about the lost world of Atlantis. Indeed a plethora of discoveries was still to be made, but, as Rudbeck lamented, there was no money to sustain the search. He could not simply rely on De la Gardie's generosity or his own resources, both of which were severely reduced, if not almost depleted. Frustrated yet not without hope, Rudbeck would be busy seeking alternative ways to pay for his book.

He tried securing loans from the Stockholm city treasury, hoping to repay the sum with copies of his book. When the city politely turned down the offer, claiming that it could not afford such a venture, Rudbeck toyed with publishing the work in the "English way," by selling subscriptions to gentlemen before publication. Some money came, too, as loans from admiring readers, including four hundred *daler kopparmynt* from the witch hunter Anders Stiernhöök. De la Gardie somehow found some funds, and a student society contributed a five-hundred-*daler-kopparmynt* loan. There was even talk of trying to make money from a tobacco company, and Rudbeck, always optimistic, still hoped that his passenger boat service might turn enough of a profit to help defray the exorbitant costs of the project.

Then, after wild swings of fortune, Rudbeck received a letter in early October 1685 that would change the nature of his search. King Charles XI had been appalled to learn how relentlessly Rudbeck had been pursued and how ruthlessly he had been treated. Less than half a year after removing him from the authority of the censor, the king now released him from the hounds of the Inquisition. After all the efforts of Schütz, Arrhenius, and the commission, they had not found any misdeed. Rather, it seems that their investigations had backfired, giving Rudbeck the opportunity to show how much he had sacrificed for the university.

During the fall of 1685, King Charles XI also came through with some promised royal subsidies, awarding Rudbeck some eight hundred *daler silvermynt*. The royal funds would later even be extended to a regular payment to the scholar. No less than two hundred *riksdaler* (four hundred *daler silvermynt*) would be given every year to ensure the publication of *Atlantica*. Following many years of economic hardship and distress, Rudbeck felt that the clang of coins was preferable to the sound of beautiful music. The year that had begun with such frightening omens ended better than he could have possibly hoped.

THE BLOWS FROM his enemies had been parried, and Rudbeck's hunt for Atlantis was, for the first time in his life, on solid financial footing. Such an unexpected turn of events enabled him to pursue his quest with all the enthusiasm of earlier times, although the recent trials had naturally drained some of his vigor. At least he was now free to investigate the mysteries of the ancient world as he saw fit, no longer forced to stay closely within the limits of monetary constraint. As he neared his fifty-fifth birthday, Rudbeck's ambitions soared, and his work swelled, and, in the end, the sequel would be even larger than the first volume.

One of the main goals in publishing the second volume was of course informing the world of the latest news about Atlantis. Rudbeck had found the comments and criticisms from readers particularly useful, helping him further refine some of the rough edges of his theories. Louis XIV's royal geographer offered some additional support for Rudbeck's vision of Atlantis, pointing to a discussion in Aelianus's *Varia Historia* between the satyr Silenus and King Midas that made Atlantis sound even more Swedish. Another scholar, Andreas Müller, a German orientalist in Berlin, had read *Atlantica* with amazement, and wondered if the Swedes had not in fact reached China.

China was in vogue in the 1680s, the decade that would see the ancient philosopher K'ung-fu Tzu first enter into Western consciousness, his name translated into the Latinate form Confucius. Müller was immersed in the discussions about China, stemming largely from his contacts with pioneering Jesuit missionaries in the forbidden land. When he read *Atlantica,* Müller was amazed at the many similarities between the Chinese and Swedish civilizations. He sent Rudbeck a list of ten comments and questions including "whether you think navigating through the north to China was an impossibility."

Rudbeck would take up this question with great enthusiasm. The National Library in Stockholm has one of Rudbeck's personal maps, full of measurements, calculations, and notes in the margins, showing how seriously he looked into this possibility. He was reading Marco Polo, following along in the medieval Venetian merchant's travels in the East, and paying close attention to the descriptions of customs, perhaps signs of a surviving Swedish presence. In volumes III and IV of *Atlantica,* the horizons expanded further, with Rudbeck taking the Swedes all the way to the banks of the Indus River, where the Swedish Buda, a figure in medieval Norse manuscripts, supposedly gave rise to the Buddha. He was also examining travel reports of the New World in the West, convinced that the Swedes had crossed the Atlantic well before Christopher Columbus (and also well before Leif Ericsson and the Viking expeditions). Similarities between words guided him in these days, with etymology rising even higher in the hierarchy of evidence and in his undisciplined speculation based on words.

The highlight of the volume, though, was elaborating on the Swedish legacy still present in the ancient Mediterranean. Worship of Sun, Moon, and Earth were considered, with wild speculations on how Swedish classical mythology really was. In one remarkable chapter, running some three hundred pages, Rudbeck discussed an array of classical myths that he believed could be explained only if they had originated in the far north. The phoenix, the elusive bird of red fire consuming itself only to be reborn of its own ashes, was a representation of the sun—its death in the wintertime, when it did in fact disappear for months, and then its return in the summer, constantly above the horizon.

Rising to a peak in popularity, Rudbeck was enjoying his own day in the sun. Adventurers, meanwhile, pledged to continue his chivalric quest. One Uppsala student, classicist Gustaf Peringer, for example, made an arduous ride of over one thousand kilometers to the far north and confirmed Rudbeck's veritable bonanza of discoveries about Atlantis. He saw Tethis Fiord, the home of the Titan Tethys, as well as Atle's Fiord, named after, he agreed, King Atle, or Atlas. The northern ports of Atlantis were also identified, as were Jupiter's marsh, Torneå (Thor's River), and other provocative place-names. Nearby, too, were the Atlas Mountains of mythology, the high plateaus where the famed Hyperborean stargazers first understood the riddles of the heavens and created the world's oldest solar calendar. Here indeed in the cold, mountainous north was the "blazing fire" of Swedish ingenuity, where the pioneer Swedes had created classical Greek mythology.

From all around Europe, visitors flocked to see the sights of Atlantis, some hoping to receive a guided tour from the "oracle of the north" himself. This had not happened before, and Rudbeck noted in jest that there was something of a minor tourist industry. Visitors were shown what was effectively touted as one of the greatest sites in the world, older than the Pyramids, more significant than the Parthenon.

On one such occasion, in the spring of 1699, a Polish diplomat received the Rudbeckian welcome. The guest is not specifically named, though it was probably F. G. Galetzski, a representative of Augustus II, the king of Poland (and father of at least 354 acknowledged illegitimate children).

With the guests scheduled to arrive on a Saturday night in late April, Rudbeck and his fellow hosts waited eagerly to receive them. The tables were set, and all preparations made, but no one came.

Then, late Sunday night, hardly a day or a time anyone expected a visitor, a student serving as a lookout rode back to Uppsala in a hurry. The Polish entourage was seen on the road from Stockholm and was very soon to arrive in town. The advance warning allowed enough time to notify the designated hosts and prepare at least some basic welcome. Rudbeck joked, "It fell upon old Rudbeck, that he would release his sweet lady from their midnight hug to cook and stew."

But since the Polish ambassador went straight to bed, the real ceremonies did not begin until the next morning. After seeing Uppsala Cathedral and the relics of the country's patron saint, Saint Erik, the guest officially met Rudbeck, who stood out among the brightly clad gentlemen in wigs with his black clothes and white collar, his long hair flowing naturally on his shoulders. When the Polish visitor learned that this old-fashioned man was the author of *Atlantica,* a book he owned and valued very much, the diplomat unleashed so many "titles of honors and held such a stately speech" that Rudbeck joked that he thought he had been mistaken for "a Roman cardinal." Galetzski made such a big deal over him that Rudbeck laughed, saying, "No one will have to do it after my death."

Escorting the guest through town, Rudbeck showed him the Gustavianum, the anatomy theater, and the library treasures with the Gothic Bible and manuscripts. They continued to the exercise house, built by Rudbeck, used for fencing, riding, and now also for the new comedy theater attached for student productions. Then they went up the hill to the palace because the diplomat wanted to see where Queen Christina had abdicated the throne. A grand feast followed that showed just how playfully and passionately Rudbeck continued to embrace life.

Guests were served by the twelve tallest Uppsala students Rudbeck could find—Hyperborean waiters with "beards down to the knees." Each toast to the king, the country, and the future was accompanied by a round of fire from the massive cannons Rudbeck had, for the occasion, stationed in the chancellor's yard. Festive as they were, the salvos did somewhat frighten the guests, and almost caused the diplomat's wife to faint. The music was of course arranged by Rudbeck, who also served as conductor with an orchestra of lutes, oboes, and violins of all sorts. Later a small orchestra played in the botanical garden, accompanied at strategic intervals, once again, by Rudbeck's favorite cannons. After the five-hour celebration, the party culminated with a trip to Atlantis.

At this point the almost seventy-year-old Rudbeck was tired, and so his son Olof junior and Professor Lundius gave the tour of the sites, presumably showing the sacred spring, the grove, the temple, the racetrack, the place of human sacrifice, and the other discoveries. This appears to have been the common itinerary, given what is known about Rudbeck's tours with other visitors, including Sweden's crown prince and future king Charles XII. The diplomat and his entourage were both impressed and grateful. "I do not know," Rudbeck said, "if my wife has kissed me so much in a year."

Diplomacy in Stockholm was, unfortunately, not as successful as the party in Uppsala. A few months after the lively occasion, Poland would join Russia; and the two powers, along with Denmark, would declare war on Sweden. The Great Northern War had begun.

NOW, WITH HIS enemies defeated and rendered powerless by the king's direct intervention, the last years of Rudbeck's life were among the most peaceful he had known. His faith in Atlantis remained undiminished, and he kept on looking for evidence, poring over ancient texts for any possible reference to ancient Sweden. By the third volume of *Atlantica,* published in 1699, Rudbeck had begun the chronology of Atlantis anew, striving in another nine hundred pages to build a stronger foundation.

Rudbeck was also still printing life-size images of the Atlantean knives and coins he had found. After publication of the third volume, he immediately started working on the fourth. He was joined

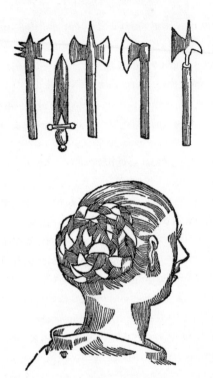

Rudbeck believed that these axes were once wielded by the Amazons, the famed women warriors of classical mythology who originally came from Scandinavia. The names of the most famous Amazon queens were found in Finland, where, incidentally, some Norse sagas had also placed fierce female warriors. Amazon hairstyles, Rudbeck added, lived on among Swedish women.

by Olof junior, who had shown interest in the quest in the last few years. Like his father, Olof junior would study medicine, develop a great passion for botany, and then spend the last decades of his life attempting to extend the frontiers of his father's lost Atlantis. Specifically, the younger Rudbeck was intrigued by the connections among Scandinavian, Asian, and Hebrew languages.

Olof junior and his sisters continued to work with their father on the botanical work *Campus Elysii,* which attempted to reproduce every plant in the world. The first volume, dealing with orchids, hyacinths, and tulips, among others, appeared in 1700, and the second, mostly on grasses, the following year. The elaborate illustrations showed the versatile talents of Olof junior, Johanna Kristina, and Vendela. Working so closely with his children, and enjoying the uncharacteristic calm at the university, Rudbeck really seems to have enjoyed the last years of his life, so full of happiness and, evidently, rich family gatherings.

One surviving portrait captures the warmth and peace of this family. It is an evening of music in the parlor. The fireplace crackles in the corner, and the elder Rudbeck sits with a pair of reading glasses on his nose. He sings in his commanding baritone, holding sheets of music in one hand and directing the family choir with the other. His wife, Vendela, sits close beside him, perhaps not very differently from the way she had when they were newlyweds, some forty years before. The sons and daughters crowd around the affectionate couple, each more or less engrossed in the fun. Johanna Kristina and Vendela sing along, while Olof junior plays the clavichord. Gustaf stands in the back with the stylish wig and scarf so playfully mocked by his father. Young Vendela would later marry a man named Petrus Nobelius, thereby making Rudbeck one ancestor of the great Swedish inventor Alfred Nobel, founder of the Nobel Prize.

Looking back on Rudbeck's extraordinary life and search, it had all corresponded so marvelously. No setback or problem, however insurmountable, had disappointed him for long. His brilliant mind found a way to crack each enigma, and then reconcile it with the larger vision of the past. Rudbeck's obsession had never lost its grip, making *Atlantica,* in the words of a nineteenth-century romantic poet, "one of the greatest insanities in the history of the world." And yet Rudbeck's madness, he continued, was "infinitely more interesting than all the wisdom of its many critics."

IN THE EARLY hours of May 16, 1702, a small fire began to burn. The dry air, wooden buildings, and great winds created a deadly combination. Within a few hours the town of Uppsala would be in flames.

The fire destroyed Rudbeck's house and almost all his possessions, including the inventions, instruments, and discoveries from his excavations. Also burned were his printing press, his curiosity cabinet, some seven thousand completed woodcuts for his *Campus Elysii,* and almost every single unsold copy of *Atlantica.* By midday, the Rudbecks were "as rich as they were when they lay in the cradle."

As his life's work turned to embers and ash, Rudbeck showed all the strength for which his long journey had prepared him. In some ways this was his finest moment. Far from complaining, losing hope, or succumbing to bitterness, Rudbeck showed the inner strength and wisdom that he always believed had existed long ago in a golden age under the North Star.

True to form, two weeks after the great fire had ravaged three-fourths of Uppsala, Rudbeck entered the council chamber with drawings of plans to rebuild his beloved town.

EPILOGUE

N SEPTEMBER 1702, only a few months after the great fire, Olof Rudbeck fell ill and died peacefully in bed. His death passed without a proper memorial, as the university was too strapped for funds and preoccupied with rebuilding the town. When a public ceremony was finally held, a year later, authorities raised a plaque over his tomb that read, "This testifies to Olof Rudbeck's mortality, but *Atlantica* his immortality." By this time, however, Rudbeck's theories were enjoying their last days of acceptance in the scholarly community.

Their demise did not, ironically, result from proven deficiencies in the theories themselves. Confidence in Rudbeck's lost civilization seems rather to have suffered more from the fall of the Swedish empire. Off to a roaring start in the Great Northern War, the last of Sweden's warrior kings, Charles XII, had won some spectacular victories, humiliating Russian armies against sometimes staggering odds. The battle of Narva in 1700, for instance, saw a heavily outnumbered Swedish force, probably about four to one, trounce Tsar Peter's Russian army. Yet, as Napoleon and Hitler would also later experience, Charles XII's invasion of Russia would ultimately bog down under the harsh attacks of General Winter and General Famine.

By the end of the Great Northern War in 1721, Sweden had been crushed, and Russia had gobbled up most of its Baltic territories. Other European neighbors, particularly Prussia, still a relatively minor power, came in for the kill. The Swedish empire was eagerly carved up, and only a few lone places were left, including a reduced Finland and a slice of Pomerania. Sweden would never again be a military power in the way that it had been in Rudbeck's lifetime, and its sudden collapse would in time make his views of ancient Sweden look absurd.

Along with these largely unforeseen military disasters, Rudbeck's once lauded theory suffered from changes in the craft of history. Historians in the Enlightenment turned increasingly to written evidence of books and documents, making Rudbeck's methods look peculiar at best. By the early eighteenth century *Atlantica* had fallen into the realm of parody. Rudbeck's name was becoming synonymous, at least in some circles, with wild theorizing—the author of *Atlantica* living on, for a time, in a new verb coined to describe such bold, uncontrolled speculation: *att Rudbeckisera,* or "to Rudbeck."

Yet, given advances in the study of history, we can now see how pioneering Rudbeck's work actually was. Despite the many etymological derivations that were indeed outrageous and hopelessly farfetched, some of his conclusions were years ahead of his time. He correctly deduced, for example, the central importance of rivers in the rise of civilization, outlining his impressive discussion in *Atlantica* some fifty years before Isaac Newton's celebrated theory. Likewise, his insights into the interconnectedness of languages were later developed and proven true when scholars discovered the Indo-European roots of many ancient and modern languages (though of course this root wasn't even close to Swedish).

Perhaps most visionary, however, were the extraordinary ways in which he advanced his search. Unlike the authors of previous efforts to locate lands relegated to the realm of myth and legend, Rudbeck was not content to speculate or theorize within the cozy confines of a library. Rather he set out to find his lost world, and chase down any remains that might have escaped the ravages of time. As he would later put it, it was the difference between sitting on a beach wondering about the mysteries of the ocean and actually hopping into the waters to find out for yourself.

Growing up between Galileo and Isaac Newton, Rudbeck also knew the value of the new scientific method for revolutionizing our knowledge and reached the conclusion that traditional historians had scarcely harnessed its potential. Painstakingly calculating, measuring, and adopting an exceptional empirical approach that stressed direct observation, Olof Rudbeck would indeed be a pioneer in using the scientific method for interpreting evidence of the distant past.

No longer could one only sit comfortably in a warm cottage, his nose in a book, and think up arguments. Rather, a true and more accurate knowledge could be obtained only with physical labor—hands blackened by experiments, back aching from closely examining plants and minerals, and eyes weary from gazing at distant stars in the night sky. This comment shows very much Rudbeck's approach to the ancient past, seeking clues wherever they might be found.

Characteristically, as Rudbeck chased Atlantis, each new discovery sparked another, and this in turn led him to undertake even bolder measures. He put his postal fleet and commercial transportation service to use in testing the possibility of an Argonaut voyage in the Baltic—a brilliant development that inaugurated what we today call experimental archaeology. But Rudbeck's most startling contribution was probably his invention of an early archaeological dating method. Field archaeologists all over the world still rely on measuring distinctions in rock and soil layers, now called stratigraphy, to determine the approximate age of objects found in the ground. Almost two hundred years before such an important method of investigation would be borrowed from geologists, Rudbeck had put it to good use on Swedish burial mounds and standing stones to date the remains of his lost civilization.

Absolutely convinced as he was of his theory, Rudbeck applied his ingenuity and enthusiasm to overcome the many difficulties he encountered. Nothing stood in his way, at least not for long. And that, essentially, is one of the main problems with his work. He had very little sense of limit and virtually no ability to accept a fact—any fact—that conflicted with his theory. Rudbeck was very much the victim of his own problem-solving talent. He succumbed, too, it must be said, to the power of his own instinct, his imagination, and his love for his country.

So, in the end, this is a very human story—the story of a dreamer whose passion took him to great extremes. His curiosity, creativity, and resourcefulness made him a great pioneer, yet all his talents and expertise, combined with his scientific methods, only took him further into the realm of fantasy. The more pioneering he became, the farther astray he went—and the more ingenuous his solutions, the more it all descended into delusion. But what a spectacular and beautiful vision, and what an adventure!

For me, the story of this adventure closes in our own backyard. In many gardens and meadows grows a lovely flower called "black-eyed Susan." This plant belongs to the family *Rudbeckia,* named in honor of Olof Rudbeck and his son. Appropriately, it is a hardy flower, capable of surviving great stress and thriving in an impressive array of conditions. This flower stands today as a cheerful reminder of Olof Rudbeck and his remarkable search.

Notes

Frequently cited works in the notes have been identified by the following abbreviations:

Atl.   Olof Rudbeck. *Olf Rudbecks Atland eller Manheim . . . Olaus Rudbecks
            Atlantica, svenska originaltexten.* Vols. I–IV. Uppsala, 1937–1950.
Bref   Claes Annerstedt, ed. *Bref af Olof Rudbeck d.ä. rörande Uppsalas universitet.*
            Vols. I–IV. Uppsala, 1893–1905.
Gylf.   Snorri Sturluson. *Edda Gylfaginning.*
KB   Kungliga biblioteket.
KVHAA   Henrik Schück. *Kgl. Vitterhets historie och antikvitets akademien. Dess förhisto-
            ria och historia.* Vols. I–IV. Stockholm, 1932–1935.
LUB   Lunds universitetsbibliotek.
RA   Riksarkivet.
RS   Royal Society.
ULA   Uppsala landsarkiv.
UUÅ   *Uppsala universitets årskrift.*
UUB   Uppsala universitetsbibliotek.
UUH   Claes Annerstedt. *Uppsala universitets historia.* Vols. I–III. Uppsala,
            1877–1914.

For readers wanting to know more about Olof Rudbeck's life, Gunnar Eriksson has written an excellent scholarly biography, *Rudbeck 1630–1702: Liv, lärdom, dröm i barockens Sverige* (2002). Its balanced analysis and rigorous treatment make the book a landmark study, and I only wish it had been available for me during the first seven years of my work. Eriksson's *Atlantic Vision* (1994) is also of great importance; special thanks to Eriksson for giving me a copy back in 1995, when I first started to be fascinated with this subject. Claes Annerstedt's *Bref* is a gold mine of information, both for its collection of primary documents and for Annerstedt's insightful commentaries. Annerstedt's history of Uppsala University, *UUH*, was also helpful, as was P. D. A. Atterbom's overview of Rudbeck's achievements, *Minne af professoren i medicinen vid Uppsala universitet Olof Rudbeck den äldre* (1850–51). Henrik Schück's history of Swedish antiquities,

KVHAA, and Sten Lindroth's *Svensk lärdomshistoria. Stormaktstiden* (1975) were likewise as indispensable to my work as they were inspiring in their scholarly expertise.

Among the many other secondary sources that have helped me understand Olof Rudbeck are Nordström's *De yverbornes ö. Bidrag till Atlanticans förhistoria* (1930), Strindberg's *Bondenöd och stormaktsdröm. Studier över skedet 1630–1718* (1937), Nelson's commentaries to the latest edition of the *Atlantica* (1937–50), Johannes Rudbeckius's *Bibliotheca Rudbeckiana* (1918), and Per Dahl's dissertation, *Svensk ingenjörskonst under stormaktstiden: Olof Rudbecks tekniska undervisning och praktiskaverksamhet* (1995). Michael Roberts, David Kirby, John Greenway, Eli Heckscher, Ingvar Andersson, Kurt Johannesson, Peter Englund, and Gunnar Broberg are also outstanding. It was John Greenway's provocative discussion of seventeenth-century Sweden that first caught my interest in Olof Rudbeck's search: *Golden Horns: Mythic Imagination and the Nordic Past* (1977), 71–82.

In addition to *Atlantica* I–IV and its accompanying Atlas volume, the present work draws on a number of primary sources housed in Scandinavian archives. The National Library (also known as the Royal Library) in Stockholm has Rudbeck's own handwritten notes about the early history of Sweden, as well as a copy of his maps with notes in his own writing (*Atland tabulae med anteckningar av O Rudbecks hand* F.m.73). Some of Rudbeck's other miscellaneous notes, including library loans, are found in *Olaus Rudbecks autografsamlingen* and *Olof Rudbeck den äldre collectanea* (F.e.16). The Swedish Riksarkivet (National Archives) has many of Rudbeck's letters in the De la Gardie collection, especially the material relating to Uppsala University (*Kanslers embetets handlingar för Uppsala universitet Arkiv* E.11:5–E. 11:8). The Swedish National Archives also has Rudbeck's letters to King Charles XI (Karl XI) and the Regency Government (6459.52, vol. 14; 1133.10, vol. 32), as well as his letters to other prominent Swedes.

Uppsala University has a wonderful survival of Rudbeck's quest—one of his own notebooks, found in *Olof Rudbecks collectanea* (R 13)—and material, too, on various aspects of Rudbeck's life: *Olof Rudbeck d.ä.* (X 240), *Rudbecks biografi* (X 208), as well as *Bibliographia Sveo-Gothica XV Palmsköld samlingen* 344, *Virorum illustrium Suec. litterae No. XVI litterae Palmsk. samlingen* 370 (W 848). Rudbeck's handwritten notes on many other matters, ranging from old runes (R 551) to astronomy, including observations of comets (A 312), are also here. Claes Annerstedt donated his notes about the history of Uppsala University (for Rudbeck, see especially U40:4, U40:5, U40:6, and U40:63). Lund University also had a sizable collection of Rudbeck's original letters to Chancellor de la Gardie in the *De la Gardiska släktarkiven: Magnus Gabriel de la Gardie* (93:1). Some of Rudbeck's other letters, particularly from later in his life, are found at Uppsala länds arkiv (*Länsstyrelsen i Uppsala län. Landskansliet biographica* I. D.IV.A, 63 and 64, as well as *Landskansliet skrivelser från akademiska konsistoriet och rektorsämbetet* D III 1). The Royal Society in London has preserved copies of its letters to Rudbeck (LBC 3.253, LBC 4.386, LBC 4.49), his letters to them (LBC. 8.273), and the actual copy of *Atlantica* sent to the society in the autumn of 1681.

A note on Swedish spelling: I have not changed or modernized Rudbeck's words. Also, some words appearing in his etymologies no longer exist in modern Swedish.

INTRODUCTION

The Uppsala fire is described in many sources, particularly Eenberg's *En utförlig relation om den grufweliga eldzwåda och skada, som sig tildrog med Uppsala stad den 16 Maii, åhr 1702* (1703), published when the city was still in ruins. Eenberg reports the especially dry spring that year (6–7), the chaos prevailing as the fire erupted (16–17), the damage to the cathedral (27ff.), and the devastation afterwards. Two of Rudbeck's letters to Chancellor Bengt Oxenstierna reveal his own perspective on the catastrophe; both are often cited as valuable eyewitness reports (17 May 1702 and 26 May 1702, published in Annerstedt's *Bref* IV, 387–90). The image of fire raining from the heavens comes from the first letter, as does Rudbeck's other personal contributions, such as loaning his horses to neighbors.

Eenberg also notes how much Rudbeck suffered from the fire, including the loss of his house and the works he had kept in the cathedral (24, 31, 41). The legend of Rudbeck climbing atop a burning building is found in many of the older secondary accounts, including Atterbom (1851), 115–17. The literal accuracy is questioned by Annerstedt, *Bref* IV, cclxxviii–cclxxix, commenting on its absence from the oldest accounts, though he notes the well-known oral tradition of Rudbeck's action and comments on how it is not contradicted by known facts. This uncertainty is why I have used the word *legend*.

Rudbeck's words on so many "unbelievable" findings come from his letter to Count Magnus Gabriel de la Gardie, 28 December 1674, *Bref* II, 98–99. The rapid pace of the discoveries was still surprising Rudbeck, with the words about uncovering "unbelievable things" found in a letter dated 3 December 1676 (RA, *Kanslers embetets handlingar för Uppsala universitet arkiv* E.11:5). Deep into the project at this point, the discoveries were coming so quickly that he hoped to publish a "small addition" or "another book." See Rudbeck's own words, for instance, in *Atl.* I, 408, or *Atl.* I, 428, and the phrase itself, *Atl.* II, 15. At about this point in the printing of the first volume, the references to future continuations become more and more frequent (*Atl.* I, 458, 460, 476, 490).

The phrase "oracle of the north," one of the many ways readers praised Rudbeck's contributions, comes from Engelbrecht Kempfer's letter to Rudbeck, 20 February 1683, printed in *Auctarium testimoniorum de Cl. Rudbeckii Atlantica* (1685), reprinted in Nelson's edition of *Atl.* IV (1950), 48. Isaac Newton's letter requesting Rudbeck's *Atlantica* was published by A. R. Hall in "Further Newton Correspondence," *Notes and Queries* 37 (1982).

The conflicts Rudbeck faced in the course of his search were enormous. Strindberg reads Rudbeck's Atlantis theories as a "romantic compensation" for his struggles and misery, *Bondenöd och stormaktsdröm* (1937), 246ff. One reason for the lack of general knowledge about Rudbeck outside Sweden is the fact that

Atlantica has never been translated into English, German, French, or any language besides Latin. Moreover, there are surprisingly few accounts about Olof Rudbeck in languages other than Scandinavian, and works in English are especially few. Apart from a couple of short studies in academic journals, Eriksson analyzes Rudbeck's methods as an experimental natural philosopher in his scholarly *Atlantic Vision* (1994), and John Greenway treats him in the context of the various images of the Nordic past in his *Golden Horns* (1977), 77–82.

Sten Lindroth notes that few printers dared to publish a work of over six or seven printer sheets in length (*Stormaktstiden,* 73–74), *Atlantica,* by contrast, with almost 900 pages on some 225 printer sheets, was a massive undertaking.

Chapter 1: Promises

Information about the intellectual and social environment of Uppsala University in the middle of the seventeenth century is found in Rudbeck's letters about Uppsala University, printed in Annerstedt, *Bref* I, xxvii ff. and Annerstedt's *UUH* I, 378–80; II, 101ff; III, 335; in Lindroth's *Uppsala universitet 1477–1977* (1976), 41–44; and in Lindroth's sweep of Swedish history of science, *Stormaktstiden,* especially volume III, 19–21, 38ff. The selected pages discuss Gustavus Adolphus's contributions to the university, as well as document the riotous student life that flourished at the time.

When Rudbeck arrived at Uppsala in February 1648, rumors of the peace ending the Thirty Years' War had been circulating for some time. They were soon confirmed when the first of many treaties, collectively known as the Peace of Westphalia, was signed in the fall of that year. The phrase "drunk with victory and bloated with booty" comes from Michael Roberts, *Essays in Swedish History* (1966), 233. Rudbeck's youth, including his attempts to follow his older brothers to Uppsala, is described in many sources, though see especially Eriksson (2002), 17–32. Another valuable discussion is K. W. Herdin's "Olof Rudbeck d.ä:s födelse och tidigare ungdom," in the collection of scholarly articles published on the three hundredth anniversary of Rudbeck's birth, *Rudbecksstudier: Festskrift vid Uppsala universitets minnesfest till högtidlighållande av 300-Årsminnet av Olof Rudbeck d.ä:s födelse* (1930).

Even though disciplines were not rigidly fixed, and polymaths moved relatively freely among them, few would argue that Uppsala's medical school in the 1650s was the best place for Rudbeck's work. His first teacher, Professor Johannes Franckenius, was busy in the alchemy lab (Lindroth, *Stormaktstiden,* 176–77). Rudbeck's work under him is discussed in Eriksson (2002), 46–47, and Lindroth, 416. Another one of Rudbeck's medical teachers at Uppsala, Olaus Stenius, was famous in his day, though trained originally as an astronomer. Rudbeck would make his discovery of the lymphatic glands with "almost no instruction" from the medical faculty, according to Eriksson (1994), 1.

One main challenge to anatomists in Rudbeck's day was how to find bodies for dissection. Cases of grave robbing, body snatching, and other macabre means to obtain specimens were well known in early modern Europe. After Rudbeck was named professor of medicine, he would write several letters to his patron, De la Gardie, trying to receive help in gaining access to bodies. See, for instance, his undated letter in 1682, *Bref* III, 187.

The discovery of the lymphatic glands was described by Rudbeck himself in an often cited letter, for instance Eriksson (2002), 58–59. The discovery is discussed in there, 59–65, as well as in Robin Fåhræus, "Rudbecks upptäckt av lymfkärlssystemet," *UUÅ* (1930), 3–9; Lindroth's *Stormaktstiden*, 416–17; and Lindroth's "Harvey, Descartes and Young Olaus Rudbeck," in the *Journal of the History of Medicine* (1957). Rudbeck's discovery of the lymphatic glands was "the first and for a long time the only significant Swedish contribution to European medical research" (*Stormaktstiden*, 414).

My discussion of Queen Christina's court is based on a number of works, particularly Susana Åkerman's *Queen Christina and Her Circle* (1991), Sven Stolpe's *Christina of Sweden* (1966), Ernst Cassirer's, *Drottning Christina och Descartes* (1940), and Lindroth's *Stormaktstiden*, 197–204, 121ff. Descriptions of Queen Christina's voice and face are from the French diplomat Pierre Chanut, and the opening of her grave is reported in von Platen's *Queen Christina of Sweden: Documents and Studies* (1966). For more on Descartes' life, see Jack Rochford Vrooman's *René Descartes: A Biography* (1970) and Richard Watson's *Cogito, ergo sum* (2002). The story of Descartes' skull remaining in Sweden after his death comes from Jerker Rosén's "Kristina's hovliv," in *Drottning Kristina: Vetenskap och kultur blomstrar*, in *Den svenska historien* VI (1979), 144.

Uppsala castle and Christina's mannerisms were described by English diplomat Bulstrode Whitelocke, who got to know the queen and the court rather well on his stay in the country 1653–54. Queen Christina's "chair of state of crimson velvet" is noted in Bulstrode Whitelocke's *A Journal of the Swedish Embassy 1653 and 1654* (1855), 23 December 1653, 231. The queen's reaction to the demonstration was, in Rudbeck's words, "fire and flames" (*eld och lågor*). The young Uppsala student described another visit to Queen Christina's court, when he sang the part of a shepherd boy and the queen a *kammarpiga* (*Atl.* I, 437; II, 442).

There is some uncertainty, actually, about which "beautiful day" in the spring of 1652 Rudbeck performed his public demonstration. He always said April, though there has been speculation that it was actually May. This is because Rudbeck *could* have been translating the Swedish Julian calendar into the Gregorian; the latter was the calendar then in use in the Netherlands, where he happened to be at the time (and this would also mean a change of ten days, no small advantage in a debate over awarding priority for the discovery of the lymphatic glands). The dispute with Bartholin would rage fiercely, with one of the Danish physician's students, Martin Bogdan, being particularly aggressive. For more on this conflict, see Eriksson (2002), 51, and Lindroth's *Stormaktstiden*,

419–21. See also Johannes Rudbeck's *"Bibliografiska anteckningar om Olof Rudbeck den äldres anatomiska skrifter och striden med Thomas Bartholin"* Samlaren (1904).

For more on the Swedish Age of Greatness, see David Kirby's *Northern Europe in the Early Modern Period: The Baltic World 1492–1772* (1990), and just about anything by Michael Roberts. The size of the Swedish empire is discussed by Roberts in *The Swedish Imperial Experience 1560–1718* (1979), 7–9, 83, 97. Sven Lundkvist's essay "The Experience of Empire: Sweden as a Great Power," in Michael Roberts, ed., *Sweden's Age of Greatness 1632–1718* (1973), 20–57, is also valuable. Roberts calls the administration "one of the best developed, most efficient and most modern administrations in Europe" in *Gustavus Adolphus: A History of Sweden 1611–1632* (1953–58), vol. I, 278.

Strindberg discusses the poverty, the beggars, and the bands of outlaws roaming the country (1937), 102–5, with the image of them filling the roads on page 112. On page 25, Strindberg paints a vivid picture of war consuming national resources, and worsening the country's social problems. The book, still controversial in some academic circles, is an opinionated and lively read. Descriptions of Stockholm in the narrative are taken from Whitelocke's *Journal* (1855): the accounts of the roads and the inns, 30 November 1653, 175ff. The forests are described in many places, including 9 December 1653, 195–96.

The Västerås wizard was Matthias Andreas Biörk (or, in his Latinized name, Biörkstadius), also known in Sweden for his mathematical work. Thanks to Gunnar Eriksson (2002), 27, for information about Biörk. Rudbeck's relationship with his father is discussed by Eriksson (2002), 17–23, and with his mother, 23–24, as well as by K. W. Herdin, "Olof Rudbeck d.ä.s födelse och tidigare ungdom," in *Rudbecksstudier* (1930). See also, among others, Hans Cnattingius, *Johannes Rudbeckius och hans europeiska bakgrund. En kyrkorätts-historisk studie* in *Uppsala universitets årsskrift* (1946), and H. Scheffer, *Johannes Rudbeckius: En kämpagestalt från Sveriges storhetstid* (1914). The stories of Rudbeck playing on a hobbyhorse and the clothes are from a letter written in 1696 and printed in several accounts. "To sit on his bottom" were Rudbeck's own words on the occasion. Rudbeck's mother as "glittering sunshine" comes from Isak Fehr's article in *Ord och Bild* (1897).

CHAPTER 2: ORACLE OF THE NORTH

Benjamin Franklin's words are cited in Edmund S. Morgan, *Benjamin Franklin* (2002), 33. Rudbeck's stay in Holland was, by all accounts, significant. Fries noted how few places would be better suited for his development than seventeenth-century Netherlands (*Den svenska odlingens stormän 1: Olof Rudbeck den äldre, Urban Hiärne och Jesper Svedberg* [1896], 7). For more on the achievements of the Dutch at this time, see, among others, Jonathon Israel, *The Dutch Republic: Its Rise, Greatness, and Fall 1477–1806* (1995); Simon Schama, *The Embarrassment of Riches: An Interpretation of Dutch Culture in the Golden Age* (1987); Paul Zumthor, *Daily Life in*

Rembrandt's Holland (1963); and Mike Dash, *Tulipmania: The Story of the World's Most Coveted Flower and the Extraordinary Passions It Aroused* (1999).

One contact Rudbeck made in the Netherlands, his former teacher the Leiden University professor of anatomy Johannes van Horne, would later encourage him to pursue his goal of writing a *Nova animalium Fabrica,* and, in effect, accomplish for animal physiology what the anatomist Vesalius had achieved for human anatomy, 12 July 1657, printed in *Auctarium Testimoniorum* (1685) in *Atl.* IV, 65, 234. He wrote again on 15 February 1666, *Atl.* IV, 240. Rudbeck's offers of employment were noted in a letter describing his early years, 9 February 1685, Annerstedt, *Bref* III, 208–9.

The early history of Uppsala's botanical garden was described in his letters, Rudbeck calling it his "firstborn son," 1 March 1685 (Annerstedt, *Bref* III, 218). For scholarly accounts, see, among others, Eriksson (2002), 198–207; Rutger Sernander, "Olof Rudbeck d.ä. i den svenska botanikens historia," *UUÅ* (1930), 10–22; and M. B. Swederus, "Olof Rudbeck den äldre: Huvudsakligen betraktad i sin verksamhet som naturforskare. En skildring," in *Nordisk Tidskrift* (1878). Rudbeck's botanical garden can be seen today most commonly in the background of the 100 Swedish kronor note. This garden is now the Linneträdgård, named after his successor Carl Linnaeus. Olof Rudbeck's son, Olof junior, played an important role in Linnaeus's early botanical career, even hiring him as a tutor for the Rudbeck children.

The reputation of a happy marriage for the Rudbecks was also confirmed by Eriksson (2002), 88 and 159, and the description of the various items in their house is from a contemporary description cited on page 170. A discussion of the alleged Caesarean section is found in O. T. Hult's "Några ord om det Rudbeckska 'kejsarsnittet," in *Rudbecksstudier* (1930), 116–20. For a sample of the reception in learned circles, see the letter to Rudbeck by Oldenburg at the Royal Society, 23 July 1670 (RS, LBC.4.49).

"When France catches cold" were the words of Klemens von Metternich, describing the revolution of 1830, and are cited in Raymond F. Betts, *Europe in Retrospect* (1979), 34. My description of Olof Rudbeck is based on many surviving portraits, including van Mijten's oil painting (1696). The single best source for seeing the various images over the years is Rudbeckius's analysis of Rudbeck portraits in *Rudbecksstudier* (1930), 35–62. The mustache is Rudbeck's own description, *Atl.* III, 517, and the fashion reference comes from Rudbeckius, *Bibliotheca Rudbeckiana* (1918), 36. Johan Esberg's speech (1703) noted the cheeks, eyes, shoulders, and clothes as well.

The contents of the Uppsala anatomy theater come from Esberg's description in his memorial speech: *"Laudatio funebris qua polyhistori magno medico longe celeberrimo, dn Olao Rudebeckio patri in regia universitate Upsaliensi . . ."* (1703). Rudbeck described one interesting skeleton with the arteries and veins colored in, kept in the theater, already made by the end of Queen Christina's reign (1654), in a letter of 9 February 1685 (Annerstedt, *Bref* III, 207). Håkan Håkansson's

Anatomens öga: Bildvärld och världsbild på kunskapens näthinna (1995) has a valuable discussion of early modern anatomy and anatomy theaters. One important primary source is a letter Rudbeck wrote on 7 March 1685 (Annerstedt, *Bref* III, 219–23). Opinion differs on the capacity of the theater; Rudbeck said it could hold as many as five hundred, and Eriksson agrees (194), though other observers have pointed to two hundred, which some have even doubted as too high.

Rudbeck's architectural work can be seen in the Atlas volume to *Atlantica*, though it must be remembered that the reproduced images do not always show the buildings as they actually appeared in Rudbeck's day. Some of the drawings were plans, never fulfilled, and others purely dream projects. See, for instance, Josephson, *Det hyperboreiska Uppsala* (1945), 11.

Rudbeck's inventions, such as a technique for improving Archimedean hydraulics, his means of recycling old screws, and a device for hoisting boats into the air in order to repair all the sides at will, are found in many of his letters, including Rudbeck to Bengt Oxenstierna, 23 April 1695 (KB, *Autograf samling*); Rudbeck to Bengt Oxenstierna, 2 December 1700 (Annerstedt, *Bref* IV, 381); Rudbeck to Baron Johan Hoghusen, 3 December 1699 (ULA, *Länsstyrelsen i Uppsala län: Landskansliet biographica* I. D.IV.A 64). The claim that Rudbeck was born under a lucky star is from Esberg's *"Laudatio funebris"* (1703).

CHAPTER 3: REMARKABLE CORRESPONDENCES

The opening quotation is taken from Fyodor Dostoyevski's *Crime and Punishment*, translated by David Magarshack (1987), 20. The reference to Tyrfing as the "keenest of all blades" comes from Christopher Tolkien's translation, *The Saga of King Heidrek the Wise* (1960), 2. Tolkien's edition also prints the opening of Verelius's Uppsala manuscript in appendix A. For more on how the *Hervararsaga* was read in the late seventeenth century, see Schück's *KVHAA* and Vilhelm Gödel's *Fornnorsk-isländsk litteratur i Sverige (till antikvitetskollegiets inrättande)* (1897).

Rudbeck's mapmaking skills were well known among his contemporaries. His work for Carl Gustav Wrangel comes from his letters of 16 May 1674 and 21 May 1674 (RA, *Skokloster samlingen* N:O 75–E 8202). In another example of how Rudbeck's expertise was valued among the Swedish elite, King Charles XI requested his help in the selection of land surveyors, mining officials, and other experts for work in the Baltic. Rudbeck's response is preserved in a letter to the king, 3 June 1688, RA, *Skrivelser till konungen Karl XI,* vol. 32.

"It was like a dream" was how Rudbeck described the sensation in a letter, 12 November 1677, KB, Engestr.*b.iv.1.30* (N:02), printed in Klemming, *Anteckningar om Rudbecks Atland* (1863), Supplement A. Another valuable source is his dedication of *Atl.* I, 3–5. On tracing the origins of the project, Johan Nordström's *De yverbornes ö* (1930), most notably, argues in favor of a connection through the legendary Hyperboreans. The narrative builds upon Nordström's thesis and a comparison with Verelius's *Hervararsaga* (1672), which Rudbeck used in making his map.

Homer's description of life in the Elysian Fields as "the dream of ease" is in the *Odyssey* IV, line 601, and the description of its games, dances, and "brilliant light" in Virgil, *Aeneid* VI, line 637, with the meadows and riverbanks, VI, lines 674–75. Rudbeck discusses the idyllic Elysian Fields most fully in *Atl.* I, 341–45, 352. Later treatments follow, developed and enlarged, including an examination of the Odödsåkern, a polar paradise in the *Hervararsaga* and broadly reminiscent of the classical Elysian Fields. The lack of snowfall, storms, or powerful rains common in classical accounts are, for Rudbeck, descriptions of the land during the summertime.

Rudbeck's words on "peace of mind" and "pen to paper" are found in his letter of 12 November 1677 in Klemming (1863), A. The time of Rudbeck's insight is not known for certain. Many older accounts simply assert, without much support, the early 1670s, but the late 1660s seems more likely. Verelius was working on the Norse *Hervararsaga* by at least 1663, lecturing regularly in the late 1660s. The work was already well enough advanced by August 1669 to have a test printing ready, and to be sent off to De la Gardie. Rudbeck's letters in the late 1660s also show a heightened interest in antiquities, and his references to the ancients become more frequent. Gunnar Eriksson is another person who believes the origins lie in the late 1660s (*Atlanticans naturalhistoria: En antologi,* 7).

The study of Norse sagas in Sweden essentially opened with Verelius, according to Gödel (1897), 216, and more in depth, 241–55. Verelius used Rugman's manuscript for *Götrek and Rolf's Saga* (251) and *Herraud and Bose's Saga* (254). Verelius's title, position, and background are summarized by Lindroth, 275–82, and more fully in *KVHAA*. Gödel also printed the official list of Verelius's duties as Professor of the Antiquities of the Fatherland (1897), 245–46. Verelius's lectures were assessed by Schück as among the "very best held at Uppsala University in the seventeenth century," *KVHAA* I, 231–32. Beginning at 8:00 A.M. and the few students in attendance come from Gödel (1897), 246. Rudbeck's appreciation of Verelius's insights can be found in many places in *Atlantica,* particularly his dedication, unpaginated in the original, page 3 in the modern 1937 edition. It is no coincidence that the first volume of *Atlantica* would be dedicated to Verelius, "its first cause" and "its beginning."

Excerpts of Verelius's letter to the chancellor on behalf of Rudbeck's project, written 20 December 1673, are cited in *Atl.* I, 3–4. Another, though smudged, copy is found at UUB, *Palmsk. samlingen* (344). Loccenius's letter in support of Rudbeck's project, 22 December 1673, can be found in the same two places. Loccenius's reaction was noted in Rudbeck's letter of 12 November 1677, in Klemming (1863), A, and Loccenius's words on *Atlantica*'s potential in his letter of 22 December 1673. As for the Saxo and Shakespeare stories, compare Amleth, Gurutha, Feng, and an unnamed "fair woman" with Hamlet, Gertrude, King Claudius, and Ophelia in *The Tragedy of Hamlet, Prince of Denmark.*

My discussion of the Norse Renaissance is based on the work of Gödel, Schück, and many others, including Thor Beck's *Northern Antiquities in French Learning and Literature 1755–1855* (1934), Anton Blanck's *Den nordiska renässansen i sjuttonhundratalets litteratur* (1911), and Frank Edgar Farley's *Scandinavian Influences in the*

English Romantic Movement (1903). Jørgensen has discussed the Danish context in *Historieforskning og historieskrivning i Danmark indtil aar 1800* (1931). Gifts, exchanges, and piracy, among other things, caused the sagas to circulate in early modern Scandinavia. The phrase "dragon brooding" comes from Lee M. Hollander's commentary (citing a contemporary) in *Poetic Edda,* xi.

The great infusion of sagas and eddas in the seventeenth century, including the seizure of Jörgen Seefeldt's library at Ringsted, and De la Gardie's purchase of Stefanus Johannes Stephanius's large collection of books and manuscripts, is discussed in many sources, e.g., Gödel (1897), 104–6, 90–95. Rugman's manuscripts are analyzed here, too, 95ff., 113–22, and 122ff. On Rugman selling many manuscripts to Verelius, see Gödel, 158. Rugman's arrival in Uppsala as a "gift of heaven" comes from Schück, *KVHAA* I, 203–4.

My account of the relationship between the Greeks and the barbarians is based on many works, including Momigliano's *Alien Wisdom: The Limits of Hellenization* (1975), Paul Cartledge's *The Greeks: A Portrait of Self and Others* (1993), and E. J. Bickerman's "Origines Gentium," in *Classical Philology* 47 (1952). Edith Hall's *Inventing the Barbarian: Greek Self-Definition Through Tragedy* (1989) shows the richness of the material by focusing on the stage of Attic tragedy. Rudbeck's analysis of the ancient term *barbarian* (βάρβαρος) is elaborated more fully in *Atl.* I, 433–34. Of the many works providing an understanding of early modern Gothic romanticism, Svennung's *Zur Geschichte des Goticismus* (1967) overviews both the European phenomenon and its impact in Sweden (68–96). Lindroth, *Stormaktstiden,* 249–74, was also very helpful, as well as his *Medeltiden: Reformationstiden,* 166–72, 288–309. Strindberg recounts the history of the phenomenon against a background of poverty and want (1937), 40–77. See also Nordström (1930); Greenway (1977), 73–82; and Kurt Johannesson, *The Renaissance of the Goths in Sixteenth-Century Sweden: Johannes and Olaus Magnus as Politicians and Historians,* translated by James Larson (1991), as well as Holmquist, *"Till Sveriges ära. Det götiska arvet," Stormaktstid. Erik Dahlbergh och bilden av Sverige* (1992).

Anatomical dissections are discussed many times in Rudbeck's letters. The comment about carrots and turnips comes from one of his letters to De la Gardie, July 1658, printed by Anders Grape, *Bref af Olof Rudbeck d.ä. rörande Uppsala universitet efterskörd* in *Uppsala universitets årskrift* (1930), 5–8. One of Rudbeck's lessons in architecture survives and was printed by Josephson, *Det Hyperboreiska Uppsala,* 85–89. Given his discussions here as well as in *Atlantica,* Josephson calls Rudbeck Sweden's "first architecture theorist," 12.

Rudbeck's love of fireworks and his collection of small cannon are related by many sources. Complaints were made about the noise coming from Rudbeck's workshops, which often disturbed the sleep of the neighbors (Fries, [1896], 11–12). Of the various descriptions of the waterworks, see Rudbeck's letter of 7 March 1685 (Annerstedt, *Bref* III, 223–26). For Rudbeck's many other activities, see Eriksson (2002). For his engineering and technical work, see Per Dahl's dissertation (1995).

CHAPTER 4: A CARTESIAN WITCH HUNT

Charlie Chaplin's words were taken from *My Autobiography* (1964), 320. The debate surrounding the introduction of Cartesian thought was one of the most passionate in Swedish history (*"starkaste strid"* in Annerstedt's words, *UUH* II, 91). "Suspect philosophy" is taken from the letter of protest written by a committee of bishops and theologians to De la Gardie, 19 July 1665.

The Cartesian struggles in Sweden are discussed in Rolf Lindborg's *Descartes i Uppsala: Striderna om "nya filosofien" 1663–1689* (1965). Lindborg gives another account in his essay "De cartesianska striderna," *17 Uppsatser i svensk idé- och lärdomshistoria* (1980). Other valuable treatments are found in Annerstedt, *UUH* II 91–101; Annerstedt, *Bref* I, xxxvi–xlii; Lindroth, *Stormaktstiden*, 447–58; and Lindroth's on the later controversies, 458–65. Richard Watson discusses the European controversies, too, in *Cogito, ergo sum* (2002), 221ff. Descartes' words "vain and useless" come from his *Discourse on the Method of Rightly Conducting the Reason and Seeking Truth in the Sciences,* translated by John Veitch (1974), 40, and "sweep them wholly away," 48.

Uppsala University, like many universities in the seventeenth century, was in service of the Church. See Eriksson (1994), 10, and Lindroth, *Stormaktstiden*, 16, 79. Rudbeck's defense in the Cartesian dispute is taken from his letter to Magnus de la Gardie, 7 September 1668, Annerstedt, *Bref* I, 48–49.

The story of the disgruntled professor of law Håkan Fegraeus comes from Annerstedt's *UUH* II, 107–8. The student rampage of destruction is related in II, 103, and the storming of the royal palace in Annerstedt, *Bref* I, xxviii–xxix. Rudbeck described the violence at the palace in a letter to De la Gardie at the end of February 1667 (Annerstedt, *Bref* I, 45–46). The sentencing of the students comes from *UUH* II, 104.

As another sign of the deteriorating economy, salaries were reduced in 1668 to about 590 a year. Uppsala University's financial problems were based in part on the sharp decline in price for grain, plummeting nearly 50 percent in 1666. This caused the university serious concern because those sales represented a large portion of its income. The economic situation was well covered by Annerstedt's *UUH* I, 330–41; II, 63; and especially II, 109–22, which chronicles the transition from a budgetary surplus to a deficit. Annerstedt also overviews the problems in *Bref* I, xliii–liv. In addition to Rudbeck's letters during the period, particularly one in 1670 (Annerstedt, *Bref* II, 78–90), additional information on the Community House is found in Annerstedt, *UUH* II, 126–34, and *Bref* II, lx–lxviii.

Arrhenius-Örnhielm's background is discussed in Lindroth's *Stormaktstiden*, 327–28. Rudbeck's lengthy defense, 1 July 1670, was printed by Annerstedt in *Bref* I, 52–73. His resignation, however, was refused, and a later direct appeal to the king was also turned down, 20 October 1670 (Annerstedt, *Bref* II, 75–76). Years later, Rudbeck was still trying to get out of his position as curator.

CHAPTER 5: FOLLOW THE FISH!

The words of the biochemist Albert Szent-Györgyi come from Royston M. Roberts's discussion of "how accidents become discoveries" in *Serendipity: Accidental Discoveries in Science* (1989), 245. Rudbeck was working with the "greatest enthusiasm" in his letter to Count de la Gardie, 23 March 1674, Annerstedt, *Bref* II, 95. "Beautiful things" was one way Rudbeck often referred to his discoveries. "One thousand curses" comes from Rudbeck's defense, 1 July 1670, Annerstedt, *Bref* I, 57. The comparison to Achilles appears in Annerstedt, *Bref* II, lv.

Rudbeck's method of investigation is elaborated in *Atl.* I, 81–92. He describes the soil used in the method—the *matjord* or *svartmylla*—in *Atl.* I, 81, and its origins on page 82. The discussion is based on my translation of Rudbeck's own words: *"All thenna Swartmylla samlar sig Årligen meer och meer, men hafwer på åtskilliga orter någon åtskilnad til sin fetma och färg," Atl.* I, 83.

Information about Rudbeck's trial with the container in his garden, his efforts to seek out difficult places, the interview with Swensson, and the tips to the reader is found in *Atl.* I, 82–85. The image of the staff and the humus comes from the Atlas volume (table 31, fig. 102). Eriksson discusses the significance of this method (1994), 15–16, 110–11. It is also treated by Eriksson (1984); Swederus, "Olof Rudbeck den äldre: Huvudsakligen betraktad i sin verksamhet som naturforskare. En skildring," in *Nordisk Tidskrift* (1878); and Sune Lindqvist's article "Olof Rudbeck d.ä. som fältarkeolog," in *Rudbecksstudier* (1930), 249–58. Translation of Rudbeck's words on pollution and reference to this early awareness come from Eriksson (1994), 110. Bruce Trigger provides a brief discussion of Rudbeck in his *History of Archaeological Thought* (1989), 49; and Ole Klindt-Jensen in *A History of Scandinavian Archaeology,* translated by G. Russell Poole (1975), 30–31.

The effects of the burial-mound investigations on his contemporaries have never been fully examined. There are many cases, though, of people who were reading closely, and taking note. The superintendent general of Pomerania, C. T. Rango, praised the "incomparable" *Atlantica,* and tried Rudbeck's methods many times at Greifswald, reporting that it led to accurate results, 8 May 1690, and printed by Nelson (1950), 101. Years before, the Kiel polyhistor D. G. Morhof also admired the "ingenious reasonings" Rudbeck drew by investigating the surface of the earth, 23 June 1681, Nelson (1950), 28. There were of course critiques as well, including a rather lengthy one in the journal *Monatliche Unterredungen einiger Guten Freunde von Allerhand Büchern* . . . appearing in the months February through July 1690.

Homer's words about the Achaean heroes at Troy were taken from the *Iliad* II, lines 472–73. Rudbeck's discussion of the golden age comes from *Atl.* I, 39. As a later addition to this theory, explaining why the Swedes were so silent about their great deeds, Rudbeck pointed to an old piece of parchment that referred to a great burning of old books and manuscripts, ordered in 1001 by King Olof Skotking (*Atl.* III, 12).

The references to the Flood are from Genesis 7:11–12, and *Atl.* I, 81 and 91. The chronology was discussed in many places in the work, for instance I, 546ff., and the calculations based on population, *Atl.* I, 34–38. Eriksson treats Rudbeck's work as an early statistician (1994), 113–17. For more on seventeenth-century views of the Flood, see D. C. Allen's *The Legend of Noah: Renaissance Rationalism in Art, Science, and Letters* (1949), though there is unfortunately nothing here on Rudbeck's theory.

Rudbeck's discussion on the importance of rivers in the development of civilization is found in *Atl.* I, 40–41. Newton's *Chronology of the Ancient Kingdoms Amended* and his "Short Chronicle from the First Memory of Things in Europe, to the Conquest of Persia by Alexander the Great" were published posthumously (1728) and discussed by Frank Manuel, *Isaac Newton, Historian* (1963). Despite many eccentricities in the natural philosopher's published and unpublished work, Manuel argues (page 9) that "the new scientific method pervaded Newton's most recondite antiquarian investigations."

No one could rival the north in fish, *Atl.* I, 56. "Sweden is the inexhaustible cradle of civilization" comes from Professor Musaeus's Latin oration on 26 April 1688 at Kiel University; the text is reprinted in Nelson (1950), 100. The description of Sweden as rich in forests, flocks, and fish also comes from this speech, as did the magnet comparison.

"Clearer than the sun" and more certain than Greek, Latin, and other literary sources references are found in *Atl.* I, 91. Rudbeck explains his certainty about why Sweden must have been one of the first lands inhabited after the Flood, *Atl.* I, 41, as well as 34–41. "The Book of Nature," a very traditional seventeenth-century metaphor, is found in many places of Rudbeck's work, calling it for instance "the greatest, the wisest and the most certain book," *Atl.* II, 49.

Verelius's letter to Count de la Gardie, 20 December 1673, is cited in *Atl.* I, 3–4, and another copy at Uppsala University, *Palmsk. samlingen* (344). Loccenius's letter was written two days later, and can be found in the same two places.

CHAPTER 6: GAZING AT THE FACE OF THOR

The opening words are from Lucius Apuleius, *The Golden Ass* (1951), translated by Robert Graves, 267. My discussion of Count de la Gardie is based on many sources, particularly Fåhraeus's *Magnus Gabriel de la Gardie* (1936), Magnusson's *Magnus Gabriel* (1993), Åslund's *De la Gardie och vältaligheten* (1992), and Rystad's "Magnus Gabriel de la Gardie," in Michael Roberts, ed., *Sweden's Age of Greatness 1632–1718* (1973), 203–36.

The description of De la Gardie's physical appearance and restless building projects is from Lorenzo Magalotti's eyewitness account, *Sverige under år 1674* (1996), 101. See also Magalotti's discussion, 24–31 and 89ff. The number of rooms and the staff in Läckö castle is in Magnusson (1993), 63 and 73–74. De la Gardie is discussed as a patron in Lindahl, *Magnus Gabriel de la Gardie, hans gods och hans folk* (1968); and Hahr, "Magnus Gabriel de la Gardie som konstmece-nat," in *Svensk Tidskrift* (1925). These works cover some of the many churches, hospitals, universities, and other institutions the count supported, as well as his fine collection of art including Titian, Tintoretto, Cranach, and Holbein the Younger. The Swedish National Museum's *Magnus Gabriel de la Gardie* (1980) also provides an overview of the Baroque atmosphere.

Queen Christina's words were translated by Bulstrode Whitelocke, *Journal of the Swedish Embassy* (1855), 344–45. When I was in Stockholm, I was able to see the actual letter Christina wrote to the count, 5 December 1653, RA, *De la Gardiska samlingen. Skrivelser till Magnus Gabriel de la Gardie* E 1371. There is another one dated 11 December 1653, RA, *De la Gardiska samlingen. Skrivelser till Magnus Gabriel de la Gardie* E 1371.

Cutting through the "tall, terrifyingly impenetrable overgrowth" is taken from *Atl.* I, 6, and Rudbeck's arguments about the lack of historical writing in a golden age are from *Atl.* I, 39–40. As he noted, historians must have something to write about, and conflict is one of history's earliest subjects. Nordström (1930) discusses the uses of the Hyperborean legend in Sweden, and other works, cited in the notes for chapter 2, outline the background to Swedish Gothicism. Rudbeck's discussion of the Hyperboreans is found mainly in *Atl.* I, 228–65. Karl Marx's words are from *The Manifesto of the Communist Party,* in *The Revolutions of 1848 Political Writings* I, edited by David Fernbach (1981), 67.

"Wondrous way" comes from Pindar's *Pythian* X, 30, which presents a vivid image of the lyres, flutes, and laurels in a Hyperborean celebration. Herodotus's words on the Hyperboreans are in his *Histories* IV, 13, and also IV, 33ff. Pliny's description of this "happy race" enjoying longevity and bliss in their "woods and groves" (as well as a little skepticism "if we can believe it") is found in *Natural History* IV, 89–91. Pliny discusses them in many other places as well, noting for instance that the "majority of authorities" situated them in Europe (VI, 34). Diodorus Siculus treats the "legendary accounts of the Hyperboreans" in his *Library of History* II, 47.

Rudbeck's mapmaking exercise to demonstrate Ptolemy's errors is re-counted in *Atl.* I, 251–52. The skeletons unearthed are noted in *Atl.* I, 400, and the legends of the giants were all over the Norse manuscripts. The story of Thor's journey comes from *Gylf.* 46. The measuring of students occurs in *Atl.* I, 400. Drawing upon his experiences as a physician, Rudbeck confirms that the Swedes rarely succumbed to the plague, typhus, leprosy, or the worst contagious diseases, which everywhere seemed to claim many victims (*Atl.* I, 58). Swedish longevity and health are also discussed in *Atl.* I, 212–13, 263–65; diet, exercise, and climate were other factors that contributed to the phenomenal health of the Hyperboreans (I, 58). Foreigners unaccustomed to this quality were, according to Rudbeck, quite impressed (*Atl.* I, 263). Evidence sent by his brother Nicholas Rudbeckius about the ages of people in Swedish villages is cited in *Atl.* I, 263. Some notes about various ages in the kingdom also survive at the National Library, *Olof Rudbeck den äldre collectanea* F.e.16.

Discussion of the difficulties of understanding the word *Hyperborean* comes from *Atl.* I, 229–33. Rudbeck's Bore or Bori is most often spelled today Buri, though the spelling of his son's name, Bor, is often still used. Buri is described as "beautiful in appearance, big and powerful" in Snorri Sturluson's *Gylf.* 6. Rudbeck's discussion of the rune outside Ekholm, the tavern song, and his comment on "strange animals," *Atl.* I, 231–33. Odin as "the greatest and most glorious that we know," *Gylf.* 7, with Bor's sons making the world, 8–9, and *Voluspá* 4. Bore place-names being found in Sweden, *Atl.* I, 231–32, with an additional comment on Bor's sons, 246. Bor, the *Bor-barn,* and the golden age are elaborated on 432–42.

Rudbeck's meeting with a "very wise peasant in Röklunda named Anders" is related in *Atl.* I, 68, and his lesson in the use of runic staffs, *Atl.* II, 650. True to form, Rudbeck inserts a formula for any curious reader who wants to make predictions on his own, *Atl.* II, 649–62 (and another one to be clipped out, 552). The survival of the wisdom in the countryside is discussed in *Atl.* I, 212.

Rudbeck was very much interested in folk customs and peasant culture, venturing into villages away from seacoasts, royal courts, markets, universities, and other cosmopolitan entrepôts where customs and languages often mix, *Atl.* III, 171–72. Oral traditions, folk customs, and popular culture help Rudbeck, again and again, interpret classical culture. No nation, Rudbeck believed, could boast of such a profound understanding of the course of the heavenly bodies as could Swedish peasants with runic staffs.

In a similar way, Rudbeck also sought out information from the Saami of the north. Rudbeck gets much of his knowledge about the indigenous peoples from Schefferus's *Lapponia* and Olaus Magnus's *Historia de Gentibus Septentrionalibus.* He also investigated matters for himself, including consulting Swedish officials who had personal acquaintance with the Saami. Rudbeck's discourse on beards appears in *Atl.* III, 516ff., and the peasant mentioned, III, 522.

CHAPTER 7: THE QUEST FOR THE GOLDEN FLEECE

John Adams's words come from Malcolm Forbes's *What Happened to Their Kids?* (1990), 13. Lorenzo Magalotti's descriptions are in his own account, *Sverige under År 1674* (1986): the purpose of his visit is on page 1; his opinions of Uppsala are on 65–68, and Rudbeck 67–68.

Information about the College of Antiquities comes from a number of sources, especially Schück's *KVHAA*; Schück's *Johan Hadorph* (1933), 64–81; and Lindroth's *Stormaktstiden,* 321–27. Runes, burial mounds, old Icelandic sagas, coins, seals, and many other antiquarian matters were part of their domain. Stiernhielm's only known meeting was the first, 25 January 1668, though the first real meeting was arguably 28 May that year (Schück, *Hadorph,* 74–75). The college's rooms are described in Magalotti, *Sverige,* 66, though they were not as appealing to members of the college. Virtually from the beginning, the institution was hoping to move into its own building. Rudbeck had been selected by De la Gardie to be its architect.

The college was called Sweden's first scientific academy, Schück, *KVHAA* II, 30, and it had the most active writers in Sweden, that is, outside of Olof Rudbeck and the legal scholar Stiernhöök, Schück, *KVHAA* III, 44. Hadorph was seen as the youngest, though already a dominant member, Schück, *KVHAA* I, 277.

Hadorph was indeed a significant figure in late-seventeenth-century Swedish cultural and intellectual life. With an assistant and two draftsmen, Hadorph rode throughout the country investigating its antiquities. Coins, medals, and gold rings were found, as well as a great collection of church silver buried in the Linköping area. His collections would eventually form the basis for Stockholm's Historical Museum (Schück, *Hadorph,* 194). Like Rudbeck, too, Hadorph wrote down old songs, including some gathered from the mother of one of his colleagues. Hadorph's many achievements are summarized in Schück, *Hadorph,* 193–265. His family is discussed in Schück, *Hadorph,* 4–7, and his educational training is noted on 7–17, as well as in Lindroth, *Stormaktstiden,* 321–27.

The law protecting Swedish antiquities is discussed by Schück in *Hadorph,* 60–64, and more elaborately in many places in his *KVHAA.* Lindroth calls the law simply the first of any country, *Stormaktstiden,* 249. Rudbeck was probably not then captivated by antiquities, Atterbom suggests (1850), 450. Arrhenius's words on the "cloud castle of hypotheses" come from KB, *Örnhielmiana* (O.20), and Annerstedt discusses the college well in many places, for instance, *UUH* I, 271–76, and II, 66. Magalotti's judgment of *Atlantica* is found in *Sverige,* 68.

My discussion of Rudbeck's theory of Jason and the Argonauts is based primarily on his account in *Atl.* I, 418–27. Helping me to understand this episode were some influential classical sources describing the quest: Apollonius of Rhodes's *Argonautica,* Ovid's *Metamorphoses,* and Pindar's *Pythian* IV, as well as shorter accounts in Apollodorus's *Library* I, 16–28; Diodorus Siculus's *Library of History* IV, 40–56; Herodotus's *Histories* IV, 179; and references in Euripides' *Medea.* That the Argonauts were the only ones known to have passed the dangerous crashing rocks is mentioned in the *Odyssey* XII, lines 85–90. Summary reviews of the Argonauts' adventure were also consulted, including Edith Hamilton's *Mythology,* 117–30; Robert Graves's *The Greek Myths* II, 215–56; W. H. D. Rouse's *Gods, Heroes and Men of Ancient Greece,* 89–108; and Lempière's *Classical Dictionary,* 70–80, 334–35. See also Mauricio Obregón's *Beyond the Edge of the Sea* (2002), as well as his earlier *From Argonauts to Astronauts: An Unconventional History of Discovery* (1977).

Rudbeck's quest was "the second Argonautick expedition" referred to by Thomas Haak, 29 March 1682, printed in *Auctarium Testimoniorum de Cl Rudbeckii Atlantica 1685,* Nelson (1950), 36.

"Terror seized him . . ." appears in Pindar's *Pythian* IV, 95, and the centaur galloping down to wave them off is in Apollonius of Rhodes's *Argonautica* I, 551–55, with baby Achilles in the arms of Chiron's wife, *Argonautica* I, 556–58. The *Argo* as the "first ship ever built" is in Ovid, *Metamorphoses* VI, 721; and its antiquity in classical mythology is mentioned in Homer, *Odyssey* XII, lines 85–90.

The following lines are in Pindar's *Pythian* IV: "locks of glorious hair fell rippling down," 83; fleece of "gleaming gold," 231; and "flower of sailing men," 189. Accounts of the crew often varied. The oldest sources are silent on Atalanta's participation, and many reviewers, including Lemprière, do not bother to mention her in the context of the Argonauts. But classical mythology seldom has only one version of a story, and it was difficult for later chroniclers to resist including this brave maiden hunter in the expedition. So, while Pindar and Ovid make no mention, she appears in later accounts from Apollodorus (I.ix.16) to Diodorus Siculus (IV.41.2).

Rudbeck's map of *Atlantica* is found in KB, *Atland tabulae med anteckningar av O Rudbecks hand* (F.m.73). This manner of sailing as "coastal navigation and island-hopping" comes from Obregón, *Beyond the Edge of the Sea*, 42. "Hugging the right side of the coast" are Rudbeck's words, *Atl.* I, 419. The various conflicting theories on the return voyage are discussed by Robert Graves in *The Greek Myths* II, 241–44, and by Timothy Gantz in *Early Greek Myth: A Guide to Literary and Artistic Sources* (1993), 362. Rudbeck's treatment comes especially from *Atl.* I, 418–27. The oldest texts as more authoritative is discussed in many places of *Atlantica*, for instance, I, 8.

The text of the *Argonautica Orphica* is reproduced with a French translation in Francis Vian's *Les Argonautiques orphiques* (1987), and John Warden has edited a collection of essays titled *Orpheus: The Metamorphoses of a Myth* (1982). The Viking paths to the east using the Russian rivers are indeed seen on Swedish runes, Sven B. F. Jansson, *The Runes of Sweden*, translated by Peter G. Foote (1962), 25ff. Rudbeck's Argonaut experiment with his yachts is related in *Atl.* I, 420ff. Hornius's account and the Russian rivers are in Eriksson (1994), 30, 111–12. Additional information comes from Rudbeck's letters, which describe Rudbeck borrowing maps of Russian rivers from the Swedish state, and even writing to ask the count about knowledge of its river systems, 20 February 1674, RA, *Kanslers embetets handlingar för Uppsala universitet Arkiv* E.11:5.

Rudbeck's yacht service was sometimes discussed in his letters, including his complaint that independent "rowing wenches" were eating into his market, 4 October 1697, ULA, *Länsstyrelsen i Uppsala län. Landskansliet biographica* I. D.IV.A, vol. 64. Rudbeck's first proposal for the postal service was published in *Historisk Tidskrift* (1899), vol. 19, 164–66. His critique of contemporary boatmen is from *Atl.* III, 341.

Thor Heyerdahl's experimental archaeology can be seen and appreciated in many of his works, and the example in the narrative is found in his *Kon-Tiki: Across the Pacific by Raft*, translated by F. H. Lyon (1964). Place-names in Sweden cited in the search for the Golden Fleece are in *Atl.* I, 424. The fact that Achilles was still a baby at the time of the Argonauts' quest is evident in Apollonius, *Argonautica* I, 556–58, and Rudbeck's words about choosing the true dreamer are found in *Atl.* I, 427.

Verelius's help to Rudbeck is described in many places, particularly the dedication to *Atl.* I, 3–5. The sources for the dispute with the eminent Danish anatomist Thomas Bartholin are cited in the notes to chapter 1. Rudbeck the Uppsala student also lost out on the discovery of the thoracic duct, just barely behind the French anatomist Jean Pecquet (Lindroth, *Stormaktstiden*, 420–21). The press is described by Annerstedt in *UUH* I, 357–60; II, 140–53, and the lawsuit continued, II, 199–202. The trial is also discussed in Annerstedt, *Bref* II, lxxii–xc. Rudbeck described the trial in his letters, for instance, relating some background to the problems from his perspective, 6 June 1681 (Annerstedt, *Bref* III, 72–73).

Odysseus's description of the approaching Underworld comes from the *Odyssey* XI, lines 14–21, and another valuable account later, when Hermes escorts the shades of the suitors there, appears at the opening of Book XXIV. Circe's "flawless bed of love" is found in the *Odyssey* X, line 390, and her advice on how Odysseus must sail to the "cold homes of Death" and hear "prophecy from the rapt shade of blind Teiresias," X, lines 540–50. The English astronomer Norman Lockyer used the Greek word in naming the element helium, "the element of the sun," first seen on the new spectroscope during the solar eclipse of 1868.

Rudbeck's discovery of the Underworld was first discussed in some detail in *Atl.* I, 332–50. The "sunless Underworld" comes from Homer, *Odyssey* IV, lines 886–88. Rudbeck overlooks Homer's words that no one had ever sailed there before, *Odyssey* X, lines 556–57 and line 597. Rudbeck believed this was contradicted by the many accounts of heroes who did in fact sail there, *Atl.* I, 332–34. Yet, as usual, Rudbeck must be watched. Perseus's trip, which he discusses, was not to the Underworld, but, as Pindar made clear, to the land of the Hyperboreans, though by now Rudbeck was convinced that this was essentially another name for the Underworld.

Explaining why Homer calls the inhabitants dead, Rudbeck offers another reason: the Swedes were called "the dead" because they tended to be fair, whiter and paler than the ancients in the Mediterranean, *Atl.* II, 388–89. Possibly, too, the idea arose from their complacency, or from the lack of action among the peaceful, prosperous civilization. Circe's instructions to Odysseus to sail north are in Homer's *Odyssey* X, 562–63. Rudbeck's discussion of the *Cimmerii*, or Cimmerians, is found in *Atl.* I, 326–32, with discussions in other places as well, including on Cimmerian darkness, I, 359, and the Cimmerian place-names, 426. Magic was discussed near his proposed Underworld in many places of the *Atlantica*—the claim of not having enough ink to record all the stories of soothsayers comes from *Atl.* I, 213. Rudbeck's treatment of the various visits to the Underworld, *Atl.* I, 213, and the Underworld as cultural center, *Atl.* I, 347. His sources agreed, with the phrase about Zoroaster found in Olaus Magnus, *Description of the Northern Peoples,* edited by Peter Fisher, Humphrey Higgens, and Peter Foote, I–III (1996–99), I, 172. Reference to the spectacular ice formations, as well as the mists around the caves, come from this source, 50–51, and Magalotti's comments on witchcraft are in *Sverige,* 68.

Tiresias was the famous seer of the Underworld, who gave Odysseus advice on how to reach home, *Odyssey* XI, line 100ff. He was so wise that even the gods asked his advice, Ovid, *Metamorphoses* III, 300. Tiresias was spelled, according to Rudbeck, in a variety of ways: Tyrisas, Turrisas, Tyreas, *Atl.* I, 357. The ancient seer was originally the Swedish Tyr, who, in the words of the *Edda*, "was so clever that a man who is clever is said to be *ty*-wise," *Gylf.* 25, and Rudbeck's discussion, *Atl.* I, 311–12. Rudbeck's expedition, led by Samuel Otto, is described in *Atl.* I, 227, 415, and images are printed in the Atlas volume (table 30, figs. 101–3).

Rudbeck's etymology of the Underworld's Charon the boatman was derived from the Swedish *bårin* or *barin,* meaning "boat" (*Atl.* I, 350). Rudbeck was possibly influenced by Diodorus Siculus, who derived the name from the Egyptian word for boat, *Library of History* I. 92. 3–4, I. 96. 8–9.

CHAPTER 8: MOUNTAINS DON'T DANCE

My discussion of Atlantis is based primarily on the oldest known accounts, Plato's *Timaeus* and *Critias* dialogues, translated by R. G. Bury for the Loeb Classical Library (1999). A century before these dialogues, the historian Herodotus wrote about a people called the Atlantes who lived in Africa and were said "to eat no living creature and never to dream," *Histories* IV, 184. Another fifth-century-B.C. historian, Thucydides, wrote about the island Atalanta, which also, incidentally, was said to have suffered an earthquake and a flood, *The Peloponnesian War* III, 89. But neither these people nor the place is demonstrably connected to Plato's more famous Atlanteans.

The Atlantis controversy is surveyed in a number of works, including Richard Ellis's *Imagining Atlantis* (1998), Paul Jordan's *Atlantis Syndrome* (2001), and L. Sprague de Camp's *Lost Continents: The Atlantis Theme in History, Science, and Literature* (1970). Among many other interesting assessments are Edwin Ramage, ed., *Atlantis, Fact or Fiction?* (1978), James Bramwell's *Lost Atlantis* (1937), and Phyllis Young Forsyth's *Atlantis: The Making of Myth* (1980). Accounts of other searches for Atlantis and theories trying to solve the riddle also helped me understand Rudbeck's early venture: Ignatius Donnelly, *Atlantis: The Antediluvian World* (1881, reprinted 1971); Otto Muck, *The Secret of Atlantis,* translated by Fred Bradley (1981); Charles Berlitz, *The Mystery of Atlantis* (1969); and others. Charles R. Pellegrino has written an absorbing account of the Thera-Crete theory in *Unearthing Atlantis: An Archaeological Odyssey* (1991), as has J. V. Luce in *The End of Atlantis* (1969). Retired Royal Air Force cartographer J. M. Allen's *Atlantis, the Andes Solution: The Discovery of South America as the Legendary Continent* (1997) is also provocative.

The discussions about the nature of justice, referred to in the text, are from Plato's *Republic,* a series of conversations that were supposed to have occurred immediately before the opening of the dialogue *Timaeus,* 17C–19A. The *Timaeus, Critias,* and *Hermocrates,* which exists today only in fragments, were intended to form a trilogy, according to Bury (1999), 3. That Critias's great-grandfather was Dropides is in *Timaeus* 20E, and the Egyptian priest's words on the Greeks as always children are from *Timaeus* 22B. The alleged old tradition is noted in *Timaeus* 20D, and the impact on Critias as a boy in *Timaeus* 26C.

In dealing with the chronology of Atlantis, there is some discrepancy in Plato's own account. In the *Timaeus* it is claimed that the history of the Egyptians stretched back eight thousand years from the time of the priests' discussion with Solon (*Timaeus* 23E), meaning that the war with Atlantis occurred sometime after 8600 B.C. But in the *Critias* it was noted that "9000 is the sum of years since the war occurred, as is recorded . . ." (108E), reckoning from the time of Socrates, Critias, Hermocrates, and Timaeus's discussions. The war with Atlantis, in other words, occurred, according to Plato, either sometime after 8600 B.C. or about 9400 B.C. (Jordan [2001], 17–20). This is why the narrative opts for a rounded 9000 B.C.

Plato's words on the truth of the story are found in *Timaeus* 20D, and Aristotle's skepticism comes indirectly, namely in a source, no longer in existence, cited by Strabo in *Geography* 2.3.6. One list of believers and critics, though incomplete, can be found in de Camp (1970), Appendix C, 314–18. The comments from Plutarch about Plato derive from his biographical portrait of Solon, printed in many available formats, for instance the compilation *The Rise and Fall of Athens* (1984), 43–76; the references to Solon, Plato, and their intentions were taken from 75–76. A "fine but undeveloped site" is a paraphrase of Plutarch's words. Herodotus's visit to Egypt is recounted in the *Histories* II. Pliny's words on Aristotle's breath are in *Natural History* VIII, 44.

"By God's Grace" comes from Rudbeck's letter to the chancellor, December 1674, Annerstedt, *Bref* II, 98. Rudbeck's discussion of Atlantis is from *Atl.* I, 92–190. Plato's "the fairest of all plains" is in *Critias* 113C, and the discussion on the fertility of Old Uppsala is from *Atl.* I, 106–7, 122, 167. Rudbeck's sources included among others Snorri's *Heimskringla* (225 and 68). The size of Atlantis is discussed in Plato's *Critias* 118A, and Rudbeck's *Atl.* I, 94ff.

The account of Rudbeck's first investigation at Old Uppsala is found in his letter of 12 November 1677, printed in Klemming (1863), A. His citing of the old hill was based on Plato's words about the mountain in the distance of the great plain, *Critias* 113C. The six mathematical students are noted in *Atl.* I, 109. Plato's description of these features comes from *Critias*: the water 113E, 117A–117C, and the racetrack 117C, with Rudbeck's discussion, including his conversations with the older gentlemen, *Atl.* I, 113ff. "Not a single point" claim comes from the letter of 12 November 1677. The map of Atlantis, with the rivers and all the sites, is reproduced in the Atlas volume (table 9, fig. 27). Rudbeck on the higher water levels and the annual recession, *Atl.* I, 116. Uppland underwater is found in Franklin D. Scott's *Sweden: The Nation's History* (1988), 4.

Plato's description of the Poseidon temple at the center of Atlantis comes from *Critias* 116C–117A, with the reference to the "encircling wall of gold" in *Critias* 116C. The "precepts of Poseidon" are in *Critias* 119C, and the rituals associated with preserving justice, including the bull hunt, the drinking of the blood-wine mixture, and the offering of the golden cup to the temple, are at 119D–120C. The sacred grove is in *Critias* 117B. Rudbeck discusses his findings, *Atl.* I, 152–65. His textual source on the Old Uppsala temple was primarily Adam of Bremen's *Gesta Hammaburgensis ecclesiae pontificum*, particularly Book IV, 26–27. He discusses the temple, the golden chain, the spring, the statues of the gods, and the ceremony with the sacrifices. The temple is also discussed by later humanists, Olaus Magnus's account, *Description of the Northern Peoples*, 156–58, being especially influential. Magnus's reconstruction, though, certainly looked very much like a late medieval or early Renaissance building: Josephson, *Det hyperboreiska Uppsala* (1945), 40.

Rudbeck's principles of source criticism, his discussion of the trip, and the unlikelihood of agreement on the details are found in *Atl.* I, 9. The example of the four apostles also comes from this passage. Had they agreed in all respects, then Rudbeck would have argued that they came from the same source, *Atl.* I, 12. Rudbeck is here using an established philological principle of source criticism. L. D. Reynolds and N. G. Wilson discuss this principle in *Scribes and Scholars: A Guide to the Transmission of Greek and Latin Literature* (1991), 208–10, as does Anthony Grafton's *Defenders of the Text: Traditions of Scholarship in an Age of Science 1450–1800* (1991), particularly in his discussion of the Renaissance humanist Poliziano.

Analysis of the Atlantis temple and the search in Old Uppsala is recounted in *Atl.* I, 152ff. and 164–165. "Every nook and cranny" comes from this last passage. Rudbeck's various outings, for instance accompanied by Professor Celsius, is told in *Atl.* I, 300. Human sacrifice and sacred groves were also noted by the Roman Tacitus observing the customs of the Germanic tribes, including the Suebi, in his *Germania*, 39.

Törnewall's figures for *Atlantica* are noted in Klemming (1863), 6, and Josephson, *Det hyperboreiska Uppsala* (1945), 9–10. Another helpful artist was one of Rudbeck's students, Samuel Otto. Rudbeck's technological students are discussed particularly by Per Dahl, *Svensk ingenjörskonst under stormaktstiden: Olof Rudbecks tekniska undervisning och praktiskaverkamhet* (1995).

Rudbeck hoped to begin printing his book, 28 December 1674, Annerstedt, *Bref* II, 98–99. The firing of Curio and the legal process are discussed in Annerstedt's *Bref* II, lxxii–lxxix, and *UUH* II, 140–44. References to the problems with the previous bookseller and Hadorph's cattle come from Eriksson (2002), 103. Among other places, the prosecution's complaints can be seen in surviving letters in the Örnhielm papers, KB, *Örnhielmiana* (O.20). Rudbeck's letter to De la Gardie, 31 March 1675, is printed in Annerstedt, *Bref* II, 107–10. The tendency to hypochondria was noted, for instance, by Strindberg, *Bondenöd och stormaktsdröm*, 248ff.

CHAPTER 9: TWELVE TRUMPETS, FOUR KETTLEDRUMS, AND A BAG OF GOLD

The epigraph is taken from *The Confessions of Jean-Jacques Rousseau*, translated by J. M. Cohen (1954), 52. De la Gardie's collection of antiquities is discussed in many works cited above, particularly Fåhraeus (1936), Gödel (1897), Schück (1932–35), and Hahr (1925). Peter Englund discusses the client-patron relationship in Stellan Dahlgren, ed., *Makt och vardag: Hur man styrde, levde och tänkte under svensk stormaktstid* (1993). Rudbeck repeatedly thanked the count for his help. His phrase on the "greatest supporter" is often repeated, for instance, 3 September 1678, Annerstedt, *Bref* II, 162.

The descriptions of King Charles XI are derived from Magalotti's observations, *Sverige*, 80ff. My discussion was also based on the studies by Göran Rystad, *Karl XI: En biografi* (2001); Anthony Upton, *Charles XI and Swedish Absolutism* (1998), and Michael Roberts, "Charles XI," in his *Essays in Swedish History* (1967). Another good description of the king comes from Robinson's *Account of Sweden 1688*, recently published and edited with an introduction by John B. Hattendorf (1998), particularly pages 30–31. Many of Rudbeck's surviving letters to the king are housed in the Swedish National Archives, for instance, *Skrivelser till konungen Karl XI* (6459.52, vol. 14, and 1133.10, vol. 32).

De la Gardie performed many valuable services for Rudbeck, and the Uppsala professor was deeply grateful, as can be seen again and again in their correspondence. Rudbeck's appreciation is obvious, for instance, in an early letter after the count was won over to the search, 17 February 1674, Annerstedt, *Bref* II, 92. De la Gardie would prove to be Rudbeck's "greatest supporter," the words coming from Rudbeck, in a letter to the count, 3 April 1677, Annerstedt, *Bref* II, 156–57, and G. Klemming (1863), Supplement E. See also Rudbeck's letter, 13 June 1681, RA, *Kanslers embetets handlingar för Uppsala universitet arkiv* E. II:7.

The count's financial gift and promise to seek support from the king are noted in Rudbeck's letter of 12 November 1677, in Klemming (1863), A. The relationship between Rudbeck and Charles XI is overviewed in Eriksson (2002), 184–85; Annerstedt's *Bref* III, clxxxii–clxxxiii; and Atterbom (1851), 98–99. The account of the university's preparations for the coronation is based upon Annerstedt's *UUH* II, 153–54. "The house of nobility" is a translation of the Swedish *riddarhus*. David Klöcker Ehrenstrahl's painting of the coronation is housed today in the Drottningholm collection. Rudbeck's part in the festivities, particularly singing over the trumpets and drums, is in Carl-Allen Moberg's "Olof Rudbeck d.ä. och musiken," in *Rudbecksstudier* (1930), 179.

Unfortunately, Rudbeck's composition for the coronation has apparently not survived, lost like his other works for weddings, funerals, and other state occasions, including Charles XII's coronation. Only one known composition exists, a funeral dirge (1654) for the chancellor Axel Oxenstierna at Stockholm's Storkyrka. It was recorded for the Royal Academy of Music's Musica Sueciae series, *Dygd och Ära: Adeln och Musiken i Stormaktstidens Sverige* (1992). The text of

Rudbeck's music took the form of a dialogue, with the lyrics largely inspired by the Book of Revelation, and performed by two sopranos or tenors. Some of Rudbeck's other compositions can only be partly imagined—for instance, Rudbeck's use of Psalms 25 for the music he wrote for De la Gardie's funeral. Carl-Allen Moberg's article (1930) is valuable for understanding Rudbeck's work as a musician and composer.

Animosity between Sweden and Denmark is well known, and Strindberg discusses *danskhat,* or hatred of the Danes (1937), 46–48, 164–168, 194ff. Kurt Johannesson recounts its flourishing in the sixteenth century (1991), 106ff. Charles X Gustav's invasion of Denmark is recounted in Alf Ålberg, "Tåget över Bält," in *Karolinska Tiden 1654–1718 Den Svenska Historien* V (1967), 30–33. The number of troops crossing the frozen Great and Little Belts in early 1658 comes from T. K. Derry, *A History of Scandinavia* (1979), 133. The charges against De la Gardie, this time, are highly unlikely. That De la Gardie would confide such treacherous comments to known enemies strains belief.

Jerker Rosén discusses the Battle of Fehrbellin in *Karolinska Tiden 1654–1718* (1967), 94–95. John Robinson called this battle "a disaster so little foreseen, or provided for, that it made a more easy way for all the miseries that ensued upon it," in his *Account of Sweden, 1688* (1998), 35, though historians tend to see its influence as more psychological than strategic. The description of the *Kronan*'s sinking is in Rystad (2001). The flagship is described by many sources, including Magalotti, *Sverige,* 22–23, and Lindquist, *Historien om Sverige: Storhet och fall* (1995), 135–47. The *Kronan* probably had 126 bronze guns on board, though most estimates put the figure between 124 and 128. Besides the cannon, a talented team of underwater archaeologists have uncovered no fewer than twenty thousand objects on the site, many now on display at the Kalmar läns museum. Anders Franzén's discovery is remarkable for understanding the Swedish Age of Greatness, though often overshadowed by his earlier and more famous discovery of the Vasa ship.

Embarrassments in the Danish war unleashed a "storm of ill will" against the chancellor (Strindberg [1937], 228–33, 240). The French would not have liked to hear that some of their subsidies to the Swedish army were being funneled by De la Gardie to the College of Antiquities.

CHAPTER 10: ALL OARS TO ATLANTIS

Rudbeck's treatment of the rivers and forests is found in *Atl.* I, 121–22. On the history of the search for Atlantis, see the notes to chapter 7. The resilience of classical texts to withstand the force of new facts is discussed by Anthony Grafton in *New Worlds, Ancient Texts: The Power of Tradition and the Shock of Discovery* (1992). Grafton shows how reluctant many Renaissance humanists and explorers were to shift out of the older classical perspective, and how easily new, apparently contradictory facts were incorporated. Ptolemy's maps underestimating the voyage are from J. H. Parry, ed., *The European Reconnaissance* (1968), 152.

Plato's words on the size of Atlantis are found in *Timaeus* 24E, and those on its wealth in *Critias* 114. The description of the Aztec gold comes from Miguel Leon-Portilla, ed., *The Broken Spears: The Aztec Account of the Conquest of Mexico* (1962), 51. The wealth is also discussed by Parry (1968), 171–231, and in *Prescott's Histories: The Rise and Decline of the Spanish Empire,* edited by Irwin R. Blacker (1963), 94–103; Cortés, 153ff.; and the capital, 184–258. The figures on the gold and silver are cited by J. H. Elliot, *The Old World and the New 1492–1650* (1992), 60–61. Montaigne's words come from his *Essays* (1580, reprinted 1958), translated by J. M. Cohen, "On Cannibals," 106. Words on Atlantis as not "fable, but veritable history" are found in Donnelly's *Atlantis: The Antediluvian World* (1881), 1–4, 217ff., and 283–86, with the pyramids, 335–42, and the obelisks, 367. The reference to museums in the future comes from Donnelly's *Atlantis,* 480, and the Jules Verne passage is from his *Twenty Thousand Leagues under the Sea,* translated by Mendor T. Brunetti (1969), 265. The Mardi Gras celebration of 1883 and the correspondence with W. E. Gladstone are in Martin Ridge, *Ignatius Donnelly: The Portrait of a Politician* (1962), 202.

Rudbeck's discussion of the lost civilization comes earliest in *Atl.* I, 92–190. The size of Atlantis as "larger than Libya and Asia" appears in Plato's *Timaeus* 24E, and *Critias* 108E–109A, and Rudbeck, *Atl.* I, 93–94. The reference to the opinion of the common boatman is in *Atl.* I, 94, and the comparison with the war between Sweden and Denmark, *Atl.* I, 12. Rudbeck's discussion of Νῆσος is found in *Atl.* I, 95–96.

Atlas, king of Atlantis, is described in Plato's *Critias* 114A. Rudbeck's comments on this ruler and the place-names around Sweden with the Atlas root are in *Atl.* I, 135–44. Atle is discussed in Norse poems, particularly the *Skaldskaparmal* in the *Edda,* and the *Atla-kviða* and *Atla-mál* in the *Poetic Edda.* The "high-builded towers" of Atle's halls is in *Atla-kviða* 14, with the "far-famed temples" and "roaring flames" in *Atla-kviða* 45. The destruction is elaborated in *Atla-mál,* 79ff. Theories still differ on this Atle figure, often spelled Atli, though many view him as a memory of Attila, king of the Huns, well known among the Goths, *Fragment of a Sigurth Lay,* in Lee M. Hollander's translation of *The Poetic Edda* (2001), 244, n. 6. The explanation of the name of King Atlas and its change from the Atlantean language to Greek is found in Plato's *Critias* 113A–113B, with Rudbeck's discussion in *Atl.* I, 123–45. The Atlas Mountains, also found in Sweden, are discussed in *Atl.* I, 215–18, 226–28, and other places.

Rudbeck's theory about the Pillars of Hercules comes from *Atl.* I, 145–50. Strabo's helpful passage is in *Geography* 3.5.5–6, and the rumor of the pillars lying in the north is in Tacitus, *Germania* 34; the Roman historian was citing the opinion of Drusus Germanicus, Nero Drusus, brother of Emperor Tiberius. Rudbeck also tells of a curious dinner party at De la Gardie's Venngarn Castle. When the French ambassador to Stockholm, Monsieur le Marquis de Feuquière, inquired about the progress of Rudbeck's work on *Atlantica,* Count de la Gardie told of the latest finding that the Pillars of Hercules were not in the Mediterranean, but in Öresund. At that point another Frenchman at the dinner, Monsieur le Picquiettiere, spoke up, noting that he, too, had reached this conclusion on their northern location (*Atl.* I, 149–50).

Rudbeck traced the Roman form of the ancient hero's name (Hercules) back to the Swedish *her* and *kulle* or *kolle,* meaning either the head or leader of an army, and the Greek Heracles to the Swedish *Herkulle* (also spelled as Hereker, Herakled, or other variants), meaning one dressed or armed as a warrior (*Atl.* I, 473–74). Rudbeck presented a list of verbs, nouns, and adjectives with variant spellings found in Norse sagas to support his theory (*Atl.* I, 471–73). Had he looked into Pindar's *Olympian* III, he would have been delighted to read about Hercules' visit to the Hyperboreans, bringing the olive tree back for the Olympian Games. The story was seconded by Pausanias, who called the Hyperborean origins a local tradition in *Description of Greece* 5.7.7.

But, despite Rudbeck's use of *Germania,* Tacitus would probably not have agreed with his interpretation of the Pillars of Hercules. The Roman historian continued: "It may be that Hercules did go there [the rumored northern pillars]; or perhaps it is only that we by common consent ascribe any remarkable achievement in any place to his famous name" (*Germania* 34). Rudbeck's discussion also overlooks many alternative explanations, including the views of writers he held in high esteem, like Diodorus Siculus's *Library of History* IV.18.4–5 or Pliny's *Natural History* III, 3–4, both of which support the more traditional location of Gibraltar.

"Not a single one" and Rudbeck's commentary on Plato's Atlantis as "looking into a mirror" are in *Atl.* I, 181. Given how well he understood Sweden, Plato was the "wisest" of the Greeks, clearly capturing the northern landscape (*Atl.* I, 335 and 485); his golden words (336). Rudbeck's words on the "102 Platonic oars" comes from *Atl.* I, 190, translated by Eriksson (1994), 23.

The war with Denmark was starting to affect Rudbeck and the town of Uppsala (21 May 1676, Annerstedt, *Bref* II, 132–33). The war was also threatening the university's income (3 September 1678, Annerstedt, *Bref* II, 161–62), not to mention the lives of many professors. Hadorph, for instance, feared that the Danes would learn from Gotland fishermen how easy it would be to move inland. Swedes were starting to hide valuables in the forests, a fact Hadorph mentioned in a letter published by Schück in *Hadorph,* 217–20.

Rudbeck had printed an invitation to a dissection in his anatomy theater in Swedish, 1 May 1677 (Annerstedt, *Bref* II, 148–49). Annerstedt also published Rudbeck's program intending to bury a dissected body, 28 May 1677 (*Bref* II, 155). On Rudbeck's building projects, see Ragnar Josephson, *Det hyperboreiska Uppsala* (1945), particularly 61–84. That the survival of Atlantis was dependent on its virtues is stated in Plato's *Critias* 120D–121C and in *Atl.* I, 187–88.

CHAPTER 11: OLYMPUS STORMED

The epigraph is from Nietzsche's *The Birth of Tragedy,* translated by Francis Golffing (1956), 29. The dimensions of the Atlantis plain, 3,000 stadia long and

2,000 wide, are found in Plato's *Critias*, 118A. One scholar who has worked meticulously to find such a large plain is J. M. Allen, though he had to cut the measurement of the stadium in half; see *Atlantis, the Andes Solution: The Discovery of South America as the Legendary Continent* (1997). The royal palace of Atlantis is discussed by Plato in *Critias* 115C–115D, and Rudbeck's connection with *Kungsgård* in *Atl.* I, 115ff., with a discussion of the use of the "Atlantis" stones to build the Uppsala castle in *Atl.* I, 180–81. On the lack of walls surfacing in his site, Rudbeck found assistance from another member of the Riksråd, Gabriel Oxenstierna, who informed him that the surrounding forests and hills were sometimes called "walls" in the past (*Atl.* I, 120).

Rudbeck's arguments on why Plato's story about the destruction of the island was not literally correct is found in *Atl.* I, 183–88. Information on the "barrier of mud" is found in *Critias* 109A. The reference to the Great Flood comes from Genesis 9:11. Two other points about Plato's account that Rudbeck said were incorrect were Atlantis's elephants and wine. The wine was actually Swedish mead, and the elephants were wolves (and later, at the suggestion of De la Gardie's son, moose) (*Atl.* I, 183–85). Rudbeck's argument based on the lunar calendar appears in *Atl.* I, 187, 485. In his interpretation of *Critias* 108E, Rudbeck counts the nine thousand years from the time of Solon's visit to Egypt, and not from the time of Socrates' Hermocrates, Timaeus, and Critias discussion about Atlantis. See notes on the chronology of Atlantis in the notes for chapter 7. Allen, who discussed how the Incans had long used the lunar calendar, is one prominent exception to the tendency noted in the text.

Everything fit so well for Rudbeck's theory, he thought that Plato's words on the "hot baths" of Atlantis were ancient references to the Swedish love of saunas (*Critias* 117B and *Atl.* I, 166, 409). As Rudbeck would later put it, "To say that Atlantis is sunk is a greater vanity than all vanity" (*Atl.* II, 28).

Complaints about Rudbeck's neglect of his teaching in these years are treated in Annerstedt, *Bref* II, cxix–cxx, and the waterworks system's not working by 1676 is noted in Annerstedt, *Bref* I, ix. For more background on the waterworks system, see Rudbeck's letter to the Inquisition, 7 March 1685, Annerstedt, *Bref* III, 219–26, especially 223–26. The need for a new roof on the anatomy theater was noted by Rudbeck in a letter to De la Gardie, 24 February 1675, printed in Annerstedt, *Bref* II, 100, and the collapsed bridge in a letter of 1 May 1677, Annerstedt, *Bref* II, 147.

Diodorus Siculus's comments on Atlantis come from his *Library of History* III, 56–61. With his discussion of King Atlas, the empire, and the many achievements, Diodorus almost offers a blueprint for Rudbeck and many other Atlantis enthusiasts: "The great majority of the most ancient heroes trace their descent back to the Atlantides" (III.60.5). Hera's words in the narrative come originally from Homer's *Iliad* XIV, lines 200–205. Hesiod describes the mythic home of the Titans "hidden under a misty gloom, in a dank place where are the ends of the huge earth" in *Theogony* 729–31, and the words "ends of gloomy earth" and "home of murky night" appear at 736–46. "The glowing Sun never looks upon them," *Theogony* 758–60.

The Norse sagas at Rudbeck's disposal included original manuscripts of the *Poetic Edda,* Snorri's *Edda,* his *Heimskringla,* and many others. Most of the Norse sagas were written during the Middle Ages, especially in the thirteenth century. Some, however, were only copies from even later times. At least a few were written down in the seventeenth century, probably before being carried over by an Icelandic student.

Hephaestus fell a few times from the sky, according to the *Iliad,* Books I and XVIII. That the ancient Greek gods came from abroad was a belief that could be read in Herodotus's *Histories,* which specifically traced them back to Egypt. The only exceptions, the historian claimed, were Hera, Hestia, Themis, the Dioscuri, the Graces, the Nereids, and Poseidon, who, he said, came from the Pelasgians or, in the case of Poseidon, Libya (II, 50). Cronos, Rhea, and the devouring of their "splendid children" is in *Theogony* 453ff. It is well known that the Titans, in ancient myth, were imprisoned after their loss in the war, but there was also a tradition of Zeus releasing them, or at least Cronos, Rhea, and Prometheus, as reported in Pindar, *Pythian* IV, 291, and Pindar, *Fragment* 35, not to mention Aeschylus's *Prometheus Bound,* which uses a chorus of Titans. Hesiod's *Works and Days* mentions it, too (173b, and *Theogony* 525ff.), though this passage seems to have been added later. (Richard Stoneman's notes to Pindar's *Odes and Selected Fragments* [1997], 143.) Setting sail with Homer was Rudbeck's phrase, *Atl.* I, 191.

Rudbeck was worrying about being only one-fourth of the way through his planned work, *Atl.* I, on page 428 of which was really page 682 in the 1679 edition. At about this point in the search (*Atl.* I, 408, or 649 in the original), the references to future continuations become more and more frequent.

Verelius's advice about the necessity of printing the work immediately and equipping it with a Latin translation is found in Rudbeck's dedication to *Atl.* I, 4–5. Scholars are virtually unanimous that the translator, an unnamed "good friend" (page 5), was Anders Norcopensis. He would later be ennobled as Nordenhielm, and appointed tutor of the future king Charles XII, according to Nelson's commentary on *Atl.* I, 567; II, 696; see also Strindberg (1937), 317; as well as R. M. Hatton's *Charles XII of Sweden* (1968), 44–45.

Rudbeck's discussion of the classical gods begins in earnest in *Atl.* I, 427–95. Worship of Apollo was exported from the Hyperboreans into Greece, or, more specifically, the Balder religion was carried over by Swedish maidens into Delphi, Delos, and Athens (*Atl.* I, 382, 477, 536–37). Apollo was pronounced Swedish (475–82). Reference to Apollo as the "most Greek" in the classical pantheon comes from Burkert, *Greek Religion, Archaic and Classical,* translated by John Raffan (1985), 143; and Cicero's words are from *The Nature of the Gods* III, 57. Balder's description and wisdom, "wisest of the Aesir and most beautifully spoken," is in *Gylf.* 21. That Balder "dreamed great dreams" is in *Gylf.* 49, and the "blessed god" is described in *Voluspá* 31–34.

Apollo was the son of Zeus and Leto (*Iliad* I, lines 8–10; and *Theogony* 917–20). According to Rudbeck, the Roman god Jupiter was originally the Greek Zeus, who in turn was first the Swedish Thor (*Atl.* I, 442–50). Like Zeus's mother Rhea, Thor's mother was Freyia (actually Frigg, but the two have long been confused). Rudbeck's derivation of Zeus from the old Swedish language is on pages 444–46, and his attempt to trace the legacy of Thor on Crete, which was often cited as the legendary birthplace of Zeus, is on pages 446–48.

The Olympians admitted that Zeus, in terms of brute strength, far surpassed the other gods (*Iliad* XV, line 101ff.). Hesiod's *Theogony* tells the story of Zeus defeating the Titans and punishing leaders such as Atlas and Prometheus (520ff.). Odin was called "All-Father" in *Gylf.* 10, and Odin's special watch over, among other things, prisoners, the slain, and the hanged is in *Gylf.* 20. Odin trading his eye for a drink at Mimir's well of wisdom is recounted in *Gylf.* 15. His drinking and eating habits, with the two ravens on his shoulder, are in *Gylf.* 38 and in Snorri's *Heimskringla Ynglingasagan* 7. Thor and the adventures in the land of the giants are in *Gylf.* 45–47. Thor was the "strongest of all the gods and men" in *Gylf.* 21. Odin and Thor's differences were revealed in many Norse works, for instance the *Poetic Edda's Lay of Hárbarth.* Rudbeck discusses Odin and Hades in *Atl.* I, 455–57.

Rudbeck's use of the Swedish language, as opposed to Latin, is related in Annerstedt, *Bref* II, xciii–xcv; and Rudbeck's words in the text, 1 May 1677, are printed in Annerstedt, *Bref* II, 148. The translation of Rudbeck's words about Cicero and Aristotle comes from G. Castrén, in Kirby (1990), 286. A stimulating treatment of Rudbeck's work as an architect is found in Hahr, "Olof Rudbeck d.ä. som arkitekt," in *Rudbecksstudier* (1930); and in Ragnar Josephson's *Det hyperboreiska Uppsala* (1945). Rudbeck had a preference for long rows of columns and round open spaces long before his interest in the Poseidon palace. Yet in many projects, the Atlantis nuances are hard to miss. Josephson compares Rudbeck's blueprints for the university building and Plato's description of the Poseidon palace on Atlantis on pages 66–72. Beyond this, Rudbeck's suspension bridge over the River Fyris was compared to a Roman aqueduct (35–36), and his work on the royal gardens near the palace was compared to the Hanging Gardens of Babylon (76–82).

The delay in the funds and the reminders of the king's money are mentioned in Rudbeck to De la Gardie, 20 March 1677, Annerstedt, *Bref* II, 142–43. Another inquiry about the status of the funds is in Rudbeck's letter of 22 April 1677, 146. The costs of the printing can be reconstructed from a number of letters. By April 1677, Rudbeck was printing two sheets a week at a cost of fifty-four *daler*: ten to the printer, eight for the paper, eighteen to the artist, and another eighteen to the engraver. By November 1677 the costs were at 2,000 *daler silvermynt* for the printer; 1,000 for paper; and 250 for the special, larger paper to be used for printing the figures (7 November 1677, Annerstedt, *Bref* II, 158–59). The total was 5,930 *daler silvermynt,* with a breakdown added as a supplement to this letter. The costs shouldered by Olof Rudbeck, not counting the research expenses, would rise to some 9,700 *daler kopparmynt,* Rudbeck to De la Gardie, 2 March 1682, RA, *Kanslers embetets handlingar för Uppsala universitet arkiv* E.11:7.

Efforts to raise money are related in Rudbeck's letters as well, including selling paper damaged in the spring flood of 1677, according to his letter to De la Gardie, 22 April 1677, Annerstedt, *Bref* II, 146. He tried to divert customs duties, as seen already in Rudbeck's letter to De la Gardie, 17 February 1674, Annerstedt, *Bref* II, 92. Securing of loans from "good friends" was admitted and described years later, Rudbeck to De la Gardie, 31 March 1685; LUB, *De la Gardie släktarkiven. Magnus Gabriel De la Gardie* 93:1. On pawning the family silver, see Rudbeck to De la Gardie, 7 November 1677, Annerstedt, *Bref* II, 58–59.

CHAPTER 12: HANGING BY A THREAD

Besides Rudbeck's letters, among the more lively sources for the dispute about Old Uppsala, my account is based primarily on Schück, *KVHAA* III, 322–66; Eriksson (2002), 271–76; Lindroth (1975), 311–15; Annerstedt, *Bref* II, xcv–xcvi; and Gödel (1897), 170–72. Schefferus's background and career are summarized in Lindroth, 206–14, and his cape was noted, 212. Schück discusses Schefferus's *Upsalia* in *KVHAA* III, 322–25, and *Epistola Defensoria* III, 340–44. As an effect of the problems with Schefferus, Atterbom reported a saying popular in Rudbeck's house: "It is as true as if it were written in Schefferus's *Lapponia*" ([1851], 36–37).

Rudbeck's use of the prisoners of war is related, among other places, in *Atl.* I, 100, 109. The stakes in the dispute are described by Rudbeck in a letter to De la Gardie, 24 May 1677 (Annerstedt, *Bref* II, 153–54). The count's letter of 17 May 1677 announcing the prohibition was printed by Schück in *KVHAA* III, 345–46. Schück outlines the problems with *Bishop Karl's Annotations* (357–60), and he, like Annerstedt, believed the controversial letter was a forgery. No one, though, as Schück notes, had accused Rudbeck of this forgery (355).

Reference to Lundius as a "worse Rudbeckian than Rudbeck himself" is found in Annerstedt, *Bref* II, cxvii. Schück's words on Lundius are in *KVHAA* III, 355–56. The anecdote of Lundius meeting the devil in his bedroom is found in many sources, for instance, Strindberg, *Bondenöd,* 224–25. The story of Zalmoxis comes first from Herodotus's *Histories* IV, 94. Lindroth's summary, (1975), 315, and the reference to Schefferus's mistake, Schück, *KVHAA* III, 329. Archaeological opinion comes from Sune Lindqvist, "Olof Rudbeck d.ä. som fältarkeolog," in *Rudbecksstudier* (1930), 249–58.

Verelius's problems with the college are discussed by Schück in *KVHAA,* as well as in his biography of Johan Hadorph (1933). His being paid only once for his many years of service as Professor of Antiquities of the Fatherland is noted, for instance, in *Hadorph,* 45.

CHAPTER 13: ET VOS HOMINES

The significance of De la Gardie's donations can still be seen today. Besides the *Uppsala Edda,* there were also the *Heimskringla, Olafssaga,* early editions of *Saxo Grammaticus,* and a codex containing a fragment of *Olof Tryggvason's Saga.* Some, however, were lost in the fire of 1702, including Snorri's *Heimskringla,* on loan at that time to Olof Rudbeck. De la Gardie's donation is discussed by Gödel (1897), 84–85; and Fåhraeus (1936), 220–23.

The Silver Bible is discussed by Lars Munkhammar, *Sílverbíbeln: Theodoriks bok* (1998); and Tönnes Kleberg, *Codex Argenteus: The Silver Bible at Uppsala* (1984). The Dutchman who owned the Silver Bible was Franciscus Junius. Rudbeck's reference to the Gothic Bible comes from *Atl.* I, 154–57, and a related derivation of the word *Uppsala* is found on page 261.

Some pages of the Silver Bible have continued to surface, including one that turned up, to considerable attention, in August 1970. Construction crews were restoring Speyer Cathedral, lowering the floor to add a more modern heating system. The page was found in a secret hiding place, in a potato sack, along with some other relics, including the bones, supposedly, of the Renaissance humanist Erasmus. As for the theft in April 1995, I was then living in Sweden and remember listening to the radio when a rather shocked disc jockey announced it. Munkhammar's account (1998) explains many of the details that, at the time, were so strange.

Lundius's specialties included, among other things, Swedish law, Roman law, and natural law theories of the influential thinker Samuel Pufendorf, who was then in Sweden as royal historiographer (Lindroth, *Stormaktstiden,* 368–70). Lindroth also discusses Lundius as a Rudbeckian (300–301). Lundius's *Zamolxis, primus getarum legislator* (1687) has been translated from Latin by Maria Crisan and into English by Honorius Crisan (available on the Web at www.dacia.org).

Outright forgeries and fabrications were circulating around Uppsala, according to Joseph Svennung in *Zur Geschichte Gothicismus,* 91–92. Svenbro discusses "veritable counterfeit workshops" in "L'idéologie 'gothisante' et l'Atlantica d' Olof Rudbeck. Le mythe platonicien de l'Atlantide au service de l'Empire suédois du XVIIe siècle," in *Quaderni di storia* 6, no. 11 (January–June 1980): 137. Gunnar Eriksson's comments on the forgery are found in (2002), 307–9. The phrase "the conscious effort to deceive" comes from Nils Ahnlund's definition of *forger* in his study *Nils Rabenius (1648–1717): Studier i svensk historiografi* (1927).

The runes were among the last findings to be incorporated into *Atlantica,* though Rudbeck had made the initial discovery at least as early as the end of 1675. The problem he faced, as usual, was how to find time for all the discoveries. His words about "how the Greeks have received their letters from us" is from chapter 38, *Atl.* I, 524. Loccenius, Verelius, and Norcopensis were reading Rudbeck's theories "with admiration," he noted in a letter to De la Gardie, 29 November 1675, Annerstedt, *Bref* II, 126.

Pliny discussed the transmission of the alphabet in *Natural History* VII, 192. Runes were "stones with old letters or unknown carved marks" overgrown with moss and not effaced by heat, cold, fire, or water (*Atl.* I, 14). The derivation of the word *runes* from "mystery" and "secret" appears in Ralph W. V. Elliot's *Runes: An Introduction* (1989), 1.

According to the *Edda,* nothing of importance escaped Heimdall, a god who could hear the wool grow on the backs of sheep. No wonder he was chosen to guard the entrance to the world of the gods at the rainbow bridge Bifrost, and send divine messages with his massive, earth-shaking horn (*Gylf.* 27).

Pan, fire, and many of the words Rudbeck chose for showing the Swedish impact on ancient Greece can be found in Plato's *Cratylus* dialogue (408C, 409D–410B). In this work, Socrates and his students discuss the roots of the Greek language, and openly admit the overwhelming barbarian, or non-Greek, influence—golden words for Olof Rudbeck, for he believed that each of Plato's words could be found in Swedish, or at least he believed that he could show they could. In either case, the words were from the barbarians, or more accurately, in his view, *bor-barn,* "children of Bor."

Discussion of world chronology, particularly the four or five hundred years after Noah, comes from *Atl.* I, 525–26. Rudbeck's dating of Swedish civilization back to 2300–200 B.C., or *Anno Mundi* 1700–1800, is found in *Atl.* I, 77–78, and *Atl.* II, 199. Rudbeck's investigations of the soil around the monuments are related in *Atl.* I, 66–79, 91, and applied to the runes on pages 525–26. The history of the ancient Greek alphabet, and its derivation from Scandinavian runes, is outlined in *Atl.* I, 527–39. The theory of Mercury's Swedish origins is argued in *Atl.* I, 457–66, and continued on 539–42. The illustration of the staff appears on page 541, and its interpretation is on 539–42. Later, Mercury's position in ancient Sweden was elaborated and, in some ways, altered (*Atl.* IV, esp. 104ff.). Hermes, Zeus's favorite son, appears as the messenger of the gods more in the *Odyssey* than in the *Iliad.* "Hermes the Wayfinder" comes from *Odyssey* V, line 48ff., and his ambrosial golden sandals, wand, and other descriptions are found here, as well as at many other places in the epic, for instance *Odyssey* I, line 123ff. Hermes leads the suitors to the Underworld in *Odyssey* XXIV, line 409.

Rudbeck thought the runic staffs were as old as the runes themselves. In Rudbeck's scheme, they were invented by Atle (Atlas) or Atin, and approved by Disa (Isis). The story of the peasant in the anatomy theater follows Rudbeck's own account in *Atl.* I, 562–63; and the gardener, on page 563, is also discussed by Eriksson (2002), 340.

CHAPTER 14: ON NOTHING

The first volume of *Atlantica,* published in March 1679 at Curio's press, appears in a number of different ways. Some have no title page, some a title page and no date, some the correct year of publication, some the year 1679 and the words "second edition," and some the publication year 1675. This last instance has led some authorities to claim, incorrectly, that *Atlantica* was published in that year, and some even to accuse Rudbeck of backdating the publication year. This is possible, but a simpler explanation is that Rudbeck started printing the work in 1675, as he in fact intended at the end of 1674. The work was not finished at the press until March 1679, as seen in Rudbeck's letter of 20 March 1679, printed in Annerstedt, *Bref* II, 164–65. One of Rudbeck's descendants, Johannes Rudbeckius, investigated the surviving copies of his ancestor's book (1918). He found a total of 111 copies of the first edition, dispersed around European libraries.

Inclement weather delayed the transport of De la Gardie's copy, Rudbeck wrote to De la Gardie, 22 March 1679, RA, *Kanslers embetets handlingar för Uppsala universitet arkiv* E.11:6.

The priest in Stockholm, Olaus Bergius, vicar of St. Clara's Church, noted Rudbeck's strengths, "immeasurable labor" and "wonderful genius," in an undated letter, probably from late 1682, inserted in the collection *Auctarium Testimoniorum de Cl Rudbeckii Atlantica,* reprinted in Nelson (1950), 43. D. G. Morhof describes his reading of *Atlantica* in a letter from Kiel, 23 June 1681 (Nelson [1950], 28). In his enthusiasm, Morhof claims that he, too, had once planned to write a book about the importance of the north in the ancient world. The title was to have been *Mysterium Septentrionis (Secrets of the North)*. Pleased that his own work "lay dormant for many years," Morhof now rejoiced that many of his suspicions had been confirmed. After reading Rudbeck's *Atlantica,* he threw away his notes, remarking how "foolish and ill-considered" it was to dance after this master. (He must have retrieved them, however, since a few years later Morhof would publish his own theory about the ancient past, with the Germans very much playing the role of Rudbeck's Swedes.)

The director of the Witchcraft Commission, Anders Stiernhöök, noted how Rudbeck had satisfied him astonishingly, 1 September 1679, Nelson (1950), 5. By November, Stiernhöök was continuing according to his plan of daily readings, and this had not changed his previously reported positive opinion of *Atlantica* (20 November 1679, Nelson [1950], 11). Information about the admiring Germans who visited Old Uppsala comes from Rudbeck's letter to De la Gardie, 5 May 1679, Annerstedt, *Bref* II, 170–71. The reference to the envy of his contemporaries is found in Lund University professor of history and poetry Stobaeus (Nelson [1950], 103). The description of the Furies comes from Aeschylus's *Libation Bearers,* 1048–49.

The Royal Society's secretary Francis Aston wrote to Rudbeck to say that *Atlantica* was "very much desired in these regions," 11 January 1682 (Nelson [1950], 34). Aston also wrote to thank Rudbeck for his copy of *Atlantica,* with his words on the "power of genius and the abundance of learning" found in the letter of 11 January 1682. This was evidently the letter President Christopher Wren asked him to write, 4 January 1681/82 (Birch, *History of the Royal Society,* 4 vols. [1756–57]).

The passage on "this deservedly famous Author" is taken from the anonymous review in *Philosophical Transactions,* 10 January 1681/2, reprinted in Nelson

(1950), 33. The reviewer also praised Rudbeck's conclusions on the location of the cradle of civilization in Sweden: "That Japhet and the first Race inhabited there, may be probable, in that it's said he possest the Isles, under which title Sweonia has gone." About the classical gods coming from Sweden, the reviewer commented on how well the Swedish language suited the names of the gods.

Rudbeck was proposed as a member of the Royal Society at the meeting on 14 December 1681. He had been mentioned as a possible candidate for membership for some time, at least since Oldenburg extended the offer as early as the late 1660s (RS, Letterbook III, Oldenburg to Rudbeck, 8 January 1668/69; RS, Letterbook III, Oldenburg to Rudbeck, 9 December 1669). But it was not until *Atlantica* was published and reviewed that the proposal of membership was official. There is some uncertainty on who reviewed *Atlantica;* Thomas Gale was asked, according to the minutes for 26 October 1681, and Cluverus on 7 December 1681.

Glad to hear the praise from London, Rudbeck informed the count of the Royal Society's view of his work (24 May 1682), and forwarded a copy of their letter (4 June 1682, RA, *Kanslers embetets handlingar för Uppsala universitet arkiv* E.11:7). The student who brought *Atlantica* to the Royal Society, Johan Heysig, is treated by Carl Harald Eugène Lewenhaupt in "Johan Heysig-Ridderstjerna," *Samlaren,* vol. 10 (1889) and vol. 14 (1893).

Atlantica was hailed as Rudbeck's own Herculean labor by G. Cuperus, 20 June 1690 (Nelson [1950], 97). The claim about the many heroic and war-like nations pouring out of Sweden like a Trojan horse comes from a speech delivered in Kiel by S. H. Musaeus, 26 April 1688 (Nelson [1950], 100). The reference to the Swedish Heracles who restored light to an area where Cimbrian darkness prevailed is in O. Bergius, undated (Nelson [1950], 43).

It would be unreasonable to expect Rudbeck's theory to sail through the learned world, especially in Uppsala, where he had so many enemies, without at least some opposition. One detailed critique of *Atlantica* appeared in W. E. Tentzel's journal, *Monatliche Unterredungen einiger Guten Freunde von Allerhand Büchern . . . ,* a 200-page review running through the February to July issues. (See Nelson IV [1950], 293, and Eriksson [2002], 425–27). Many other critiques are noted in the later volumes of *Atlantica.*

Notice of Rudbeck's lecture series "On Nothing," appearing in Uppsala University's catalog in October 1679, was printed in Annerstedt's *Bref* II, 177, and discussed in Eriksson's article "Om Ingenting: Olof Rudbecks föreläsnings-program 1679," *Lychnos* (1979–80). Rudbeck's explanation is found in a letter to De la Gardie, 3 November 1679 (Annerstedt, *Bref* II, 178–79). Annerstedt discusses this episode in *Bref* II, ci–ciii; and Eriksson (2002), 146, interprets *De Nihilo* as serious, joking, and having fun with the enemies all at the same time. The description of Schefferus's reaction is in Rudbeck's letter to Count de la Gardie, 5 April 1679, printed in Annerstedt, *Bref* II, 166. The rest of Schefferus's words were taken from Elias Palmsköld, *Palmsk. samlingen* XV: T.15, 557; thanks to Annerstedt for this information, *Bref* II, cxxv, n. 2.

The slow sales were already noted in Rudbeck's letter to De la Gardie, 5 April 1679, Annerstedt, *Bref* II, 165–69. The continued slow rate is seen in his letter of 14 September 1679, Annerstedt, *Bref* II, 173–75. Two hundred forty copies were sold by March 1682. This did not count the twenty that were lost at sea when the ship carrying them went down outside of Rostock. Rudbeck to De la Gardie, 2 March 1682, RA, *Kanslers embetets handlingar för Uppsala universitet arkiv* E.11:7.

Verelius was showing signs of ill health at least by the late 1670s, and Rudbeck described his friend standing at the doorway short of breath, exhausted by even a short walk, 5 April 1679, Annerstedt, *Bref* II, 168. Punishment of Norcopensis for allegedly neglecting university duties is in Arrhenius's letter to De la Gardie, 2 January 1683, copied in *UUB*, U40:5. The last years of De la Gardie's life were "full of misfortunes, sorrows, and humiliations" (*"olyckor, sorger, och förödmjukelser"*), Annerstedt, *Bref* III, clxxxvi. This episode is discussed in Fåhraeus (1936), 282–319; and Magnusson (1993), 132ff. Rudbeck's loyalty to the count is well known and was praised by Atterbom, who saw this as one of the "more beautiful" sides of Rudbeck's character ([1851], 82).

The reduction is defined by Anthony Upton in *Charles XI and Swedish Absolutism* (1998), ix, as "a legal process, based on the principle of the inalienability of the crown's lands and revenues. The principle meant that even if a ruler made a grant to a subject in perpetuity from these lands and revenues, he, or his successors, could recall the grant at any time on grounds of public necessity." Information about the political culture of this period also comes from Kurt Ågren's "The reduktion," in Roberts (1973). Strindberg (1937), 79–87, discusses the Crown properties sold, bestowed, and dispersed to meet the needs of Swedish warfare, and the background to the reduction, 110ff.

Many aristocratic families were ruined in the reduction, literally reduced to begging for clemency at the palace gates where they had formerly been welcomed as guests. Voltaire described this sight in his *History of Charles XII,* translated by Winifred Todhunter (1908), 13, and many others have noted it as well. Michael Roberts has printed many documents about this period in his *Sweden as a Great Power 1611–1697: Government, Society, Foreign Policy* (1968). Besides the effects of the war on morale, the council was losing influence through the deaths of its prominent members and the king's slow replacement of them (and then with his own favorites). Surviving members were often sick and elderly, if not also away from the capital on various activities (Rystad, *Karl XI: En biografi* [2001], 147–48). The council's demotion was already a fact before 1680 (179).

In addition to Makalös, De la Gardie owned the following castles and properties at one time or the other: "Drottningholm, Karlberg, Jakobsdal (Ulriksdal), Venngarn, Ekolsund, and Ekholmen in Uppland; Frövdi with Hinseberg in Västmanland, Kägleholm in Närke. Läckö, Traneberg, Mariedal, Katrineberg, Höjentorp, Synnerby hospital, Slädene, Magnusberg, Råda ladugård and Jönslunda in Västergötland. Along with these came large areas in

Finland and Livonia, among others Pernau and Arensburg on the island of Ösel. He also had property in Pomerania and Mecklenburg" (Gunda Magnusson, *Magnus Gabriel* [1993], 62). See Fåhraeus (1936), 236–62; and Sten Karling's "Slott och trädgårdar," in *Magnus Gabriel de la Gardie: Nationalmusei utställningskatalog* nr.434 (1980), 29–40. De la Gardie's words from the Swedish hymnal were translated by Göran Rystad in Roberts, ed., *Sweden's Age of Greatness 1632–1718* (1973), 236.

In contrast to Rudbeck, Hadorph and the College of Antiquities were quickly choosing other powerful men as patrons, including De la Gardie's own rivals, Sten Bielke, Göran Gyllenstierna, and Claes Fleming (Schück, *Hadorph,* 160–62).

CHAPTER 15: AND THEN THE SNAKE THAWED

Olof Rudbeck's words forming the epigraph to this chapter are found in his letter to Count de la Gardie, 29 November 1670, Annerstedt, *Bref* II, 77. Professor Henrik Schütz's background comes from Annerstedt, *UUH* II, 207–8, as well as Annerstedt, *Bref* III, cxxxvi ff. The students' dislike of Schütz is discussed by Annerstedt, including their chanting outside his window, *Bref* IV, ccviii, n. 1. Rudbeck's appeal for the library position appears in his letter of 13 January 1682, Annerstedt, *Bref* III, 188–89. Jonas Rugman's manuscript-hunting missions are analyzed in Schück, *KVHAA* I, 203ff., and in Lindroth, *Stormaktstiden,* 280; Hadorph and the College of Antiquities are treated also by Schück *KVHAA* and also *Hadorph.* Annerstedt's *UUH* II, 208–13, discusses the struggle for the library.

That Hadorph began to see Rudbeck as the main opponent for the college, and fear that he would put the college's work "in the shadows," is shown by Schück in *Hadorph,* 167–68. Hadorph's vanity is also discussed, though Schück believed it was not as pronounced as in others of the day, such as Verelius, *Hadorph,* 87–89. The praise of *Atlantica,* however, "jarred the ears" of the College of Antiquities members Örnhielm and Hadorph, 170.

Schütz's attempt to obtain Verelius's position and Schütz's trip to Stockholm while Verelius was on his deathbed are found in Annerstedt, *Bref* III, cxxxvii. The relative who probably helped him gain the position was Johan Bergenhielm, one of the royal secretaries in Stockholm. Rudbeck's clashes in the consistory and his defeat are shown in Annerstedt, *Bref* III, cxxxvii–cxxxv. Rudbeck's hiding of the keys is in Annerstedt, *Bref* III, cxxxix, n. 1. According to Annerstedt, Uppsala was in a "true state of war" (cxxxviii).

Rudbeck's words in the narrative come from his letter dated 13 January 1682, printed in Annerstedt, *Bref* III, 73–74. Rudbeck's answer to Schütz's demand that he return the manuscripts was printed by Gödel (1897), 168. Rudbeck's arguments for a chance to defend himself against the charges of forged documents are found in, among other places, his letter of 26 February 1684. Some of Rudbeck's responses to the Inquisition Commission were published in Annerstedt, *Bref* III, 206–26, 256–65. Another response to the chancellor, full of information about the university, is on 226–51. Rudbeck's requests for access to university records appear as supplements to this letter. Annerstedt saw the creation of the Inquisition as a response of Rudbeck's angered enemies (*Bref* III, cil). Strindberg basically agrees on this point, claiming that Schütz and Arrhenius intended to use the Inquisition to blame Rudbeck for the university's problems (254).

All the Inquisition's demands are outlined by Annerstedt, *Bref* III, cil–cl; *UUH* II, 223–35; and Rudbeck was treated as their main goal, II, 230. Annerstedt called Schütz the "grand inquisitor," *Bref* III, cxxxxvii; and Atterbom ([1850], 423) made a comparison to the Spanish Inquisition, not least in turning on its own members. Rudbeck's irony about their honor is found in Annerstedt, *Bref* III, cil ff.

Rudbeck describes Schütz storming the press in an undated letter of 1685, LUB, *De la Gardie släktarkiven: Magnus Gabriel De la Gardie* 93:1, reprinted in Annerstedt, *Bref* III, 266–69. Sithellius's letter, 20 May 1684, was published in Nelson (1950), 51. Although originally written in Swedish, this letter had been translated into Latin and its claims intensified. The dispute with the College of Antiquities is found in Annerstedt's *UUH* II, 235–40, and *Bref* III, clxii–clxvi, as well as in Schück, *KVHAA* III, 366–401; Atterbom, *Minne* II, 41ff.; Lindroth, *Stormaktstiden*, 299–300; and Strindberg, *Bondenöd och stormaktsdröm*, 259.

Rudbeck paid the expenses for the publication of the Collections. The first one, *De viri clarissimi Olavi Rudbeckii Atlantica Diversorum Testimonia*, appeared in 1681; and the second, *Auctarium Testimoniorum*, in 1685 (Rudbeck to De la Gardie, 25 March 1685, Supplement, printed in Annerstedt, *Bref* III, 226–51, particularly 251). Another controversial letter in the collection was from Jena professor of law Schubartus, who claimed that Rudbeck's theories would correct some of Schefferus's errors about the Goths, 18 January 1683, printed in Nelson (1950), 46.

The right to censorship was found in the 1655 constitution (Schück, *KVHAA* III, 373). All of these challenges set Rudbeck back in his plans. Before the crisis erupted, for instance, Rudbeck believed that the second volume would be done by the summer of 1684 (letter of 26 February 1684, RA, *Kanslers embetets handlingar för Uppsala universitet arkiv* E.11:8).

Rudbeck's economic sacrifices are clear from glancing at his letters at this time, including, for instance, 27 March 1683, RA, *Kanslers embetets handlingar för Uppsala universitet arkiv* E.11:8, and 23 March 1682, E.11:7. The expenses and Rudbeck's own contributions are noted in his supplements to a letter dated 25 March 1685 (Annerstedt, *Bref* III, esp. 240–51). Rudbeck's words on being too shy to beg and having no strength to quarrel come from a letter to De la Gardie, 31 March 1685, reprinted 254–56. This is also the source for not daring to string the bow any tighter. In 1685, when Rudbeck was in bad economic straits, a merchant refused to extend him any further credit. In outrage, Rudbeck immediately took off his coat in the market and used it as collateral (Rudbeck to De la Gardie, 16 July 1685, LUB, *De la Gardie släktarkiven: Magnus Gabriel De la Gardie* 93:1.

On threatening to sink a second time like Plato's Atlantis, Rudbeck certainly feared the risks of De la Gardie's planned retirement (Rudbeck to De la Gardie, 22 October 1684, reprinted in Annerstedt, *Bref* III, 204).

Jacob Arrhenius as a treasurer, Annerstedt's *UUH* II, 204–7; his comments to the *Bref* III, cxxxv–cxxxvi. Rudbeck had moved more quickly in his career than Hadorph, and then helped him (Schück, *Hadorph,* 57–58, also 98). The relationship between Rudbeck and Hadorph, however, was under great strain even before the conflict over antiquities (Rudbeck's letter of 14 December 1679, copy in KB, *Örnhielmiana,* and printed in Annerstedt, *Bref* II, 179–82). Part of the background, too, was the hostility between Verelius and Hadorph. Their relationship had moved from positive to disintegration: salary disputes, antiquarian rivalries, the Curio lawsuit, and the dispute over Verelius's support of his nephew, Isthemius-Reenhielm, as a member of the college (as Hadorph wanted his son Johannes). Schück, *Hadorph,* 97–108, and the Isthemius dispute, 119–22.

Rudbeck described his carriage accident and vertigo in a letter to the chancellor, 24 May 1684, Annerstedt, *Bref* III, 199. As the crisis deepened, Rudbeck's dizziness became worse (9 May 1685, Annerstedt, *Bref* III, 274). Rudbeck's great disappointment and the image of the snake come from his letter to the chancellor dated 1 July 1684, Annerstedt, *Bref* III, 202. This story is also found in an Aesop fable, in Olivia and Robert Temple's edition of Aesop, *The Complete Fables* (1998), fable 82, 65.

CHAPTER 16: THE ELYSIAN FIELDS

This struggle is outlined in Annerstedt's *UUH* II, 235–43, and *Bref* III, clxii–clxvi; Atterbom (1850), 425ff.; Schück's *Hadorph,* 174–82; and many places in Schück's *KVHAA.* Hadorph's intentions for printing Stiernhielm's work, *De Hyperboreis,* come from Schück, *KVHAA* III, 320; and Lindroth, *Stormaktstiden,* 269. Like Atterbom ([1851], 58–59), I think it would have been interesting to see what Hadorph and his friends, including the royal historiographer and natural law theorist Samuel Pufendorf, would have written.

Arrhenius's comparison of Rudbeck to a crow is an old device, found in Aesop, *The Complete Fables,* translated by R. and O. Temple (1998), fable 162, 119. Credit for founding the College of Antiquities was disputed, and both Hadorph and Rudbeck claimed the distinction. One possible resolution, offered by Schück, is that Hadorph proposed the institution and Rudbeck secured De la Gardie's support (*KVHAA* II, 2–3; and *Hadorph,* 65).

Rudbeck's comparison of his response to the college's letter and drinking the best liquor is found in his letter of 11 June 1685, Annerstedt, *Bref* III, 285. His response to the college attack came three days later (Rudbeck to De la Gardie, 14 June 1685, printed in Annerstedt, *Bref* III, 287–93). The words about the French ambassador and other praise also come from this letter (289). The king freeing Rudbeck from the censorship is noted by Annerstedt, *Bref* III, clxiv; and Atterbom (1851), 38–39. The college's accusations are in a letter from the Collegium Antiquitatum Patriae to De la Gardie, 4 June 1685, copy, KB, *Örnhielmiana* O.20. Rudbeck's defense was taken from his own letter to the count, 14 June 1685, in Annerstedt, *Bref* III, 287–93. Rudbeck's words on the college, not wanting to obtain their subsidies, which Schück cited and believed, are on pages 173–74. De la Gardie's response, dated 18 June 1685, was printed in C. C. Gjörwell, ed., *Den svenske Mercurius,* February 1760, 105–14.

The clash between Rudbeck and the College of Antiquities is treated in Schück, *KVHAA* III, 366–401; Schück, *Hadorph,* 174–82; and Annerstedt, *Bref* III, clxii–clxvi. The college's move to Stockholm was perhaps not as radical as it might seem today. After the deaths of many older members and the move of others to the capital, few were still in Uppsala (Schück, *Hadorph,* 118). This was not the way it appeared to De la Gardie, however.

The *tryckeritunna* was a considerable fund for antiquities, the money based on 2,221 *kyrkohärbärgen* across the country contributing a bushel of grain (valued at three *daler silvermynt*) to equal some 6,000 a year. The problem, of course, was collecting the money in the large country, where many people resented the tax, if they did not outright resist it. Many disputed its legality, "revocerad" back in 1637 (Schück, *Hadorph,* 111–15, 122–26). Additional insight on the history of the *tryckeritunna* is found in Abel Ahlquist's "The History of the Swedish Bible," in *Scandinavian Studies,* vol. 9 (1926).

Hadorph was one of the best-paid officials in Sweden, earning theoretically over 2,200 *daler silvermynt,* compared with a professor at 700, an assessor in court at 900, and even a *landshövding* at 1,500 (Schück, *Hadorph,* 117 and 127). A *landshövding* was a local governor whose power in most parts of Sweden could be compared, in the words of one observer, with a combined lord lieutenant and sheriff (John Robinson, *Account of Sweden, 1688* [1998], 13). Hadorph's official salary, though, was in reality somewhat less. Teachers reduced to begging are described in Schück, *Hadorph,* 188.

The conclusion of the Curio lawsuit is described in Annerstedt, *Bref* III, clxvi–clxix, and the printer's fate in *Bref* IV, ccx–ccxi. Valuable information on the press comes also from supplements AZ, AA, and AAA to Rudbeck's letter of 25 March 1685 (Annerstedt, *Bref* III, 247–51). Rudbeck's support of Curio is described in many places, particularly a letter of 3 August 1685, Annerstedt, *Bref* III, 295, and another letter with the same date, 296–97. Rudbeck's pawning of copies of *Atlantica* comes from a letter dated 12 October 1685 (Annerstedt, *Bref* III, 305). The descriptions of Arrhenius and Schütz's efforts to block Curio come from an undated letter in September 1685, probably written around the middle of the month. By 16 September, Rudbeck was writing to ask the chancellor to seek help from the king in the Curio conflict (Annerstedt, *Bref* III, 301).

Rudbeck's letters shed some light on his work with the sagas, for instance, 2 June 1680, RA, *Kanslers embetets handlingar för Uppsala universitet arkiv* E.11:7. Rudbeck's printing of the Norse sagas is listed in Rudbeckius's *Bibliotheca Rudbeckiana* (1918). Before printing the sagas, Rudbeck was urging manual copying to protect the manuscripts from too much handling, according to Rudbeck's letter to De la Gardie, 20 March 1682, RA, *Kanslers embetets handlingar för Uppsala universitet arkiv* E.11:7.

The attempt to secure funds from the Stockholm city treasury is discussed in Rudbeck's letter to De la Gardie, 9 May 1685, printed in Annerstedt, *Bref* III, 276. His hope of following the English example by publishing *Atlantica* in installments and the report on the state of his debts are from a letter to De la Gardie, 9 May 1685, Annerstedt, *Bref* III, 274–76. Other fund-raising attempts, including loans from students and readers, are found in a letter dated 12 October 1685 (Annerstedt, *Bref* III, 306). Rumors of possible royal support were noted by Rudbeck in a letter to De la Gardie, 11 June 1685, Annerstedt, *Bref* III, 284–86. Both the archbishop and the *landshöfding* were privately assuring Rudbeck of success. See also Rudbeck to De la Gardie, 13 September 1685, Annerstedt, *Bref* III, 298–99. The king's letter of 6 October 1685 and his opinion of Rudbeck's Atlantis project are cited in part in *Atl.* II, 4–5, 8. The second volume of the *Atlantica* was dedicated to Charles XI, just as the third would be to be dedicated to his son and successor, Charles XII, with more words on Rudbeck's appreciation (III, 4).

State funding put the search on a solid financial basis: a 200-*riksdaler* award, with "annually" scribbled in the margins, 13 July 1693 copy, KB, *Autografsamling*, printed in Annerstedt, *Bref* IV, 340–42; and Rasmus Nyerup, *Olof Rudbeck den ældre. Et biographisk omrids. Sœrskilt aftrykt af det skandinaviske litteratur selskabs-skrifter for 1813* (1814), 59–63. The level of support is also seen in a supplement to Rudbeck's letter to Bengt Oxenstierna, dated 13 January 1697, Annerstedt, *Bref* IV, 353–57. The reference to the clinking of coins was used first for De la Gardie's subsidy, which galvanized Rudbeck back into action (Rudbeck to De la Gardie, 21 April 1685, Annerstedt, *Bref* III, 269).

The president of the Chancery, Bengt Oxenstierna, was, at this time, a great supporter. According to Oxenstierna's secretary, Rudbeck's theories were "frequently the running topic" of discussion and the president "repeatedly punctuated his solemn public charges" with the reading of *Atlantica*. In fact he claimed that Oxenstierna's reading of *Atlantica* was so vigorous that he often did not heed pressing matters of state. C. Staude, 11 November 1689, Nelson (1950), 93. Rudbeck's victory in the Inquisition is discussed in Annerstedt, *Bref* III, cli–clii.

Confucius was introduced into learned Europe with Philippe Couplet's translation of the Analects, *Confucius Sinarum Philosophus* (1687). The questions about China were from the German oriental scholar Professor Müller (Mullerus Greiffenhagius), November 1685 in Nelson (1950), 89. See also Rudbeck's own investigations about Swedes in China, for instance, KB, *Atland tabulae med anteckningar av O Rudbecks hand* (F.m.73). Rudbeck acknowledges the comments of the royal geographer Sanson, citing the discussion between Silenus and King Midas on Atlantis, found in Aelianus's *Varia Historia* (*Atl.* II, 138). Among the reasons for Swedes in India were the Swedish names for many places he saw (*Atl.* III, 471–86). Rudbeck's discussion of the various representations of the sun is the longest chapter in the entire *Atlantica* (II, 148–449).

Rudbeck's hopes for sending Peringer out on another, even more ambitious, journey around Europe were noted in a letter to Bengt Rosenhane, 20 November 1683, Annerstedt, *Bref* III, 194. Peringer would later succeed Örnhielm as a member of the College of Antiquities, in 1689, and publish his influential edition of Snorri's *Heimskringla*. Many other trips were taken, or at least planned. The German traveler Engelbrecht Kempfer, for one, hoped to use the opportunity of accompanying the Swedish embassy to Japan to explore the Far East for more evidence of Rudbeck's theories. His letter, dated 20 February 1683, asks Rudbeck for an itinerary (printed in Nelson [1950], 48). Visitors seeking out Rudbeck and a trip to Old Uppsala are noted by Annerstedt, *Bref* IV, cclxiii. The Polish resident was identified as possibly F. G. Galetzki, Annerstedt, *Bref* IV, cclxiv, n. 1. Rudbeck's letter to Bengt Oxenstierna elaborates on the colorful occasion (372–74), which was discussed in Annerstedt, *Bref* IV, cclxiv–cclxvii; and Eriksson (2002), 614–17. The reference to the tourist industry is in Rudbeck's letter to De la Gardie, 2 October 1685, Annerstedt, *Bref* III, 302.

Rudbeck's *Campus Elysii* is treated in Eriksson (2002), 250–54, and Lindroth (1975), 429–32. The romantic poet in question was P. D. A. Atterbom, his words on the *Atlantica* coming from Atterbom (1850), 281. The great fire of 1702 is described in Eenberg's *En utförlig relation om den grufweliga eldzwåda och skada, som sig tildrog med Uppsala stad den 16 Maii, åhr 1702* (1703), as well as in two of Rudbeck's letters to Oxenstierna: 17 May 1702 and 26 May 1702, printed in Annerstedt, *Bref* IV, 387–88 and 389–90. The fire is also described in Annerstedt, *Bref* IV, cclxxviii–cclxxi; and Annerstedt, *UUH* II, 350–52. Some manuscripts at Rudbeck's house were lost, including an early Latin manuscript of Saxo Grammaticus, which Rudbeck refers to in various places in *Atlantica,* such as II, 83, and III, 675–76. Klemming (1863) has noted a list of manuscripts cited in Rudbeck's work that are no longer in existence. Another manuscript lost in the fire was a codex of *Heimskringla* (Gödel [1897], 166).

Rudbeck's part in rebuilding Uppsala is noted in Eriksson (2002), 620; Annerstedt, *Bref* IV, cclxxxi–cclxxxii; Annerstedt, *UUH* II, 353; Atterbom (1851), 117; and Fries (1896), 30.

EPILOGUE

Charles XII had grown up with Norse sagas and Rudbeck's *Atlantica* (Atterbom [1851], 64; Strindberg [1937], 316ff.). Victories of this warrior king were sometimes celebrated in Rudbeckian terms, for instance making him Sweden's Hyperborean king (Strindberg, 329–30); Charles XII's officers searching for Rudbeck's theories are noted (401). The Battle of Narva has received quite a bit of attention in Swedish and European sources, as noted, for instance, by Hatton (1968), especially 152–54, and Voltaire, 48–54. Rudbeck's words on the hands black from chemistry and the back aching from stargazing come from a letter cited in Annerstedt, *Bref* IV, cxcv. *Rudbeckia* was named by Carl Linnaeus in honor of the Rudbecks, Olof and Olof junior.

Select Bibliography

Ahnlund, Nils. *Nils Rabenius (1648–1717): Studier i svensk historiografi*. Stockholm: Geber, 1927.

Åkerman, Susanna. *Queen Christina and Her Circle: The Transformation of a Seventeenth-Century Philosophical Libertine. Brill's Studies in Intellectual History.* Leiden and New York: E. J. Brill, 1991.

Annerstedt, Claes. *Uppsala universitets historia.* 3 volumes. Uppsala: Uppsala Universitet, 1877–1914.

Åslund, Leif. *De la Gardie och vältaligheten.* Uppsala: Avdelningen för retorik, 1992.

Atterbom, P. D. A. *Minne af professoren i medicinen vid Uppsala universitet Olof Rudbeck den äldre: Svenska akademiens handlingar ifrån år 1796. Del 23–24* (1850–51).

Bickerman, E. J. "Origines Gentium." *Classical Philology* 47 (1952).

Bramwell, James. *Lost Atlantis.* London: Cobden-Sanderson, 1937.

Broberg, Gunnar. *Gyllene äpplen. Svensk idéhistorisk läsebok.* Stockholm: Atlantis, 1991.

Broberg, Gunnar, Gunnar Eriksson, and Karin Johannisson, eds. *Kunskapens trädgårdar: Om institutioner och institutionaliseringar i vetenskapen och livet.* Stockholm: Atlantis, 1988.

Burkert, Walter. *Greek Religion, Archaic and Classical.* Translated by John Raffan. Oxford, England: Blackwell, 1985.

Dahl, Per. *Svensk ingenjörskonst under stormaktstiden: Olof Rudbecks tekniska undervisning och praktiska verksamhet.* Uppsala: Institutionen för idé- och lärdomshistoria, 1995.

de Camp, L. Sprague. *Lost Continents: The Atlantis Theme in History, Science, and Literature.* New York: Dover Publications, 1970.

Derry, T. K. *A History of Scandinavia: Norway, Sweden, Denmark, Finland, and Iceland.* Minneapolis: University of Minnesota Press, 1979.

Eenberg, Johan. *En utförlig relation om den grufweliga eldzwåda och skada, som sig tildrog med Uppsala stad den 16 Maii, åhr 1702.* Uppsala, 1703.

Ellis, Richard. *Imagining Atlantis.* New York: Alfred A. Knopf, 1998.

Englund, Peter. *Ofredsår: Om den svenska stormaktstiden och en man i dess mitt.* Stockholm: Atlantis, 1994.

———. "Om klienter och deras patroner." In *Makt och vardag. Hur man styrde, levde och tänkte under svensk stormaktstid,* edited by Stellan Dahlgren, Anders Florén, and Åsa Karlsson. Stockholm: Atlantis, 1993.

Eriksson, Gunnar. *The Atlantic Vision: Olaus Rudbeck and Baroque Science.* Vol. 19, *Uppsala Studies in History of Science.* Canton, MA: Science History Publications, 1994.

———. "Olof Rudbeck d.ä." *Lychnos* (1984).

———. "Om ingenting: Olof Rudbecks föreläsningsprogram 1679." *Lychnos* (1979–80).

———. *Rudbeck 1630–1702. Liv, lärdom och dröm i barockens Sverige.* Stockholm: Atlantis, 2002.

Esberg, Johan. *"Laudatio funebris qua polyhistori magno medico longe celeberrimo, dn Olao Rudebeckio patri in regia universitate Upsaliensi . . ."* Uppsala, 1703.

Fåhraeus, Rudolf. *Magnus Gabriel de la Gardie.* Stockholm: Geber, 1936.

Fant, E. M. *Observationes in Atlanticam Olai Rudbeckii senioris.* Uppsala, 1800.

Fehr, Isak. "En underbar man från vår storhetstid." *Ord and Bild* (1897).

Forsyth, Phyllis Young. *Atlantis: The Making of Myth.* Montreal: McGill–Queen's University, 1980.

Fries, Ellen. *Den svenska odlingens stormän 1: Olof Rudbeck den äldre, Urban Hiärne och Jesper Svedberg.* Stockholm: Norstedt, 1896.

Gantz, Timothy. *Early Greek Myth: A Guide to Literary and Artistic Sources.* Baltimore: Johns Hopkins University Press, 1993.

Gödel, Vilhelm. *Fornnorsk-isländsk litteratur i Sverige (till antikvitetskollegiets inrättande).* Stockholm, 1897.

Grafton, Anthony. "The World of the Polyhistors: Humanism and Ency- clopedism." *Central European History* 18 (1985).

Grape, Anders. *Bref af Olof Rudbeck d.ä. rörande Uppsala Universitet efterskörd: Uppsala Universitets Årskrift* (1930).

Graves, Robert. *The Greek Myths.* 2 volumes. Baltimore: Penguin Books, 1955.

Greenway, John. *Golden Horns: Mythic Imagination and the Nordic Past.* Athens, GA: University of Georgia Press, 1977.

Hahr, August. "Magnus Gabriel de la Gardie som konstmecenat." *Svensk Tidskrift* (1925).

———. "Olof Rudbeck d.ä. som arkitekt." In *Rudbecksstudier. Festskrift vid Uppsala uni- versitets minnesfest till högtidlighållande av 300-Årsminnet av Olof Rudbeck d.ä:s födelse.* Uppsala: Almqvist & Wiksells boktryckeri, 1930.

Hamilton, Edith. *Mythology.* Boston: Little, Brown, 1942.

Hatton, R. M. *Charles XII of Sweden.* London: Weidenfeld and Nicolson, 1968.

Heckscher, Eli. *Sveriges ekonomiska historia, 1600–1720.* Stockholm: Bonnier, 1936.

Holmquist, Bengt M. "Till Sveriges ära. Det götiska arvet." In *Stormaktstid: Erik Dahlbergh och bilden av Sverige.* Lidköping: Stiftelsen Läckö Institutet, 1992.

Jacobowsky, C. V. "Johan Gabriel Sparwenfeld, en vittberest stormaktstida lärd." *Svenska humanistiska förbundet* (1939).

Jansson, Sven B. F. *The Runes of Sweden.* Translated by Peter G. Foote. New York: Bedminster Press, 1962.

Johannesson, Kurt. *I polstjärnans tecken: Studier i svensk barock.* Stockholm: Almqvist & Wiksell, 1968.

———. *The Renaissance of the Goths in Sixteenth-Century Sweden: Johannes and Olaus Magnus as Politicians and Historians.* Translated by James Larson. Berkeley: University of California Press, 1991.

Jordan, Paul. *The Atlantis Syndrome.* Stroud, England: Sutton, 2001.

Josephson, Ragnar. *Det hyperboreiska Uppsala.* Stockholm: Norstedts, 1945.

Kirby, David. *Northern Europe in the Early Modern Period: The Baltic World 1492–1772.* London: Longman, 1990.

Kleberg, Tönnes. *Codex Argenteus: The Silver Bible at Uppsala.* Uppsala: University Library, 1984.

Klemming, Gustaf Edvard. *Anteckningar om Rudbecks Atland.* Stockholm, 1863.

Klindt-Jensen, Ole. *A History of Scandinavian Archaeology.* Translated by G. Russell Poole. London: Thames & Hudson, 1975.

Lewenhaupt, Carl Harald Eugène. "Johan Heysig-Ridderstjerna." *Samlaren: Tidskrift för svensk litteraturveten-skaplig forskaing,* vol. 10 (1889), vol. 14 (1893).

Lindahl, Göran. *Magnus Gabriel De la Gardie, hans gods och hans folk.* Stockholm: Arkitekturmuseum, 1968.

Lindborg, Rolf. "De cartesianska striderna." In *17 Uppsatser i svensk idé-och lärdomshistoria.* Uppsala: Bokförlaget Carmina, 1980.

———. *Descartes i Uppsala: Striderna om "nya filosofien" 1663–1689.* Uppsala: Lychnos-bibliotek, 1965.

Lindroth, Sten. *Svensk lärdomshistoria II: Stormaktstiden.* Stockholm: Norstedts, 1975.

———. *Uppsala universitet 1477–1977.* Uppsala: Uppsala Universitet, 1976.

Luce, J. V. *The End of Atlantis: New Light on an Old Legend.* London: Thames & Hudson, 1969.

Löw, Gustav. *Sveriges forntid i svensk historieskrivning,* vol. 1. Stockholm, 1908.

Magalotti, Lorenzo. *Sverige under år 1674.* Stockholm: Rediviva, 1996.

Magnusson, Gunda. *Magnus Gabriel.* Stockholm: Timbro, 1993.

Momigliano, Arnaldo. *Alien Wisdom: The Limits of Hellenization.* Cambridge, England: Cambridge University Press, 1975.

Munkhammer, Lars. *Silverbibeln: Theodoriks bok.* Stockholm: Carlsson, 1998.

Nordström, Johan. *De yverbornes ö: Bidrag till Atlanticans förhistoria.* Uppsala, 1930.

Nyerup, Rasmus. *Olof Rudbeck den ældre. Et biographisk omrids: Særskilt aftrykt af det skandinaviske litteratur selskabs-skrifter for 1813.* Copenhagen, 1814.

Obregón, Mauricio. *Beyond the Edge of the Sea: Sailing with Jason and the Argonauts, Ulysses, the Vikings, and Other Explorers of the Ancient World.* New York: Modern Library, 2001.

———. *From Argonauts to Astronauts: An Unconventional History of Discovery.* New York: HarperCollins, 1977.

Pellegrino, C. *Unearthing Atlantis: An Archaeological Odyssey.* New York: Random House, 1991.

Ramage, Edwin S., ed. *Atlantis, Fact or Fiction?* Bloomington: Indiana University Press, 1978.

Roberts, Michael. *Essays in Swedish History.* London: Weidenfeld & Nicolson, 1966.

————. *Gustavus Adolphus: A History of Sweden 1611–1632.* 2 volumes. London: Longman, 1953–58.

————, ed. *Sweden as a Great Power 1611–1697: Government, Society, Foreign Policy.* London: Edward Arnold Ltd., 1968.

————, ed. *Sweden's Age of Greatness 1632–1718.* New York: St. Martin's Press, 1973.

————. *The Swedish Imperial Experience 1560–1718.* Cambridge, England: Cambridge University Press, 1979.

Robinson, John. *Account of Sweden, 1688: The Original 1688 Manuscript, Edited and Collated with the 1693 Manuscript and the Published Editions from 1694 with an Introduction by John B Hattendorf.* Stockholm: Karolinska Förbundet, 1998.

Rudbeck, Olof. *Bref af Olof Rudbeck d.ä. rörande Uppsalas universitet,* I–IV. Edited by Claes Annerstedt. Uppsala: Akademiska boktryckeriet, 1893–1905.

————. *Olavi Rudbeckii Atlantica sive Manheim: Olf Rudbeks Atland eller Manheim,* I–IV. Uppsala, 1679–1702.

————. *Olof Rudbecks Atland eller Manheim . . . Olaus Rudbecks Atlantica, svenska originaltexten,* I–IV. Edited by Axel Nelson. Uppsala: Almqvist & Wiksells boktryckeri, 1937–50.

Rudbeckius, Johannes. *Bibliotheca Rudbeckiana: Beskrivande förteckning över tryckta arbeten, vilka författats eller utgivits av medlemmar av släkten Rudbeckius-Rudbeck samt handla om dem eller deras skrifter: En släkthistoria i elva led från 1600–1900–talen.* Stockholm, 1918.

Rudbecksstudier. Festskrift vid Uppsala universitets minnesfest till högtidlighållande av 300-Årsminnet av Olof Rudbeck d.ä:s födelse. Uppsala: Almqvist & Wiksells boktryckeri, 1930.

Rystad, Göran. *Karl XI. En biografi.* Lund: Historiska media, 2001.

————. "Magnus Gabriel de la Gardie." In *Sweden's Age of Greatness 1632–1718,* edited by Michael Roberts. New York: St. Martin's Press, 1973.

Schück, Henrik. *Johan Hadorph: Minnesteckning.* Stockholm: Norstedts, 1933.

————. *Kgl. Vitterhets historie och antikvitets akademien. Dess förhistoria och historia.* 4 volumes. Stockholm: Wahlström & Widstrand, 1932–35.

Stolpe, Sven. *Christina of Sweden.* Translated by Sir Alec Randall and Ruth Mary Bethell. New York: Macmillan, 1966.

Strindberg, Axel. *Bondenöd och stormaktsdröm. Studier över skedet 1630–1718.* Stockholm: Albert Bonniers Förlag, 1937.

Swederus, M. B. "Olof Rudbeck den äldre. Huvudsakligen betraktad i sin verksamhet som naturforskare. En skildring." *Nordisk Tidskrift* (1878).

Turville-Petre, E. O. G. *Myth and Religion of the North: The Religion of Ancient Scandinavia.* Westport, CT: Greenwood Press, 1975.

Upton, A. F. *Charles XI and Swedish Absolutism.* Cambridge, England: Cambridge University Press, 1998.

Voltaire. *History of Charles XII.* Translated by Winifred Todhunter. London: J. M. Dent Co., 1908.

Whitelocke, Bulstrode. *A Journal of the Swedish Embassy 1653 and 1654.* London: Longman, 1855.

Acknowledgments

It is a great pleasure to thank everyone who has contributed so much to this book. First I would like to thank Suzanne Gluck at the William Morris Agency for all her brilliant and enthusiastic support. She is absolutely amazing—the very best agent anyone could hope to have, and I know how fortunate I am to be able to work with her. My deepest gratitude also goes to my editor, Kim Kanner Meisner. She read the manuscript with passion and insight, and her comments were phenomenal. Thank you again for all your help, which has wonderfully improved the book.

I would also like to thank Jake Morrissey, Teryn Johnson, and Shaye Areheart for their support of this project, and Diane White for reading the manuscript with great encouragement. Thank you, Raymond Betts and David Olster, for showing just how exciting history really can be, and John Greenway for first introducing me to Olof Rudbeck. Thanks, too, to Gunnar Broberg, Gustav Holmberg, Ulla Järlfors, and Jane Vance. Russell Hargreaves kindly looked over my Latin translations, Birgit Zetinigg my German, Richard Turner my French, and my wife, Sara, my Swedish. Even if all the translations did not in the end appear, they certainly helped inform the narrative. All errors in the translations, as well as in the story itself, are mine alone.

Special thanks to the many people who helped make my stays in Sweden so memorable. Ingvor Gerner showed again and again that Swedish hospitality truly reaches Rudbeckian proportions. She went out of her way to make sure I had a great time in Stockholm, and I certainly did. Thank you, Annika, Pär, and Jacob Levander for my home on the west coast. At Lund, I enjoyed the stimulating intellectual and cultural climate at the Department of History of Ideas and Science. Jan, Gunnel, Rakel, Lisa, and Tove Fagius made me feel just as welcome in Uppsala. Gunnar Eriksson gave timely support, including a copy of his *Atlantic Vision,* when I was just starting my fascination with Rudbeck. Years later, on another trip to Uppsala, Karin Johannisson presented me with copies of Rudbeck's second, third, and fourth volumes, another kind, thoughtful gesture that greatly helped my work. All researchers should feel such a warm welcome.

In his delightful book *Banvard's Folly,* Paul Collins called libraries "the most heroic of human creations," and I am inclined to agree. I would like to thank the librarians and archivists at a number of institutions: the National Library in Stockholm, Riksarkivet in Stockholm, Uppsala University, Lund University, Uppsala landsarkiv, Anglia University, Cambridge University, and the Royal Society in London. My thanks, too, to the interlibrary loan team at the Young Library at the University of Kentucky, who always responded graciously to my urgent 3:30 a.m. e-mail pleas for yet more obscure treatises from the nineteenth century and available only in Swedish. Remarkably, they managed to track down almost every single one.

I would very much like to thank the J. William Fulbright Commission in Washington and Stockholm for an unforgettable year and a half in Sweden—it was enough to turn me into a raging Swedophile. The American Scandinavian Foundation Fellowship was of tremendous help, deepening my obsession with all things Swedish, while also allowing me to spend more time in the archives reading the rest of Rudbeck's letters and notes. I would also like to thank the Cambridge Overseas Trust, London's Overseas Research Award Scheme, and the Emmanuel Research Award for their support, years ago, of my interests in European history. Thanks to everyone who helped make my stay in England so enjoyable, including the entire Cambridge University Baseball Team. At my age and ability, I had come to think my days of playing first base were long over. And even if they probably should have been, it sure was a blast.

As always, my parents, Van and Cheryl King, have offered valuable advice, support, and encouragement at just the right time, all of which helped me stay focused and on the right track. You are a source of unbelievable love and inspiration—thanks! Thanks, too, to my grandmother, Ella King; my brother, Brent; and his wife, Lindsay.

Following Rudbeck in his quest for Atlantis has certainly led to some surprises. Best of all, my passion for this search led to finding the love of my life, a wonderful Swedish girl named Sara, and today we are married. As far as this story was concerned, you were its first critic, reading every page a frightening number of times and making so many fantastic suggestions. I always looked forward to our book nights, which were fun and at the same time outrageously helpful. Thank you for sharing the story with me! I am so happy for everything you do in my life, and I am overwhelmed with joy as I look at the very special addition to our family, our beautiful three-week-old daughter, Julia. Sara, I am so glad to dedicate this book to you with all my love.

Index

Page numbers in *italics* refer to illustrations.

About the Author

DAVID KING currently teaches European history at the University of Kentucky. A Fulbright Scholar with a master's degree from Cambridge University, he spent several years in Europe gathering information to write *Finding Atlantis*. He lives in Lexington, Kentucky, with his wife, their baby daughter, and their twenty-two goldfish.